A Faithful Guide
to Peace with God

Being Excerpts from the Writings of
C. O. ROSENIUS

ARRANGED AS DAILY MEDITATIONS
TO COVER A PERIOD OF TWO MONTHS

With the Assistance of
BISHOP N. J. LAACHE

Reproduced by
GEORGE TAYLOR RYGH

1923
AUGSBURG PUBLISHING HOUSE
MINNEAPOLIS, MINNESOTA

Originally published by Augsburg Publishing House in 1923.
Reprinted in 1990 by
The Board of Parish Education
The Association of Free Lutheran Congregations
3110 East Medicine Lake Boulevard
Minneapolis, Minnesota 55441

CONTENTS

THE FIRST SERIES

THE SECOND SERIES

Page

PREFACE

CARL OLOF ROSENIUS occupies a place in the history of Sweden similar to that occupied by John Wesley in England, John Knox in Scotland, Christian Scriver in Germany, and Hans Nielsen Hauge in Norway. In the day of these holy men of God, rationalism, externalism and worldliness threatened the life of the Church, even as they do this day. As orthodoxy sank into orthodoxism; as the Spirit was quenched by the letter; as the spiritual life of the Church was being choked by forms and ordinances, God raised up living witnesses to translate profession into practice, to call men to repentance, to faith in the atoning blood of the Son of God, and to a new walk of life after the Spirit.

Like the prophets of old, they demanded truth in the inward parts. They fearlessly denounced the sins of their day and generation. Their testimony has come down through later generations and, please God, it shall ring in the ears of men to the end of time. Their sermons and other writings have been a leaven which to-day is as effective for the conversion and spiritual stabilization of men as ever it was in the day of their authors' earthly pilgrimage. "The words that I speak unto you," says Christ, "they are spirit, and they are life" (John 6: 63). Men die and pass away, but the words of Christ live and shall never pass away.

Carl Olof Rosenius was born in the year 1816
in Nysätra (New Chalet), Province of Norrland,
Sweden, where his father was a pastor in the Lutheran State Church. Spiritually, the days were dark
and the night of inky blackness. Nearly all the
pastors were simon-pure rationalists, discoursing
from their pulpits on the value of honesty, thrift,
and other virtues, giving detailed information on
the correct feeding of cattle, and the proper treatment of the soil. If a layman essayed to preach
the living Word of God to his fellows, he was ac-
cused by the clergy, arrested and jailed under the
provisions of the law against conventicles. The first
half of the last century was characterized by shameless persecutions of all who dared to confess Christ.

One of the few pastors who proved themselves
to be shepherds indeed, was Rosenius' father. He
was a veritable John the Baptist, a voice crying in
the wilderness, "Repent ye, the axe is laid to the
root of the trees." People began to read their Bibles, and all who persisted in the practice were nick-
named "readers." The rationalist clergy disap-
proved and complained of the strange pastor to the
authorities. He was removed willy-nilly to another
parish, where the same experience befell the intrepid
witness for Christ. From parish to parish he was
shunted, but the movement he had started would
not down. The more vigorously the learned and
the mighty labored to put out the fire, the more the
sparks scattered. Soon all of Western Bothnia was
aflame with the revival.

A home of such vital Christianity was a blessing

to the thoughtful lad Carl Olof. Early in life he understood that the Spirit of God was at work in his heart. When his brothers and sisters and other playmates were engaged in their games and sports, he would frequently separate himself from the merry company, steal off into the woods or the fields and there quietly meditate upon the mysteries of God, of himself and the universe. He yearned to come into closer communion with God, but God was so great and seemed so far away.

At times the lad's faith was sifted by the devil, who has no more mercy on the young than he has upon the old. He was tempted to doubt the existence of God. One day the little fellow decided to find out for sure if there is a God. Back of the barn was a yard. Blindfolded he determined to walk across the barnyard diagonally toward the corner of a granary. If he hit the corner, he would conclude that God had led his steps. He tied a kerchief about his eyes and started out upon his experiment. He had walked a while when suddenly he was halted by a paralyzing fear. An invisible power seemed to hold him back. He dared not take another step forward. He tore the kerchief from his eyes and saw to his horror that he stood on the very edge of a deep well. Another step and he would have been hurled into eternity. He instantly realized that the hand of God had held him back and saved his life. From that moment his doubts as to the existence of God vanished and never came to trouble him again.

When the father was removed to the village of

Sæfwar, Carl Olof and his brother Anton were sent to school in Umea. Carl Olof was a quiet, thoughtful boy, with a profound veneration for the Word of God. His desire was to become a minister, and when he read about the martyrs of the faith, he would be as one of them. At the age of fifteen years he came to a conscious, living faith in Christ. He rejoiced in God his Savior. Besides reading the Bible assiduously, he studied carefully the writings of Luther.

When Rosenius at the age of sixteen left the school at Umea, he conducted his first Bible meeting. At a service which he led some time later, there were not more than seven or eight persons present, but outside of the meeting-house a crowd of schoolmates had assembled. With cat-calls and the throwing of rubbish through the open windows into the little audience they attempted to break up the meeting of the "readers." But the young evangelist was undaunted and continued the service to its close.

In the fall of the year 1833 Rosenius entered college in the city of Hernösand. Here he remained during a period of four years, suffering poignantly from the sneers of his fellow-students on account of his fellowship with the handful of young men who loved the Lord and occasionally met in prayer meetings.

In 1834 his father was removed to the parish of Burtresk, some sixty or seventy miles north of the city of Umea. Here the young student made the acquaintance of an itinerant woman evangelist, whom he jokingly designated as "the prophetess from Great Rapids." She was of large spiritual help to him as a wise and experienced Christian. In later years Rosenius frequently corresponded with her.

On Good Friday and Easter, 1836, Rosenius delivered his first public sermons in the parish of Stigsjö. But the sermons displeased the parish priest, who complained that the young man had demeaned the pulpit by using the dialect of the common people. Nor did the contents of the sermons satisfy his reverence. Rosenius had referred to the union of the believer with Christ, and this was dubbed as "mystical fanaticism" by the parish priest.

Graduating from college in 1837, he returned to the home of his parents in Burtresk. He assisted his father in the pulpit, in prayer-meetings and sick visitations. With the permission of the bishop he made a missionary journey among the Lapps, an experience which made a deep impression upon him.

In the fall of 1838 Rosenius matriculated at the University of Uppsala in the department of theology. On the day before leaving his home he wrote his faithful friend and guide, "the prophetess": "To-morrow I start for the place where the throne of Satan has been erected. How should I dare to go there if the Defender of Israel were not my sure defense? He has so willed it. Let Him have the responsibility." The student life was wild and shameless. "The darkness here is appalling," he writes, "more dense than that of Egypt. The place is a veritable Sodom. Drunkenness, immorality, oaths and all other kinds of vice flourish freely. When the learned, who are the leaders of Israel, live thus abominably in sin, what may be expected of the common people who from childhood have been taught to follow their steps?"

Under such conditions it is not to be wondered at that the spiritual life of the young theolog at times was below par. He did not long remain at the university, however. Lack of means, illness, and an ever increasing aversion to the life which he saw all about him, caused him to arrive at the determination to quit the university. A final reason was his desire to go out and witness for the Savior. He lost all interest in the secular studies required of him. He concentrated more and more upon the things concerning the Kingdom of God. His friends advised him to break off his course at Uppsala and advertise for a position as a private tutor. He soon found what he wanted. In the summer of 1839 he became the family tutor on the estate of Lenna, near Stockholm. His pupils were the two sons of the Countess Lenna.

Presently he heard rumors of a great revival passing over the capital city like "the sound in the tops of the mulberry-trees." He bestirred himself to visit the evangelist, an Englishman of the name of Scott. Scott was a Methodist, and without emphasizing the idiosyncracies of Methodist doctrine, labored zealously for the salvation of souls. He was a man of faith and firm in his convictions. He served to strengthen the weak young Lutheran theologian in the fundamentals. God had led Rosenius to this man, who in turn was to lead him into the labor of the Vineyard. He felt within him the call of the prophet, and refused ordination on the ground that it would bind him to a certain parish.

His close affiliation with the Methodist revivalist from England naturally provoked censure from various quarters. He was warned against the sects and the sectarians. But Rosenius continued his evangelical activities in alliance with the Englishman. Without being influenced in the least by the false doctrines of Methodism, Rosenius held immovably fast to the Lutheran Confessions in all his preaching, teaching and writing. He remained a staunch Lutheran to the end of his life.

After having written a number of articles published in *The Missionary Times* of Stockholm, Rosenius became the editor of that periodical at New Year's, 1842. Simultaneously he and Mr. Scott began the publication of a monthly paper called *The Pietist*. Through this periodical Rosenius was enabled to reach the people all over the country. Its columns contain the greater part of his life-work. Thousands and tens of thousands of souls have been blessed thereby.

Rosenius was now thoroughly happy. He had found a vehicle through which he could find free and unhindered utterance. He was surrounded by loyal and capable associates in the work of calling the dead bones of the Church to life. His life was filled with work for the salvation of sinners by the Gospel of the Crucified and Risen Christ. A dark cloud eventually overshadowed his joy, however.

The rising tide of ill will and hostility against Mr. Scott culminated on Palm Sunday, 1842, in a mob attack upon the church in which he was preaching that evening. He was forced to save his life by escaping through an open window and barricading himself in his rooms. The authorities notified him that they could no longer be held responsible for his life and advised him to flee the country.

Shortly after the departure of his friend and colaborer, Rosenius made a visit to his home in Norrland. His old father was dead, and he comforted his aged mother. His visit was short, however. By mid-summer he was back in Stockholm editing his two religious journals. In the following year he married. When the "Evangeliska Fosterlandsstiftelsen" was organized, in 1856, Rosenius became one of the most active members of the directorate. He remained faithful at his post of duty as writer and preacher to the end of his days. He died February 28, 1868, in Stockholm. The present volume, as his other books, has been compiled from his writings in *The Pietist*. Beyond the borders of his native land, in Norway, Denmark and America, his writings have brought light, comfort and joy to numberless souls.

We trust that this volume in its English version may be similarly useful in leading many souls to peace with God.

G. T. R.

THE FIRST SERIES

THE HOLY LAW OF GOD

*We know that the Law is good,
if a man use it lawfully.*

(1 TIMOTHY 1: 8.)

THE FIRST DAY

DOCTOR SWEBELIUS says: "The Law is fairly well known by nature; the Gospel, however, is a mystery concealed from reason." This is true, and strikingly expressed. And yet the greatest misapprehension and misuse of the Law are frequently found within the bounds of Christendom, a misapprehension and a misuse which render the whole Law and the entire Word of God without power and benefit, thereby destroying souls in their helplessness. By the gracious assistance of God, we shall consider the gravest of these misapprehensions and misuses.

We do not speak of the despisers of the Law, whose condemnation is swift and easily understood. For everybody understands well enough that God does not admit into His heaven such as are not only sinful, but also contemners of His holy will. What is the Law but the will of God? He who despises the will of God despises God, and surely no one has ever found a single promise that God would be merciful to those who despise Him. You may be weak and sinful; you may have transgressed the Law of God; yet His mercy is great enough to forgive your sin and guilt for the sake of Christ. But if you despise God and His will, not even trying to love and obey Him, how can you expect that such utter contempt of God and His Word shall be forgiven? How can you believe that you are on the way to heaven? Stop a moment and consider.

We have, then, a matter before us which may not be brushed aside as of no importance. It is a matter which involves the eternal destiny of your soul. We shall soon discover, however, that it is not enough to respect the Law of God and to make some sort of use of it. What is required is, that we use it "lawfully," that is, rightly, or as God wants us to use the Law.

The Apostle Paul writes concerning his brethren in Israel, that "they have a zeal of God, but not according to knowledge" (Romans 10: 2); that they "followed after the Law of righteousness" (Romans 9: 31); that "they go about to establish their own righteousness" (Romans 10: 3); but that for their sakes he had "great heaviness and continual sorrow" in his heart (Romans 9: 2), and that he could wish himself "accursed from Christ for my brethren, my kinsmen according to the flesh" (Romans 9: 3), if thereby they might be saved. What, then, was the fault with Israel? The fault was, the apostle says, that "when Moses was read, the veil was upon their heart" (2 Corinthians 3: 15), so that "they went about to establish their own righteousness" (Romans 10: 3). "But Israel, which followed after the Law of righteousness, have not attained to the Law of righteousness" (Romans 9: 31). They did not permit the Law to serve them by condemning them, convicting them, driving them to Christ: they made the Law a way of salvation. They failed to understand the purpose of the Law and as a result, made a wrong use of the Law.

The essential purpose of the Law is to arouse and drive sinners to Christ, who is "the end of the Law for righteousness to every one that believeth" (Romans 10: 4). "For what the Law could not do, in that it was weak through the flesh, God sending His own Son in the likeness of sinful flesh, and for sin, condemned sin in the flesh" (Romans 8: 3). "He that hath the Son hath life, and he that hath not the Son, hath not life" (John 5: 12). "Wherefore the Law is our schoolmaster to bring us unto Christ" (Galatians 3: 24). Such is the purpose of God's holy Law. The Law is a Boanerges, a son of thunder (Mark 3: 17), who indeed does not baptize with Spirit and with fire, but with "the Baptism of repentance," thus presenting unto the Lord a well-prepared people. The Law is the prison-house wherein "we were kept under the Law, shut up unto the faith which should afterwards be revealed" (Galatians 3: 23-24).

This, then, is the first, greatest and most dangerous misuse of the Law. It renders the entire Law useless. It misses its purpose altogether. When the Law is thus made useless, "when the salt has lost his savor" (Matthew 5: 13), wherewith shall souls be aroused and humbled? When the heart has no experience of the power of the Law to its abasement, the Gospel also remains ineffective; Christ, with all His merit, remains ineffective. For "they that be whole need not a physician, but the sick" (Matthew 9: 12), that is to say, they that have been made sick through the harsh dominion of the Law. But when both Law and Gospel, that is, the whole Word of God, no longer exert any influence upon the human heart, the soul is hopelessly lost; it cannot be saved.

Let us, however, consider how it happens that the Law, and thereby the entire Word of God, is rendered futile. It happens in this way: You make the Law a way of salvation, while it should be a condemning judge, a schoolmaster to bring you to Christ. This comes to pass when any one modifies, mitigates and whittles down the commandments and judgments of the Lord, in order that they may agree with the sinner's opinions, or, at all events, correspond with his natural powers. It is sometimes said: "No mortal man can meet this or that requirement of the Law. Therefore, it cannot be God's purpose to demand strict fulfilment of the Law in every respect; for God cannot demand more than we can do." This is the fundamental error. In this way "every mouth" is not "stopped," and "all the world" does not "become guilty before God" (Romans 3: 19). If a single human being could fulfil all the demands of the Law, his mouth would not be stopped; he would be able to "boast" before God.

He who would understand why the Law requires more than we are able to perform, and also how far the Law goes in its requirements, must consider

what the Law is. The Law is nothing else than
God's holiness, God's holy will expressed in human
words and in men's consciences. Therefore the Law
reaches as far in its demands as God's holiness
reaches. It is the Law which says to you, This and
that God requires of you; this and that He forbids.
Now it is clear that this will of God must demand
a constantly increasing righteousness before you become as holy as God Himself. For what He Himself will not do, He does not ask you to do. Consequently, He never says: This or that I do not wish
you to do, but since you ask me for permission, I
will give you leave to do this thing. But He says:
"Be ye holy, even as I, the Lord your God, am holy"
(Leviticus 19:2). When we consider that the Law
is simply the holiness of God, the will of God, we
understand why the Law may not be changed or
modified in a single letter to suit the weaknesses of
the fallen race; for in that case God's holiness would
have an end. He who receives the grace rightly to
discern the holiness of Gods Law, can no longer
hope to become perfect before God, that is, to become as holy as God Himself is. On the contrary,
he will surely be humbled and crushed. He who
hopes to gain righteousness by the Law, has a "veil"
before his eyes: he is blind, and does not realize
what the Law demands of him.

But you say: "True, no man can become perfect
as God is perfect. But we can do as much as we
are able to do in the way of fulfilling His holy
Law." God does not accept that sort of righteousness. You must keep the Law perfectly, or you

are condemned. The Law says distinctly: "Cursed be he that confirmeth not all the words of this Law to do them" (Deuteronomy 27: 26). And an apostle says in the New Testament: "For whosoever shall keep the whole Law and yet offend in one point, he is guilty of all" (James 2: 10).

You say, however: "But God is merciful for the sake of Christ. He will forgive me if I do not perfectly keep His Law." God is by no means merciful to him who is guilty of violating the Law. The matter is quite different with them who through faith possess the righteousness of Christ. They are not in the least indebted to the Law, for through Christ they have the righteousness which the Law demands (Romans 8: 4), the righteousness to which the apostle refers when he says: "For what the Law could not do, in that it was weak through the flesh, God sending His own Son in the likeness of sinful flesh, and for sin, condemned sin in the flesh" (Romans 8: 3). In short, "they are not under the Law, but under grace" (Romans 6: 14-15). But he who is under the Law has no remission of sin, as Jesus Himself declares: "For verily I say unto you, Till heaven and earth pass, one jot or one tittle shall in no wise pass from the Law, till all be fulfilled" (Matthew 5: 18). O what injury is done to the soul when we do not remember that there are those who are under the Law, while others are not under the Law, but under grace (Romans 3: 19; 6: 14; and 7: 4, 6).

These two classes of men are under quite different judgment. It is true that the grace of God in Christ

is boundless, but it can do them no good whatever
who are under the Law and desire to remain "the
disciples of Moses" (John 9: 28). The Apostle
Paul says: "For as many as are of the works of
the Law are under the curse" (Galatians 3: 10).
To suppress this truth, and to preach in its stead the
gospel of the flesh; to detract from the Law that
which the sinner regards as too severe; to lower the
goal of the striving after holiness down to such a
plane that the sinner may reach up to it, creating in
the sinner self-satisfaction, self-righteousness and
carnal security—this is the most dangerous misuse
of the Law. In this way, the entire purpose of the
Law is frustrated. For that purpose was to drive
and chastise the soul, not to the yoke of bondage,
but into the slough of despair, and thence to Christ,
who is "the end of the Law unto righteousness to
every one that believeth" (Romans 10: 4).

But this levelling down of the Law, this breaking
off of the point of the Law, may also be accomplished by persuading oneself or others to hope for
the future: that which is still lacking in the fulfilment of the Law may be accomplished by the
grace of God later on. When the victory has been
won, the time is come to appropriate to oneself the
merit of Christ in all its fulness. Alas, what a Sa-
tanic deception! Remember that if death should
come to you this night, you would be condemned,
since you are not holy as God's Law requires of
you. You reply: "I have this hope that God will
not call me away before I am prepared for heaven."
It is all very well that you have such fine thoughts

about God. But where is it written that God will hold death back from you until you are as holy as the Law requires? In that case you would never die.

We ask: Have you not received the help of God's Spirit? Are you certain that you have rightly made use of His grace, rightly prayed for His help, watched and fought in the power of God as strenuously as you should have watched and fought? If you consider this, you shall possibly find that you have nothing to expect which God has not already given you. If you realize that according to the Law you are lost, the answer is: That is precisely what the Law would show you, in order that you might take refuge in Christ.

You need not wait for the future. The Kingdom of God is near you. You shall learn that the righteousness which the Law demands, but which you cannot produce, will be found in another way, namely, through faith in the blood of Jesus.

THE HOLY LAW OF GOD
(Continued)

We know the Law is good, if a man use it lawfully.
(1 Timothy 1:8.)

THE SECOND DAY

IT behooves us to beware of the false interpretation of the Law to the effect that we are able to keep it perfectly. We must likewise beware of

the thought that we can not be saved before we
have fulfilled the Law and become pure and perfect.
For under this thought lies a concealed assassin of
souls, an anti-Christ, who would render the blood of
Christ unnecessary and tell us that the blood of
Christ is of no avail whatever; or, at the most, that
it is only a means of sanctification, not the atonement for sin; an assassin who destroys the soul
either with a false confidence in its own righteousness, or with a tormenting spirit of bondage. On
the contrary, the more threatening the thunderings
of Mount Sinai, and the more clearly the demands
of God's Law press upon our souls, the better; for
the sooner shall we find that comfort which abides.
We shall be deprived of the false consolation which
lies in the hope of justification by the Law. We shall
be driven to seek help of Him whose name is Jesus.
In Him we shall find joy and peace.

Many a soul, ignorant of this truth, says: "If
I am driven so strenuously and condemned so un-
mercifully, I shall lose courage. I shall not be able
to find consolation in Christ nor love for Him."
Reply: Have we any right to modify or annul what
God has commanded? Who dares to alter the commandments and judgments of God? It must be remembered that the sinner does not need consolation
first of all; he needs a broken and a contrite heart.
The consolation which a soul draws from the righteousness of the Law is accursed—it is a false consolation. It is this consolation which misleads the
soul into bondage, self-righteousness and hypocrisy.

It is the very road to hell. It is this consolation which the Law must take away from us.

Note, furthermore, that there is no better means to advance souls to true comfort than to present the Law in all its severity; for until they are deprived of all comfort in their own righteousness by the Law, they are not ready to accept the righteousness of Christ in the Gospel. When John says: "Who hath warned you to flee from the wrath to come? The axe lieth at the root of the trees: Therefore every tree which bringeth not forth good fruit is hewn down, and cast into the fire," he struck at the pride of their hearts. Thereupon he said: "Behold the Lamb of God which taketh away the sin of the world." At once he lifted up the valleys, the dejected souls, and prepared the way for the Lord. (Matthew 3; Luke 3; John 1.)

Since we have found that the first work of the Law is to bring the sinner to humility and the recognition of sin, we ask: What should be the nature of this knowledge of sin, in order that it may be acceptable to God? *Reply*: It is not enough to know our sins of commission; for with such knowledge you may still comfort yourself with your good intentions and hope of amendment. The feeling of your sinfulness must be profound and thorough. You must know the root of your sinful depravity, which consists in carnal security, hypocrisy, hardness of heart, contempt of God. You must realize that for these reasons you are a lost and condemned sinner. As long as you do not recognize this depravity of the heart, your self-sufficiency will assert itself. You will continue to say: "I shall save myself." Your own righteousness and carnal security will live on. You will never apprehend Christ and rest upon His merit alone.

To this fundamental knowledge of self, few come immediately through their awakening. It is true that the soul becomes terrified. But it is not embarrassed; for it argues: "I know a way out. I will repent." Then begins the labor under the Law in the attempt to convert oneself, to lay aside sin and sinful habits. As long as you see nothing but external righteousness and your conversion seems to be complete, you become hopeful and remain in your self-righteousness. But if you look upon the inner sanctification and realize that God requires your heart, and that you desire its cleansing, you are very quickly disappointed. For when now you determine to love God above all, you feel that you have an idolatrous heart. When you desire to pray and to fight earnestly against your sins, you find that you lie down in the mire of sin. You are not even able to regret your sins and weep over them. Then you are startled and exclaim: "I am a lost soul. I am a hardened sinner. I am a hypocrite. For neither do I fight earnestly against sin, nor do I sincerely repent."

Behold now, this was precisely what the Law set out to accomplish in you. What is it that you now recognize? Is it not the security of your heart, your hypocrisy, your contempt of God? The purpose of the Law is that you learn to know the evil of sin. In this condition you find no comfort, for it is a terrible thing to be hard-hearted, secure and hypo-critical. But did you not desire this knowledge of your heart? Certainly you did, only you desired nothing more than the knowledge of your corruption, not the vileness of the corruption itself. How was it possible that such was the result? You do not need to feel an evil that you have not, but only the evil which you have. Now it seems to you, however, that you have no conscious feeling of your sins, but that you are obsessed with sin itself. You see your sins, but do not feel them.

But was it not this lack of sorrow for sin which you should recognize? Was it not the purpose of the Law to deprive you of every comfort, in order that you might be compelled to go to Christ, so that He might become your only consolation? It is no easy matter, however, to seek refuge with Him. It is not an easy matter to believe. Now it becomes necessary that you receive the grace of God, without which you still remain a lost sinner in spite of all the experiences of sin which you have had. He stands before you, gently calling: "Come unto me all ye that labor and are heavy laden, and I will give you rest." If only you close your eyes to hindrances and throw yourself as you are in His arms, you shall be saved as a brand from the burning, cleansed in His blood, justified, rejoicing. Now you understand what is meant by the Scripture declaration: "Christ is the end of the Law unto every one that believeth" (Romans 10: 4).

We have seen that the Law is good, if any one use it lawfully. We have shown the correct and the incorrect use of the Law in the conversion of souls. But the Law also has its use in the daily renewal; partly to show the regenerated, justified and pardoned soul how it should conduct itself in all respects; and partly, when the heart is in danger of becoming worldly, to correct and drive the soul to seek Christ daily.

There is still another error to be pointed out. This error has made its appearance in different localities of our country (Sweden). We refer to the Anti-nomians (rejecters of the Law), who regard the Law as superfluous both in conversion and in the daily renewal. By this we would not express the same fear as that which obtains with the disciples of Moses, who say now, as was said in the time of Paul, when the works of the Law were discarded as competent to produce righteousness, that we "abolish the Law through faith."

They who thus treat the Law are people who have never learned to distinguish between justification and sanctification, Law and Gospel, spirit and flesh. It seems to them that Paul at times is too evangelical, that he opens the door to the Mercy-seat too widely. At times they think that he is too severe, that he requires too much of human nature. They say that he denounces what they regard as innocent. We are not speaking of these people here. We speak of the real Anti-nomians, who assert that the Law is unnecessary to conversion. To prove this, they adduce as evidence that only the Gospel operates upon their hearts. A deplorable error! What effect would grace have upon the heart if sin were not acknowledged and felt? That which chastises sin is the Law, even when it speaks through the wounds of Christ. The Law works as a rule in an unknown and secret way. For "I had not known sin but by the Law" (Romans 7:7). Though the Law does not give life, it nevertheless brings about the result, that the Gospel gives light. The Law is the plowing, the Gospel is the seed. It is true that the growing does not come by the plowing only, but also requires the seed. Still, if the ground is not plowed, the seed remains useless, lies upon the surface, dries up, and is picked away by the birds. But those who regard the Law as superfluous for regenerated souls who have an obedient mind, quite misunderstand Scripture passages such as these: "Now when faith has come, you are no longer under the schoolmaster"; and, "You shall not bind the conscience by the Law." *Reply*: I did not mean your conscience, but your flesh, if so be that you are under grace. If your heart is not right with God, so that you have your delight in God's Law according to the inner man, and you still wish to retain this or that sin intact, your conscience will be bound, yea, your soul and your body will be bound in hell. For what is bound upon earth shall likewise be bound in hell. "If ye live after the flesh, ye shall die" (Romans 8:3). But if you are a true Christian, the spirit is indeed willing, and does not need to be chastised by the Law. The flesh is weak, secure and evil. It needs to be chastised, as Luther said: "Bit and bridle do not belong to the marriage chamber, but to the stable and to the horse." Remain, therefore, steadfast in the liberty with which Christ hath set you free, but do not make use of your liberty to sin. "Stand fast therefore in the liberty wherewith Christ hath made us free, and be not entangled again with the yoke of bondage" (Galatians 5 : 1, 13).

THE LAW AND ITS PURPOSE

THE THIRD DAY

THE Word of God with reference to its content is of two kinds: Law and Gospel. If we correctly understand these two divisions of the Word of God which requires something of us, whether it God in its essential character, since there is not one word referring to the will and counsel of God unto our salvation which does not belong to one or the other of these two divisions.

To the Law belongs all that Word of God which teaches what we are to be and to do; all that Word of God which requires something of us, whether it be inner qualifications or external deeds. For God's Law lays claim to the entire man, his inmost character, his heart, thoughts and desires. Therefore, the commandment does not read: Your head, your mouth, your tongue must do this and refrain from doing that, but it says: "Thou," "Thou,"—that is, the Law speaks to the entire man. Take, for example, the First Commandment only. How does it not demand our entire heart and soul and all our powers and all our mind! (Luke 10 :27.) Consider the scope of Luther's explanation of the First Commandment: "That we above all things fear and love God, and trust in God alone." That I am to fear God above all things involves the injunction that I am not to be carnally-minded, secure and indifferent concerning God and my soul; that I am not to sin lightly, but that I am to fear to do anything displeasing to God, in such a spirit that I am willing to suffer everything, even death itself, rather than to sin against my God. It implies that I watch and fight against sin earnestly, zealously and effectively. It implies that I watch and pray and fight, not only one hour and then yield to the temptation the next hour, but that I watch and fight and pray without ceasing.

That I am to "love God above all things" implies that I am not to be cold in my relationship to God, and disinclined to prayer, but that I am to live with God as my greatest joy and desire. I am above all things to think about Him, speak of Him, and cheerfully do all that which He asks of me. I am to be willing to suffer anything which He permits to come upon me. All these things we do for the person whom we love.

"To trust in God above all things," requires true faith and confidence in Him. It forbids all trust in myself or in any other created being or thing. It forbids self-sufficiency and selffishness. It forbids all distrust, all pagan care and unbelief. In a word, if you carefully study God's commandments, you shall find that they demand of you not only this or that deed, this or that member of your body—the hand, the foot or the tongue: they demand the entire person. For which reason Christ, in the fifth chapter of the Gospel according to Saint Matthew, explains that he who is but angry with his neighbor is of God regarded as a murderer. He who but looks upon a woman with unclean lust in his heart is judged of God as an adulterer.

From these considerations, we find, in the first place, that God's Law not only demands deeds, not only says what we are to do and how we are to do, but that it requires above all else our inner personality. It demands a God-pleasing spiritual condition, good inner qualities. It instructs us as to what we are to be, and how we are to be. As a consequence, the Law includes also the words of God which deal with our intellect and character. Hence, when I am reprimanded for my spiritual carelessness, hardness of heart, frivolity, pride, selfishness, sluggishness in the use of the Word of God and prayer, it is the Law of God which chastises me.

Nor is this all. We find that this inner spiritual condition, the heart, the mind, and the soul's desire, is the supreme requirement, that which God demands above all else. Hence, though I live an outwardly pious life, do a great deal of good in the world, and refrain from all evil, but in my heart cherish such thoughts and desires as "war against the Spirit," I am of God regarded on an equal footing with those who brazenly in actual deed commit the same sin. Therefore, if I am in a spiritual condition in which I do that which is good from compulsion, moved by the threatenings of the Law, then I am not doing one single deed pleasing to God.

Such is God, and such is His holy Law. The Law of God is nothing more nor less than God's holiness, God's nature and God's will, expressed in words. As He Himself is, He would have us be. What He loves, He would have us love. What He hates, He would have us hate. He is not content with us if we hate what He loves, or love what He hates. As little as He Himself can be reconciled with sin and the devil, even so can He not endure that we serve sin and the devil. For this reason He presents Himself as our pattern. He requires of us that we be holy and perfect as He Himself is. For He says: "Ye shall be holy: for I the Lord your God am holy" (Leviticus 19: 2). Christ says: "Be ye therefore perfect, even as your Father which is in heaven is perfect" (Matthew 5:48). What fools are they who say: God has no right to demand of us more than we are able to perform. The words of God just quoted are clear and incontrovertible. If God did not require more of us than we are able to perform, then every mouth would not be stopped and the world would not be guilty before God (Romans 3:19). Then there would have been no necessity of Christ's suffering death for us.

What is the essential purpose and meaning of the Law? What is its right use? What is its wrong use? These are vital questions. The correct answers would resolve a thousand spiritual difficulties if accepted with a thoughtful mind. Here is the criterion which separates true Christians from false Christians.

What, then, is the essential meaning, purpose and function of the Law in the matter of the soul's salvation? Paul, among his many testimonies, writes the following words: "Now we know that what things soever the Law saith, it saith to them who are under the Law: that every mouth may be stopped, and all the world may become guilty before God. Therefore by the deeds of the Law, there shall no flesh be justified in His sight; for by the Law is the knowledge of sin" (Romans 3:19-20).

Here no interpretation is necessary. We only need to take the words as they are written; for it is the aim of the apostle in this place to express the purpose of the Law. The purpose of God's holy Law is not that the world by it is to become pious, righteous and blessed, but "guilty," "that every mouth may be stopped," that "no flesh can be justified by the work of the Law, for by the Law cometh the knowledge of sin." Still another Scripture passage: "Moreover the Law entered, that the offense might abound. But where sin abounded, grace did much more abound" (Romans 5:20).

THE PURPOSE OF THE LAW
(*Continued*)

THE FOURTH DAY

BUT you say: "I did not mean that the Law only makes me sinful and guilty. I meant that if I earnestly took the Law to heart, sin would eventually come to an end and be destroyed as by fire. I would learn to abandon my sins. I meant that the Law entered that the offense might abound. Does not this abundance of sin signify the abundance of the knowledge of sin, sorrow for sin, tears of contrition? Not that sin should become more abundant actually, but that by the commandment sin becomes less and contrition becomes more intense?" Thus it may seem. But see what the apostle says: "What shall we say then? Is the Law sin? God forbid. Nay, I had not known sin, but by the Law: for I had not known lust, except the Law had said, Thou shalt not covet. But sin, taking occasion by the commandment, wrought in me all manner of concupiscence. For without the Law sin was dead. For I was alive without the Law once: but when the commandment came, sin revived, and I died. And the commandment, which was ordained to life, I found to be unto death. For sin, taking occasion by the commandment, deceived me, and by it slew me" (Romans 7:7-11).

These words are clear and decisive. The apostle says expressly that sin "takes occasion" from the commandment and kindles concupiscence, that without the Law, sin is dead. The inner concupiscence, the real sin, is more hidden when it is free and unhindered, than when the Law offers resistance.

Dr. Gezelius says concerning these words: "Without of the Law, sin is dead. Sin is 'dead,' since it does not assert itself as violently, nor does it struggle as determinedly against God's Law, neither does it show its power as formerly, since it does not regard as sin that which it does later."

This sad consolation is reached in the following manner: When sin is unhindered by the Law, the concupiscence, the real sin, lies asleep, indolent and inoperative within the heart. But as soon as the Law comes and resists the sin, the hidden evil of the heart rouses itself to conflict. It becomes more active and consequently also more manifest, just as the contrary spirit of a naughty child is aroused and manifests itself when its will is opposed, or as a stream, when it is dammed, overflows its banks. Such is the case with sin and the Law. The idea that the Law by its prohibitions has the effect of deadening the evil desires and of making the heart, the will, and the lusts good, is precisely the idea which the apostle here refutes. He says that the evil desires in the heart are enkindled and increased the more the Law prohibits them.

Above all, God wants our inner life to be good and holy. He desires in us the love of that which is good; for this love is the condition, the life and soul in every good act. Where this inner goodness is lacking, this love for that which is good, there is no good; for "God looketh to the heart." When the character has grown worse, sin has grown stronger. For what good is there in offering God the hand or the deed, while the heart, the will and the desire incline to sin? What is that but giving God the shell and sin the kernel? What is that but giving God the chaff and sin the wheat?

But here is another consideration: A new sin develops in the heart, which was not there before the commandment came: the soul becomes embittered

by the Law itself. It complains about the Holy
Spirit as if He were an oppressor. The soul complains against God Himself, who has given the Law.
The heart says: "Would that God had never given
such a Law! Why does God forbid me to do this
or that? Why may I not be free to follow my inclinations?" This language is a very climax of evil. In
such a spirit, a man has not only the desire for that
which is evil, but his heart also harbors bitterness
against God and His holy Law.

Every sincere Christian will testify that this actually happens. Sin increases in the heart in proportion as the commandments would hinder its development. At the moment when by the grace of
God he was awakened from his sleep in sin to a
deep concern for his salvation and sincerely turned
to repentance, the commandment, which threaten-
ingly chastened him, while he felt his lack of serious purpose, made him more unhappy than before.
Never had he been so exposed to sin; never had sin
so violently raged in his flesh, with its lusts and evil
desires. Yea, it often happens in such a case that
all the piety which he had strived to build up, possibly during many years, with great solicitude and
many serious resolutions, a piety which he cherished,
and over which he watched as his most precious
treasure, now tumbles about him like a dam built
of straw upon the quicksands. His righteousness is
shattered. He commits sin as he never sinned before. He struggles spiritually; he prays; he rouses
himself, but falls again. He finds himself a terrified witness to the death of his own soul, a spiritual

shipwreck, which no human wisdom, not even the Law of God, could have prevented, since it was that Law which brought about the disaster.

"What shall we say then? Is the Law sin? God forbid. Nay, I had not known sin, but by the Law: for I had not known lust, except the Law had said, Thou shalt not covet. But sin, taking occasion by the commandment, wrought in me all manner of concupiscence. For without the Law sin was dead . . . Wherefore the Law is holy, and the commandment holy, and just, and good.. . . Was then that which is good made death unto me? God forbid. But sin, that it might appear sin, working death in me by that which is good; that sin by the commandment might become exceedingly sinful. For we know that the Law is spiritual: but I am carnal, sold under sin. For that which I do I allow not: for what I would, that do I not; but what I hate, that I do" (Romans 7: 7, 8, 12-15). Note the words: "I am carnal, sold under sin. For that which I do I allow not, for what I would, that do I not; but what I hate, that do I." This is precisely the lesson we are to learn. Since we cannot believe the Word which teaches it, we shall have to learn it through sad experience. If the Apostle Peter had as thoroughly believed the Word of Christ concerning his weakness as he learned to know it by experience a few hours later, when he had denied and forsworn his Lord and Savior, he would have escaped the bitter anguish of soul when "he went out and wept bitterly."

Oh, how difficult it is, how many sorry experiences the soul must pass through before it becomes so thoroughly convinced of its own lost and condemned condition that it no longer attempts to save itself, or tries to do something in that direction. As long as a man finds something which he himself must become or something he must do, Christ cannot become his Savior. As long as a man remains under the yoke of the Law, he remains unhelped and unhappy. Until he has worn himself out and staggers under the burden of his sins, gives up all confidence in his own efforts, and falls exhausted before the feet of Jesus, then, and not till then, will his spiritual condition improve.

This blessed despair of one's own powers of conversion would be advanced if he would contemplate his inherent corruption and consider that God looks to the heart, the thoughts, the mind and the desires. If he would consider that no one is regarded of God as pious so long as the good deed is forced by the Law. The chief elements of a human soul— heart, mind and desires—are devoted to sin. He becomes embittered against the compulsion, against the Law, and against God. Not even this embitterment can the Law take away: it rather arouses it.

If all this is rightly considered, a man will soon despair of salvation by the Law. He will condemn himself, give up all effort at fulfilling the Law, and surrender to God's judgment. Then is fulfilled in him the word that says: "Every mouth shall be stopped and the world is become guilty before God."

Conviction, then, is the chief purpose of the Law.

God desires nothing more of the sinner than that he as a lost and condemned sinner permits Him to grant him grace from the fulness of Christ, believing and accepting that which Christ Jesus has wrought for him. Then behold! everything is corrected. All is well. Then is demonstrated the force of the words of Scripture:

"Moreover the Law entered, that the offense might abound. But where sin abounded, grace did much more abound" (Romans 5:20).

"Wherefore the Law was our schoolmaster to bring us unto Christ, that we might be justified by faith" (Galatians 3:24).

"For Christ is the end of the Law unto righteousness to every one that believeth" (Romans 10:4).

"For what the Law could not do, in that it was weak through the flesh, God sending His own Son in the likeness of sinful flesh, and for sin, condemned sin in the flesh" (Romans 8:3).

"Christ hath redeemed us from the curse of the Law, being made a curse for us: for it is written, Cursed is every one that hangeth on a tree" (Galatians 3:13).

———

THE PURPOSE OF THE LAW
(Continued)

THE FIFTH DAY

WE have seen the first and chief end of the Law Besides producing conviction of sin and guilt, the Law also produces this result that ungodly people are held in check from fear of punishment and restrained from disturbing the common peace. Finally, the believers, who are the free children of grace, possess in the Law a faithful guide, a good and reliable chart, a clear vision of the spiritual temple which is building in their hearts by faith and love. But we shall not deal with these functions of the Law at present. Since we have seen the chief purposes of the Law, it is easy to understand what is the right use of the Law and what is the wrong use.

The Law has been given that "every mouth should be stopped and all the world be guilty before God." Yet there are innumerable people within the bounds of Christendom who make the Law their way of salvation, and seek by the Law to be justified and saved. Herein lies the first, the greatest and most common misuse of the Law. From such misuse of God's holy Law, two kinds of unhappy souls proceed: First, the common, vulgar Pharisees, who, while they perform sundry external deeds of the Law, imagine that they are Christians, pious and just. They know, to be sure, that the Pharisees were not Christians. They believe sincerely enough, as the Apostle Paul teaches, that no man can be justified by the deeds of the Law. Their purpose is not to take that way to salvation. What has happened to them may be described as follows: They have been awakened from the vanity of the world to seek their soul's salvation. They have begun the work of conversion. They read the Word of God. They pray. They shun the world. They do that

which is good. All of which is required plainly
enough in the Word of God. They have succeeded
in a measure. For all this they praise God alone
(Luke 17:11), and they have found peace.

These people, who thus have become better by
degrees, who have had the deceptive joy of finding
peace in their own improvement, have arrived at
this spiritual state in the following manner: In the
first place, they were possibly never truly awakened
from their sins. They were only convinced of the
fact that the broad primrose path followed by
worldlings does not lead to life. Therefore, they
have entered upon another way. Soon they come
to believe that since they walk in a different way
from the way of the world, all must be well with
them. They have rid themselves of a number of
ordinary sins and sinful habits. They have adopted
certain Christian customs and ways, but they are unable to comprehend the important consideration that
God looks to the heart, and requires a mind and a
will to do that which pleases Him. Neither did they
understand nor care anything about the necessity of
regeneration. They were satisfied with their artificial betterment and tinsel piety. While at times
they were not quite content with this external godliness, they thought immediately: "The Christians,
too, have their shortcomings; but God is merciful."
They were, as they thought, "not under the Law
but under grace." Furthermore, they had become
accustomed to haggling with the Law. They said:
"No human being can keep this commandment or
that commandment. Surely God will not require

that of us." Thus they arranged their own way of salvation. They placed the goal of their salvation at an attainable height, in order that they might not feel themselves "guilty before God."

If they had only understood that the chief aim of the Law is to produce the knowledge of sin, to create repentance and contrition, they would also have reasoned that, since they have suffered agonies of conscience over this or that particular sin—a knowledge of sin which Cain also had—comforting themselves with this or that good quality, their good will, their good heart, they really had never been under the wrath and the judgment of God.

This is the principal element in a false conversion.

It is impossible to enumerate the various methods and ways by which this false conversion is reached. But the matter may be presented thus: As long as men have not entirely lost the false hope of God's grace; never have realized that they come short of the glory of God in their conversion; never have felt themselves condemned and under the judgment of God, the chief element in a true conversion has been lacking. Dr. Luther says concerning this matter in the first sermon on the Third Day after Easter:

"By true contrition and sorrow for sin, the Scripture does not mean an imaginary notion, which has been called *contritio* and *attritio*, a whole or a half repentance. True contrition grips a soul when the conscience begins to lacerate and oppress it, and when the heart earnestly feels the wrath and judgment of God, not only on account of open and coarse sins, but also on account of the strong inclinations to sin which you feel within yourself; namely, unbelief, contempt of God and disobedience, as Paul says: 'The carnal mind is enmity to God,' with all its lusts and evil desires, wherein you are guilty, and whereby you have deserved the wrath of God, so that in eternity you should be cast away from His presence and burned in the flames of hell.

"This contrition and sorrow for sin does not comprise simply a few evil deeds which one has committed openly against the Ten Commandments, and wherein one makes a distinction in order to find something creditable. Thorough contrition embraces your entire personality, your entire life and character, your entire being. It shows you that you are under the wrath of God, condemned to hell. Even though such contrition may begin with sorrow over one particular sin, as when David was chastened by his conscience for adultery and murder, true contrition covers your whole life and conduct. It casts you to earth as by a bolt of lightning, leaving you utterly under the wrath of God. It says to you: You are a child of hell. Your heart is so terrified that the world becomes too small for you."

The other class of men who make the Law a way of salvation, creating their own righteousness by the deeds of the Law, are these doubting and unhappy souls who realize that something is lacking in their conversion, but who still hope that by persistent prayer and struggle they will win out in time, conquer the evil in themselves and finally appropriate the grace of God in Christ. These people are not so ignorant as to think that they may be justified by the deeds of the Law (by which expression they mean external deeds). They think in their heart: "My heart needs the Lord, needs love, needs sorrow for sin, humility, prayer. Now, behold, these works of mine are the sacrifices which are pleasing to the Lord." By these inner deeds of the Law they seek to become more pleasing to God. They will not have it said that they seek a righteousness which is by the Law. They imagine that their conversion is a true conversion, such as God expressly requires. In this way the contagion of self-righteousness has laid itself upon their soul, and a more serious and painful disease has been the result.

But has not God demanded your inmost being? Has He not demanded of you repentance, contrition and prayer? *Reply*: Has He not also demanded the outward deeds? This is not the question. On the contrary, God in His holy Word above all requires your inmost being. Such is the chief doctrine of the Law, especially of the First Commandment. But the fault lies in this that men seek by external or internal works of the Law to render themselves pleasing to God, to make this betterment their way of salvation. Even though men do not realize this, it is, nevertheless, a fact, since the heart says: "If I could only repent, pray and live rightly; if I were not so indifferent, so hardhearted and lifeless, I should believe that God is merciful to me." Thus the wretched heart struggles after the Lord and His wise purpose with us.

It was God's intention with the requirements of the Law, that you should find that you are guilty before God in your inmost soul. For it is easier to perform the outward deed. But you had hoped to find yourself pleasing to God according to the inner man. This is the reason why you never have found true peace, never have come to a clear relationship with God. You are cast hither and thither, for you are not willing to recognize that all within you is sinful and condemned. You are bent upon winning salvation by your struggles under the Law. By the way of the Law, however, you will never reach the goal. "Every mouth shall be stopped, and all the world shall be guilty before God." Otherwise, Christ will never be your Savior, for He is the Savior of sinners. Otherwise "Christ died in vain" (Galatians 2:21).

THE PURPOSE OF THE LAW
(*Continued*)

THE SIXTH DAY

THERE is still another grievous error in regard to the purpose and power of the Law. Beside those who seek justification by the Law, there are those who strive after perfection by the Law. Frequently an otherwise intelligent Christian, with a pessimistic turn of mind, may be heard to say: "Yes, I know very well that 'no flesh is justified before God by the Law,' but that Christ alone is the 'Lord of righteousness.' I know that we are justified by grace to the uttermost through the redemption which is in Christ Jesus. Nevertheless, the Word of God says expressly: 'But of Him are ye in Christ Jesus, who of God is made unto us wisdom, and righteousness, and sanctification' (1 Corinthians 1: 30), and furthermore that 'without holiness no man shall see the Lord' (Hebrews 12: 14). Wretched sinner that I am, I am never able to apply the Law of God to my heart so that it leads to my sanctification. I am too dull and spiritually sluggish. Oh, that the hammer of the Law might crush my hard heart, so that I might feel the bitterness of sin in all its depth and learn to shun all evil."

This lamentation is nothing but a new form of the deeply rooted delusion concerning the power which we imagine lies in ourselves, if only the Law might call it into activity. What confusion arises in the soul of such a contrite sinner when, simultaneously with this cry of anguish, he calls to mind the truth that Christ is of God made unto us "justification and sanctification" (1 Corinthians 1:30). How unhappy is the soul that imagines itself to possess powers of true conversion, and at the same time complains that the lack of sanctification comes from the lack of the threatening and condemning knowledge of the Law! How unhappy is he who imagines that this knowledge of the Law supplies the deficiency that one need not believe so much in Christ, but rather wallow in greater spiritual agony and sorrow for sin, in order to attain holiness!

Dear friend, will you not note the sacred words of the Scripture and ponder upon them? The Word of God does not say that the Law is made of God unto us for righteousness and sanctification. It says that Christ is our righteousness and sanctification. But Christ is not the same as the Law, with its threatenings and damnations.

That Christ is of God made unto us for sanctification, comes about in this way: Through faith in Him and His righteousness, we are freed from the Law, its judgments, its agonies in our conscience. We have peace with God through the remission of sins. While in this state of faith and spiritual blessedness, we receive a child-heart toward God. We have a joyful desire to so conduct our lives as to be acceptable unto Him. Now I do the good, not because I am driven by the demands, judgments and threatenings of the Law, nor yet by my damning conviction of sin, but because God desires me to do that which is good, and to do it from the free choice and love of God and His will. Thus Christ works through faith in our hearts. For Christ is made of God unto us both righteousness and sanctification. The Law never produces such results. Nor is the Law given for that purpose. Its purpose is to arouse and reveal sin (Romans 7: 7-11). The purpose of the Law is that sin might "abound" (Romans 7:13), that "every mouth should be stopped and all the world become guilty before God" (Romans 3:19). Therefore the Law is called "the ministration of condemnation" (2 Corinthians 3:9), the "yoke of bondage" (Galatians 5:1) and "a schoolmaster to bring us unto Christ" (Galatians 3:24).

Such are the purposes of the Law. That which essentially belongs to our sanctification, the life itself, the desire and strength to do that which is good, the Law can never create in us. Nor has the Law ever promised this effect. That does not come within the scope of the Law, nor does it belong to the "ministration" of the Law; "for if there had been a Law given which could have given life, verily righteousness should have been by the Law" (Galatians 3:21). It is true, I am sorry to say, that there are a species of heroes who deserve to be attacked and crushed in their consciences. These frivolous abusers of the grace of God and the Gospel of Christ, who never worry about their sins and derelictions, but rather trusting in their evangelical liberty, claim and defend the liberty of the flesh, the liberty to live according to the pleasure of the world, are deceived by a dead faith which is never disturbed; but a perverted faith which never accomplishes anything. The heart remains unbroken, secure and self-justified, in the midst of the practise of their favorite sins. The faith of such people overrides the Word of God and gives clear evidence that their faith is a dead faith. What they need is to be aroused and awakened. The Law has not accomplished its work in them. It has not condemned and humbled their hearts.

Furthermore, it is true that believing Christians are also benefited by the Law. The Law renders them large service, but not this service that through the terrors of conscience you are to learn to avoid sin and in this manner arrive at a greater degree of

sanctification. No, that this is the work of the Law,
we never intend to say when we speak of true sanctification. The Law rather increases the inner evil,
as we already have shown. A believer uses the Law
to his own good. As to the manner in which this
takes place, the following considerations should be
noted: The Christian applies the Law best of all
when in his conscience he is most free from the Law,
its judgments, threatenings and terrors. He makes
the best use of the Law when he is sure and happy
in faith and regards the righteousness of Christ as
sufficient. For then his heart is childlike, grateful
and desirous of doing the will of God. He has the
purpose of pleasing God. The Law becomes a well-
beloved guide. It does not drive him nor compel
him. It does not threaten him nor give him the
power to do that which is good, but it serves him
as the plan of a house serves the builder.

In the second place, the believer makes the best
use of the Law in applying it to his daily conduct,
not to the question as to his relationship with God.
Then he says to the Law, as Luther used to express it: "In regard to my life, or how I am to be
and what I am to do, I shall gladly hear and obey
the commandments of the Law. But if you try to
force yourself into my conscience or into my relationship with God, then I will have nothing to do
with you. It is settled beforehand that in the presence of the Law I am thoroughly ashamed and
stand condemned. But in order to stand justified
before God, I have another kind of justification. It
is true, I am bound to do that which is good, and

I am willing and ready to take counsel from you
and follow your directions. I am furthermore an
obstinate creature. I have an obdurate and wicked
heart, disinclined to that which is good. My flesh
is sluggish, constantly warring against the spirit.
Help me against my evil nature. Be a bit and a
scourge to my flesh."

By such use of the Law, a Christian is kept awake
and active. He is constantly poor. He hungers for
the mercy of God. In that condition, he always
needs the Savior. He needs the Gospel. He needs
prayer. He needs the Sacrament of the Lord's Supper. Such is a good and right use of the Law.

It is quite a different thing when a poor soul, disappointed with its own life and humbled regarding
its slow progress in sanctification, groans within itself and thinks: "If only I could lay the Law to my
conscience rightly, if I could only feel the bitterness
of sin, I surely would learn how to guard against
sin."

This is an error in every respect. It is not in this
manner that the Law can be of service to us. If
you had been self-satisfied and carnally secure, the
Law might possibly serve to your humiliation. If
you had been free of the Law and happy in faith
in Christ, the Law might have served as a guide for
your conduct and life and as a warning to keep you
in a humble state of mind. But by its judgments in
your conscience to eradicate sin and advance your
sanctification, your desire to do that which is good
in free and cheerful conformity with the commandments of God, that is a work which the Law can

never perform. The Law does nothing more than to arouse and increase the love of sin. It makes you all the more helpless and sinful.

THE PURPOSE OF THE LAW
(*Continued*)

THE SEVENTH DAY

IT is not faith in Christ which makes you ungodly, but it is the lack of faith, the secret bondage under the Law, "because the Law worketh wrath" (Romans 4:15). The Law causes sin to be aroused. For even though you may have come to faith, the Law will constantly force itself into your conscience. It complains about your shortcomings and derelictions. It makes you depressed and cheerless. It drives faith and peace in Christ out of your heart. Behold! the Law once more holds its own place in your soul and proceeds to awaken and arouse sin within you. Have you not learned by experience when you came to faith—if otherwise you have been set free through faith in Christ—have you not learned by experience that you became a new creature, willing and prepared to do your heavenly Father's will? That you condemned your former sins, and with cheerfulness and alacrity lived the life which formerly had been so difficult and impossible? The same faith still has the same power.

But what, on the other hand, did the Law accomplish when it thundered in your heart? Was not the result that you became more sinful than you ever had been before? Was not the result that "sin took occasion from the commandment" and awakened "concupiscence" in you? Was not the result that "sin abounded?" But the Law has the same power and effect now as then. It will always have this result whenever it is permitted to enter your conscience. It expels your faith, your childlike trust and peace in Christ.

Have you never understood and thought upon the teaching contained in the important narrative which we read in Exodus 19? God gave His holy Law amid "thunders and lightnings while a thick cloud rested upon the mount and the voice of the trumpet was exceedingly loud; and all the people that was in the camp trembled. And Mount Sinai was altogether on a smoke, because the Lord descended upon it in fire," and "the smoke thereof ascended as the smoke of a furnace and the whole mount quaked greatly" (Exodus 19:16, 18). Under such terrifying signs of the zealousness which God had in demanding conformity to His Word, He declared His holy Law. The first and greatest commandment was the following: "Thou shalt have no other gods before me. Thou shalt not make unto thee any graven image or any likeness of anything that is in heaven above, or that is in the earth beneath, or that is in the water under the earth" (Exodus 20: 3, 4). This commandment He repeated, as recorded in verse 23 of the same chapter: "Ye shall not make with me gods of silver, neither shall ye make unto you gods of gold." "And all the people saw the thunderings, and the lightnings, and the noise of the trumpet, and the mountain smoking: and when the people saw it, they removed, and stood afar off" (Exodus 20:18). Now, the people, to be sure, were terrified by the Law, but what do we read in the twentieth chapter of Exodus? Moses had no sooner come down from the mount than he found the people constructing a golden calf and proclaiming it as their god. So little did the Law and the terrors of Mount Sinai suffice to sanctify the heart or even to prevent the breaking forth of sin.

The result presents a constant reminder to all that there never was given a law which could create life. The bitterest sorrow for sin, the most violent outbreakings of sin, are often united with a wretched contrition, moving along after this fashion: We sin, we are terrified. We sin again, and we are again terrified. Once more we commit sin, and again are agonized. We weep and pray, but sin anew. That is the way matters turn out under Mount Sinai. That shows how little the threatenings and the terrors of the Law succeed in coercing the heart to sanctification.

The Law is incompetent to create holiness by its threatenings and terrors. The apostle goes so far as to say that we must be free of the Law in our conscience. Yea, we are to be "dead unto the Law" before we are prepared for sanctification. In Romans 7: 4, he writes: "Wherefore, my brethren, ye also are become dead to the Law by the body of Christ; that ye should be married to another, even to Him who is raised from the dead, that we should bring forth fruit unto God." In chapter 6, verse

14, we read: "For sin shall not have dominion over you: for ye are not under the Law, but under grace." And in Galatians 2:19, we read further: "For I through the Law am dead to the Law, that I might live unto God."

Consider these words well. The apostle says that we are dead to the Law; that is, separated from the Law, in order that we may "bring forth fruit to God," that "we may live unto God," that sin for this reason shall have "no dominion" over us, because "we are not under the Law, but under grace." Consequently, we cannot bear fruit for God and live for God before we are dead to the Law. Who would have thought of such a thing? I should rather reason in this way: If only I could lay the Law upon my conscience, I should live unto God. Here in Romans 7, the apostle says that, first of all, I must be free from the Law as a woman is free from her husband when he is dead (verses 1-4). I must be free from the Law before I can live unto God. He shows in verses 7 and 19 of the same chapter the reason for this condition. As long as the Law with its commands and threatenings holds dominion in the conscience, and not grace, faith and the happy, childlike spirit, sin is only aroused to strength and vitality.

Furthermore, even if I perform a few outward deeds according to the letter of the Law, I am not doing them "unto God." I am not doing them from love to God and the delight in doing His will. But I perform such acts from fear of the commands, threatenings and promises of the Law. Rightly, then, such deeds are not called my acts, but the "deeds of the Law" (Galatians 4:10), because I have to thank the Law for doing them.

All this does not result in sanctification. For unto sanctification is required, first of all, holiness of the heart, its free desire and delight in that which is good. But this delight in doing God's will comes only through faith. In faith I have the exceeding joy of realizing that I am free from the guilt of my sins, and that in Christ I am justified and saved. In a word, I am free from the Law. Christ has also taught us this same truth, when He says: "Abide in me, and I in you. As the branch cannot bear fruit of itself, except it abide in the vine; so neither can ye, except ye abide in me. I am the vine, ye are the branches: He that abideth in me, and I in him, the same bringeth forth much fruit: for without me ye can do nothing" (John 15:4, 5). This, then, is the meaning of that word of Paul which says that "Christ is made of God unto us for righteousness and sanctification."

THE GOSPEL

Behold, I bring you good tidings of great joy (LUKE 2:10). *For what the Law could not do, in that it was weak through the flesh, God, sending His own Son in the likeness of sinful flesh, and for sin, condemned sin in the flesh* (ROMANS 8:3).

THE EIGHTH DAY

HOW glorious is the angel's proclamation: "Behold, I bring you good tidings of great joy: for unto you is born this day a Savior"; and then later: "Glory be to God in the highest, and on earth peace, good will toward men." This is a glorious message, and yet there is many a soul who in the midst of the Christmas joy has had no benefit whatever from the birth of this Wonder-Child. Most regrettable it is, however, when pious, well-meaning souls, who in deep earnestness try to celebrate the birth of their Savior in a worthy manner because they have heard that men should rejoice as little children on the occasion of so important an event, yet go on year by year making these desperate attempts to keep the Festival of Christ's Nativity worthily without ever experiencing what use His birth has been to them or why they ought to rejoice. No sooner is the Christmas sentiment passed, no sooner are the Christmas lights gone out, than their Christmas joy is likewise gone and quite evaporated.

If you but realized what Christ has done for you,

you would keep Christmas the year round and all your life. Yea, throughout eternity you would praise God for the wonder of His grace in sending His only-begotten Son to earth. O that we might try to comprehend what the purpose is in the coming to earth of the Son of God and what service and use I might receive daily from Him. Then, too, we should daily beseech God for the gift of the Holy Ghost.

If, now, He will be merciful and guide our meditation, we shall be greatly blessed. Otherwise we shall go away as poor as we were when we came. The longer we are in this school, the more we shall become convinced of the truth that it depends entirely upon the grace of God whether we shall be enlightened concerning Christ. Otherwise it shall avail us nothing that He is clearly presented to us. He Himself has said: "No man knoweth the Son but by the Father, neither knoweth any man the Father save the Son and he to whomsoever the Son will reveal Him" (Matthew 11:27).

What is God's great purpose in sending His Son to the world? What is the chief errand of the Son of God in thus coming to us? What does He wish to accomplish? Among the many Scripture passages which give answer to these questions, one of the most remarkable is Romans 8:3: "For what the Law could not do, in that it was weak through the flesh, God sending His own Son in the likeness of sinful flesh, and for sin, condemned sin in the flesh."

It is true that we have heard the same message from the Prophet Isaiah in his wonderful Christmas

joy, when he speaks of the "Child" which is born
unto us, the "Son" that is given to us: "They joy before Thee according to the joy of harvest, and as
men rejoice when they divide the spoil. For Thou
hast broken the yoke of his burden, and the staff of
his shoulder, the rod of his oppressor, as in the day
of Midian" (Isaiah 9: 3-4). What is meant by the
expression: "the yoke of his burden" but the Law,
which binds the burden of sin upon our shoulders?
What is "the staff of his shoulder" and "the rod of
the oppressor" but the threatening, smiting and condemning Law, which continually torments the conscience? Therefore the Apostle Paul expressly calls
the Law "the yoke of bondage" (Galatians 5 :1).
The terms: "yoke," "the staff of the shoulder," "the
rod of the oppressor," are all taken from the service of slavery, in which state the poor slaves are
driven by whips and goads to go under the yoke and
drag stones and other heavy loads.

As we have already said: The Spirit of the same
Lord has told us the same truth as that which the
apostle here so emphatically declares. But the words
of the prophet are clothed in figurative language,
and the thought is not so clearly expressed as it is
in this passage by the great apostle. When our false,
artificial peace is shattered and the Ancient Enemy
no longer praises our peace, but rather assails it as
a delusion and a snare, then we become so skeptical
of the promises of God, that He must speak very
distinctly and emphatically in order to make us believe that such is really His meaning—the truth
seems altogether too comforting.

In the second place, the words of the apostle which we are considering give expression to a content so comforting and gripping, that its like is scarcely found anywhere else in the New Testament. Christians with some experience know that the following strange confusion at times comes into our minds: We readily admit that Christ has accomplished all for our salvation; that He "was made under the Law that He might redeem them that were under the Law," and that He has saved us from the curse of the Law in that He became a curse for us. But while we contemplate all this with pious devotion, this consolation crumbles into dust in the twinkling of an eye in the following manner: "All this is true and glorious, but of what help is it to me, since I know in myself that in this or that matter I am not what I ought to be, nor do I do what He would have me do? This or that God has expressly forbidden me to do, but I am unable to rid myself of a certain sin or sinful habit. How can I under these circumstances take to myself any comfort from the words of Christ?"

Against this confusion of thought, our passage from the Apostle Paul is a most powerful antidote. Only read what he says. He says that it is precisely that which the Law could not do that God has done when He sent His Son in the likeness of sinful flesh. Precisely that which yesterday or to-day you thought of with much anxiety as impossible for the Law to perform, is what the Son of God has done for you. He was sent to be the fulfiller of the Law and the bearer of sin for us in every respect, "made of a woman, and made under the Law" (Galatians 4:4). Then you shall find that Christ becomes of great and blessed use to you. Then you shall understand why He is to be our "exceeding great joy."

Is it singular that souls who have such actual use of the Savior rejoice in Him and magnify His name? Is it possible to wish for anything more desirable and blessed? If a soul who knows the misery of its sin should stop to wish, it could wish for nothing better than this: "O that God had given us some one who for us and in our stead would fulfil the Law and suffer the punishment for our sins! O that God had given us some one who by his obedience would procure a perfect righteousness for us, so that God in him might be perfectly satisfied with us and might love us without let or hindrance, even as in the beginning He loved all that He had created, and man in particular, whom He made in His own image! What if God had concluded such a counsel for our salvation? Is it possible that such is in reality the fact?"

Well, the Apostle Paul seems to have thought so, when he wrote these words: "That which the Law could not do, in that it was weak through the flesh, that God has done, in sending His Son in the likeness of sinful flesh." The same wonderful truth seems to lie in the words of Paul where he writes: "For as by one man's obedience many were made sinners, so by the obedience of one shall many be made righteous" (Romans 5:19). Again, the words of Christ read thus: "For their sakes I sanctify myself, that they also might be sanctified through the truth" (John 17:19). "The Son of Man came not to be ministered unto, but to minister, and to give His life a ransom for many" (Matthew 20: 28). O Thou Eternal Love of God, who shall be able rightly to praise Thee? O thou wearisome Darkness of Unbelief, which does not permit us to behold the glory of God!

The chief content of the Gospel is that God has sent His Son to the world to accomplish that which the Law in us could not do. All the prophets testify to this truth. All the prototypes in the Old Testament—persons and ordinances and institutions— testify to the same truth. Hence Saint Paul writes in another connection: "When the fulness of time was come, God sent forth His Son, made of a woman, made under the Law, to redeem them that were under the Law" (Galatians 4:4). And finally: "For Christ is the end of the Law for righteousness to every one that believeth" (Romans 10:4).

THE GOSPEL
(*Continued*)

THE NINTH DAY

LET us now see what the apostle means by saying that the Law was powerless on account of the flesh. Is then the flesh so strong? Is not the flesh weak? Yes, the flesh is strong in that which is evil, and weak in temptations. For this reason the demands of God's Law upon us remain futile and without result. The statement that the Law is powerless on account of the flesh may be readily illustrated as follows: If I desire to have a fine piece of furniture made by an excellent artisan, whose tools also are in excellent condition, but I give him a rotten piece of wood as material, a stick of wood that is full of worm-holes everywhere, all his skill and workmanship will fail, because the material was of such a character that it could not be worked but fell apart in his hands. His workmanship failed on account of the wretched quality of the material.

Even so here. The Law is holy and good. Its commandments are peremptory and its threatenings terrible. Before the will of God, all creation, all the heavenly bodies and all the angelic hosts must bow. But the righteous Law of God is not able to bend or conform man to the will of God. There is in human nature a looseness, an irresponsibility which makes it impossible to say whither our best resolutions will lead us. The material falls to pieces in the hands of the workman. God says concerning the heart of man: "The heart of the sons of men is full of evil" (Ecclesiastes 7: 3). A man may fear, weep, struggle, sweat and pray for power to keep the Law, and yet when the temptation comes, he violates that same Law as flagrantly as if he never had heard of its threatenings. Yes, he may even give way to despair, and still commit the sin. There is nothing to hold him back, as many a bond-servant under the Law plainly shows. He grows desperate from dread of the damnation of the Law, and yet he frivolously continues to sin; he is terrified, and goes on sinning.

Since, then, the Law is incapable of checking the

carnal mind permanently, and of creating a true and lasting repentance, as old and worn-out slaves under the Law demonstrate by the fact that they no longer mourn their sins—they despair and continue in sin— it may be truly said that the material is unfit, and that it crumbles to pieces. That which the Law demands is not to be found in man. It is difficult to give what one does not possess.

"But," you remonstrate, "have we not a free will? Otherwise what is the sense in the commandments, if we lack the power to do what God demands of us?" *Reply*: The term "free will" is a memory-word from the happy days of Paradise before the Fall. Then man had a free will. But since the day when Adam and Eve ate of the forbidden fruit, it has nowhere existed in the human race. Paul says: "I am carnal, sold under sin." Note the word "sold." He who has been sold into slavery has no freedom to do as he pleases. The apostle says even more. Not only is the Law incompetent to make us holy—the apostle even says that the Law increases the sin in our lives, since by the commandment comes the knowledge of sin (Romans 7: 7). The Law arouses man to hostility against God, since he can not be subject to the Law of God (Romans 8: 7).

Consider the result when the Law augments the sin and simultaneously condemns it, augments and forbids, augments sin and damns the sinner—what misery! Thus it comes about that "the Law worketh wrath" (Romans 4: 15). As long as a man does not believe that he is by nature thoroughly corrupt and incapable of fulfilling the Law of God; as long as he imagines that he has the power to keep the Law to perfection, if only he might be terrified into making the right use of his natural abilities —a foolish notion which lies deeply imbedded in all human nature owing to the poisonous seed injected into the heart of man by the Serpent when he said, "Ye shall be like God"—he runs after a will-o'-the-wisp. A man who does not believe that he is utterly lost, the Law being entirely incapable of saving him, finds himself in a wretched and endless struggle, in which many awakened souls are nigh to perishing, while they continue to run after the phantom of law-fulfilment in their own strength. They constantly see before them the vision of what they ought to be. But when they would grasp it, it flees from them, causing them renewed pain and anguish. They will not permit themselves to be told that their delusion is a picture of what we were at one time in the garden of Paradise, and that the perfect holiness of God has been found in no man save in the man Christ Jesus.

The wise and gracious order of God, however, is that the Law is to present before us the perfect holiness of God, in order that we may learn to mourn over that which we have lost and to seek after Him who is what we lack. But the self-righteous man turns this to his own hurt. He believes that he still possesses the power to fulfil God's demands. He struggles and torments himself in the desperate effort until he sinks to defeat and surrenders as a sinner completely lost, ready to receive grace for grace. Such is the strait gate. Only when conscience is "dead to the Law," set free and made blessed in Christ, does the soul begin to take note of the powers of the new-born life to love God and keep His commandments—yet always in proportion to its abiding in this liberated and believing mind.

THE GOSPEL
(*Continued*)

THE TENTH DAY

AS against this flagrant self-righteousness and tormenting disbelief, resulting from the recognition of the deep corruption and depravity of your heart, there would be a fine remedy, if only you could realize what God has provided for just such misery, if only you would ponder the words of the apostle: "God sent His only-begotten Son in the likeness of sinful flesh, and for sin, and condemned sin in the flesh" (Romans 8: 3). Will you not hear, as if for the first time in your life, the great and glorious message: God has sent forth His own Son? Have you ever really considered and believed that God sent His Son to the world? Why should you doubt the truth of the message? If only we could believe that God has given His Son to be our brother and the fulfiller of the Law in our stead, we should scarcely survive for pure joy and wonder. Do you believe that the great God, who in the beginning created the heavens and the earth and all that therein is, and all this for the service of man, His image and heir—do you believe that God has sent His Son to earth to fulfil that which it was impossible for the Law to fulfil? It is an old and trite saying—even the little children know it—and yet, have you ever truly believed it?

He who can easily believe this has never realized what the statement of the apostle contains. Consider that the Son of God, who was with the Father from eternity, even as John declares: "In the beginning was the Word, and the Word was with God, and the Word was God," who created all things—this Word "was made flesh." God became man and dwelt among us. Not as some hold, that God was man from eternity, which they try to prove by the statement that "God made man in His own image." No, John says expressly: "The Word was made flesh." The Holy Spirit declares the same thing in the remarkable words of the Prophet Micah, 5 : 2, where He foretells the town wherein Christ was to be born: "But thou, Bethlehem Ephratah, though thou be little among the thousands of Judah, yet out of thee shall He come forth unto me that is to be ruler in Israel; whose goings forth have been from old, from everlasting." Note the words! He who is "from everlasting" is to "come forth out" of Bethlehem: there He is to be born; there He is to become man.

The historical fact that God in the fulness of time became man is replete with promise for mankind. It proves His thoughts of mercy and His loving purposes for men. Can you believe that this took place for the very purpose that He do for us that

which it was impossible for the Law to accomplish,
and then for one moment trust in your own righteousness? Can you for one moment still remain in
the spirit of bondage? Can you really believe that
God sent His Son to be our Servant, to fulfil the
Law and shed His blood for us and for the guilt of
the world, and still for a moment remain disquieted
in your soul? Do you think that you count more
than the eternal Son of God? Ought not rather all
your sorrows vanish in the presence of this great
revelation? Should not rather all your misgivings
be changed into never-ending praise?

Pray God for an open heart. Pray that He may
drive away the black clouds of unbelief. Then shall
your heart be filled with peace. Devoutly you shall
exclaim: "I surrender to God's wonderful love. It
is true that my unworthiness is great. Even if it
were a thousandfold greater, it reduces itself to
nothing, now that God has sent His Son. Him
only will I praise."

Look further at the words of the apostle: God
sent His Son "in the likeness of sinful flesh," that
is to say, like us in our sinful state. As Moses
fashioned a serpent in the desert, outwardly like
that venomous brood but yet containing no poison
in itself, even thus Christ was to be like our sinful
race, in order that we should discern His purpose in
coming to earth, for whose sake He came. He was
to be "like His brethren in all things, except in sin."

"And condemned sin in the flesh," that is, our
sin, which He had taken upon Himself and made
His own sin, sacrificing it in His own body "on the

tree," and condemning sin in so thorough a manner that sin no more should condemn us. Or, to speak still more plainly: When Christ for us endured the condemnation of sin, He deprived sin of its damning power. There is a marvellous mystery in the term used by the apostle, which nevertheless precisely expresses the relationship. Christ has not removed sin from the world. By His assumption of sin, He has placed all sin under the sentence, that it no longer is effective for our condemnation. As a murderer, condemned to death, no longer counts as a member of society, but even while he lives in prison, awaiting the day of his execution, is dead to society—physical life he still has, so that if anyone comes near enough, he might commit another murder—; but he has no rights; he is nothing more to society than he would be if he were already dead—thus it is with sin. By the sin which Christ bore for us and sacrificed in His body, sin is condemned as being without the power of condemnation. Sin has lost its vote or voice. Sin has no right to condemn those who are in possession of the sacrifice which Christ has made for sin. Sin may still live in our sinful flesh. We experience this fact every day to our sorrow. It is still capable of murdering souls. But this it can accomplish only by separating us from God, not by any inherent power of condemnation. For sin is powerless to condemn those "who are in Christ" (verse 1). "There is therefore now no condemnation to them who are in Christ Jesus." The sin that still dwells in them has lost its damning power by virtue of the atoning death of Christ.

Such is the meaning of the statement of the apostle. For this reason Saint Paul uses this phrase in expounding that which he has said in verse 1, namely: "There is therefore now no condemnation to them who are in Christ Jesus." This is a marvellous statement, full of comfort. How does he explain it? "Christ Jesus hath made me free," he says (verse 2), "from the Law of sin and death" (Romans 8: 2).

THE GOSPEL
(*Continued*)

THE ELEVENTH DAY

"I AM made free from the Law," says the Apostle. How does this come to pass? In the following manner: "For what the Law could not do, in that it was weak through the flesh, God sending His own Son in the likeness of sinful flesh, and for sin, condemned sin in the flesh" (Romans 8: 3). In this Scripture passage the phrase "condemned sin in the flesh" is an explanation of the statement that "there is now no condemnation for them who are in Christ Jesus." For Christ "condemned" sin by the sin which condemned Him.

As the apostle does not say concerning sin that it has been removed from the world or from our flesh, but only that its condemning power has been taken away by the fact that Christ has suffered the condemnation of sin for us and in our stead, so the apostle says concerning the Law, that "Christ hath redeemed us from the curse of the Law, being made a curse for us" (Galatians 3: 13). The Law has not been annulled. It still speaks to us. It declares the will of God. It demands obedience. From its condemnation, however, we are set free. The Law can never condemn those who are in Christ Jesus. Owing to the weakness of faith, we do not always understand this truth. We permit ourselves to be terrorized by the judgments of the Law. But in truth no believer is judged by the Law. For if we still were judged by the Law, the merits of Christ would be of no avail.

In the same manner the Scriptures also speak of death: "O death, where is thy sting?" Death itself is a fact, to be sure, but its frightful sting, its significance as the wages of sin, has been broken. Sin, death and the Law still survive, in the same manner as the murderer sentenced to death. But they have lost their power. Sin in the believer does not count as sin. "There is no condemnation to them that are in Christ Jesus." The condemnation of the Law is as if it did not exist. It is able to frighten us and threaten us, but it is not permitted to condemn us. Death is able to lay the body in the earth, but it is unable to keep it there. Like a faithful servant, death only helps us to a good rest.

The important thing is that we be well-grounded in the Word of God and true believers in Christ. Then we shall not allow ourselves to become confused, as we note that sin still lives, the Law still threatens, and death still assaults us. The vital thing is to remember what Christ has done in taking our sin upon

Himself and condemning our sin in His own body, in becoming a curse for our sakes, in redeeming us from the condemnation of the Law, and in rendering death harmless by His death.

All this has been accomplished by Christ's great victory over sin, death, devil and hell, for which reason the apostle defies these tyrants of humanity and exclaims: "O death, where is thy sting? O grave, where is thy victory? The sting of death is sin; the strength of sin is the Law. But thanks be to God, which giveth us the victory through our Lord Jesus Christ" (1 Corinthians 15: 55-57). Luther says that as the Jews defied Christ, when He had been nailed to the cross, and shouted: "If Thou be the Son of God, come down from the cross" (Matthew 27: 40), so should we now to the glory of Christ defy everything that would terrify us and say: "Thou wicked devil, thou dost still live in my flesh, it is true; but thou shalt not condemn me. That power has been taken from thee, since Christ has condemned sin in His flesh. Thou holy, terrifying Law, thou hast with good right punished me. I am a sinner. But thy condemnation shall not condemn me. He who redeemed me from the curse of the Law by becoming a curse for me, forbids thee from condemning me to death. Thou death, who art always trying to frighten my foolish heart, thou shalt lay my body in the dust, I admit; but thou shalt do me no harm whatever. On the contrary, thou shalt do me a great service. For even though my ignorant flesh doth not love thee, thou art nevertheless a blessing to me, because thou dost bring me rest.

For I know and believe in Him who has said: 'I am the resurrection and the life. He that believeth in me, though he were dead, yet shall he live' (John 11: 25). The Lord of life and death can not lie. He has not shed His blood to secure for us only a material good. Thou grave and thou hell, where is now your victory? Thanks be to God which giveth us the victory through our Lord Jesus Christ."

Behold here a gleam of the inexpressible boon which we may have in this Savior, concerning whose birth the angel announced: "Behold, I bring you good tidings of great joy." O that we might daily make use of this blessed truth in all the perplexities which come from the fact that the Law grants no strength to fulfil that which it requires; that sin still lives and rages in the flesh, and that conscience therefore continues to condemn us. When temptations to unbelief would undermine our faith, we should learn to come before God and say: I know that sin still lives and that it has not been removed from the world. But sin is under condemnation. It is as if it were dead. It is as if it did not exist. It can not condemn me before God. Even if I do not always remember this, such is nevertheless the fact. For God knows how to evaluate that which His only-begotten Son has accomplished by His innocent suffering and death. Precisely that which the Law could not do, God has done in the sending of His Son to earth.

If now, for instance, I were so wearied and callous to-day that I am unable to dwell upon the Word of God, that I have no delight in the Word, no taste for it, but feel myself like a dead tree, does it follow that what Christ has done is not true and is of no validity? "But what good does the work of Christ do me," you ask, "since I am so torpid and do not feel the life of faith in me?" You do not "feel" your faith? What do you mean? Do you suppose that our changeable feelings have the power to overthrow the state of grace in which we are through faith in Christ? Shall our defective feelings and varying emotions annihilate Christ and bring His work to naught?

It is by just such side considerations that you hinder the life of faith in your heart. If, rather, you thought and pondered more upon these great and comforting truths, your faith would revive and be restored to strength and vigor. The fact remains unmovable, that what was impossible for the Law, God has done by the sending to earth of His Son. I am, for example, disinclined to prayer and defer my prayers to a later season. Does that imply that the merits of Christ are rendered of no avail for me? Am I not still in the same grace with God? Or is the Lord Christ only a partial and an imperfect Savior, so that my reconciliation with God depends in some degree upon what I may do? May God defend us from robbing the Savior of His honor by such imaginary cooperation with Him!

Since Christ "in the days of His flesh has offered up prayers and supplications with strong crying and tears" (Hebrews 5: 7), I shall not even with my prayers attempt to complete my redemption. Rather than that, I would never pray at all. No one but "the Lamb slain from the foundation of the world" (Revelation 13: 8), is worthy of glory and honor. In thus having all things in Christ, I, too, shall begin to pray, and to pray in faith. In this way I shall, in all possible wretchedness, possess the comfort and joy, that Christ has accomplished that which I could not do, and performed that which was impossible for me to do by the Law. I am unable rightly to love God. My heart is cold and hard. This is what the Law castigates in me. But exactly this fulfilment of the Law, which I never could attain, is what God has done in sending His own Son. I am unable rightly to mourn my sins. This also Christ has done for me, when He sweat "great drops of blood" in the garden. Shall not Christ be my only comfort? Or must my love, my holiness, my contrition and my prayers work together meritoriously with the merits of Christ to bring about my redemption?

If to-day I realize my lack of all this, if I feel that there is much of sin and much of deficiency in my contrition and prayers, is therefore my acceptance to grace with God to be shaken? In that case, what would be the value of faith and justification by faith? No, I will go on praising Christ. When this becomes a really strong faith in my heart, I can not do otherwise than love Him, who has done me this inestimable service of bearing the guilt and penalty of my sin, whereby I have come into possession of God's abiding grace. Then I shall love God's holy will. Then I repent, hate and curse all sin, because sin displeases God. Then my life shall harmonize with the song of the angelic host on the morn of Christ's nativity: God receives all the glory, on earth there will be peace, and goodwill toward men. Amen.

"HE IS FAITHFUL AND JUST TO FORGIVE US OUR SINS"

(1 John 1:9)

Not as though I had already attained (Philippians 3: 12).

THE TWELFTH DAY

WHEN the aged hero of faith, our Church Father Luther, had gone gray in the service of the Lord, in the study of God's Word, in prayer, in writing and sermonizing, upon all matters of faith, he said: "Through much practice I have now arrived at the point, thanks be to God, that I almost begin to believe that God is the Creator of heaven and earth." A remarkable utterance! Is the old church father so weak in the faith? "I almost begin to believe that God is the Creator of heaven and earth." Why, children at seven years of age believe that. That is something which belongs to the ABC's of faith.

But what shall be said of Luther, when the great Apostle Paul, the greatest preacher of faith the world has ever seen, confesses that he had not yet learned the art of faith? For he says: "I follow after," "I reach forth," "I press toward the mark," "that I may apprehend that for which also I am apprehended of Christ Jesus"—that is, the grace of God in Christ. But "the man after God's heart" explains the mystery. "In my prosperity I said: I shall never be moved; but when Thou didst hide Thy face, and I was troubled, I cried unto Thee, O Lord; and unto the Lord I made supplication." See, here is the point. Paul and Luther are not speaking of the easy faith of assent, which comes of itself in our days of prosperity and success. But they speak of that faith which is a great reality in the soul, that faith which develops into a power in the time of tribulation, a mighty struggling principle of life.

It is an easy matter to believe when there are no trials and temptations. When Luther, however, speaks about his faith in the Creator, he means a faith by which he, alone and undefended, might dare engage in battle with a world of enemies; might dare, for instance, to enter the great court room at Worms, dare to face the emperor and the wrathful Duke George, and all the secular and spiritual princes, through whom the entire power of the devil and the pope sought to compass his death. When external support no longer was of any avail, and he must comfort himself with the protection of God Almighty alone, then it was for him earnestly to believe that God is the Creator of heaven and earth and that He has the power over all created things, and that not a hair falls from the head of any one of us but by His sovereign will. Concerning such a faith it is that Luther speaks.

After the same manner, faith in Christ and the grace of God in Christ are to serve us. When all is well, when the heart is spiritually-minded, strengthened by the Word and by prayer, when one's life corresponds in some measure with one's profession, then one may believe as much as one desires (if such faith deserves to be called faith). But when one is in spiritual darkness; when the heart is ungodly; when sin and distress overwhelm the soul like a mighty flood, and God appears before the soul as a holy and righteous judge, then are we called upon truly to believe. In such circumstances it will develop whether we have a sure anchorage for our soul.

They whose Christianity consists merely in a Christian philosophy of life have soon exhausted the subject. Many of us might thus readily learn the science of faith. But they who need faith as a fighting force against the cares and trials of life possess not one whit more than they sorely need even after they have grown gray in the practice of it. We have made reference to the faith-hero Martin Luther. Another man of God, known for his joyous faith, Christian Scriver, begins a fine sermon with these very words of Luther and thereby shows that neither he had attained to more in the way of faith.

What is in reality the quality of the faith of such Christians as thus speedily have learned all about the Gospel and believe so easily, since we see that the heroes of faith are so weak? We are not speaking of the common crowd and their easy faith. We refer to the many pious souls who marvel at these weak, static Christians who constantly need to hear and ponder the Word of grace and faith, while they themselves have had more than enough of it. They have the same taste for the Gospel as Israel had for the manna, which they called "this light bread" —their souls "loathed" it (Numbers 21:5).

Others again talk a great deal about faith and the Gospel, but reveal the suspicious trait that they are always strong and unafraid, always able to believe as much as they want to believe. They speak of faith as if faith were a matter of our own strength and creation. What does such language demonstrate? Occasionally such sentiments may be heard upon the lips of the true Christian. But if your entire life is characterized by that sort of bombast, you certainly ought to understand that your faith is not the right faith and that you are not living under the correction and discipline of the Holy Ghost. For in that case the Spirit of God would so assault the depravity of your heart that you would find it exceedingly difficult to believe the forgiveness of your sins and your state of childhood with God. You would have the same experience as the greatest saints have had. You have a faith and a Christianity which the devil does not attack or disturb. He leaves you in your fatal delusion.

It is really this spurious faith which Luther in burning zeal would expose in speaking thus drastically concerning the weakness of his own faith; for to the words of Luther which we have cited, he adds the following: "This matter of faith has at all times been too easily understood and believed by everybody, excepting by me and certain poor sinners, such as Moses, David, Isaiah and others, who scarcely have begun to believe. An old disciple and superannuated doctor of theology like myself only wonders that people who barely have turned the leaves in a book know as much as the Holy Ghost knows."

Luther in other places warns against the same delusion especially in connection with faith in the forgiveness of sin and the friendship of God: "This matter of faith," he writes, "is the most difficult science on earth; but it has the wretched feature that nothing seems easier to learn. For as soon as one has read or heard a little about faith, he regards himself a graduate from the school of faith, and now desires to hear something new and better." Again he says: "I therefore admonish all who would be Christians, whether they be teachers or auditors, that they above all else beware of this harmful delusion. They should know that in the matter of faith they must remain humble disciples as long as they live. Even if they have the true faith, they may a thousand times lose their courage in the warfare against the world, the flesh and the devil." This is the first topic in our meditation.

The second matter, which also is of great moment, is that we need faith and the Gospel in the evil day, in dark and troubled times. Faith is a firm confidence in the words of Almighty God when life is most complicated and desperate. In times of weakness and spiritual distress, when we see our sins, on account of which we deserve to be condemned and are near to desperation; or in times of spiritual darkness and dullness, when we feel nothing and seem spiritually dead, then to overcome all discouraging contradictions and to believe in the grace and love of God, solely and only on the foundation of the redemption wrought by Christ and His faithful promises—this is the true, living faith. Faith is to believe that God became man; that He alone is our righteousness, so that while I "cry for sorrow of heart and howl for vexation of spirit" on account of my sin and unfaithfulness, I nevertheless believingly hear God say to me: "Behold, I this day cleanse you from all your iniquities and blot out all your transgressions" (Ezekiel 36:33). Such faith is true faith. But this faith is not common property. Faith is a most difficult science. Happy is the man who at such times of tribulation can say with Luther that he "almost believes"; that he almost believes that the Son of God was born "in the flesh"; that "Christ is my only righteousness"; "I almost believe that the Son of God has shed His blood for me, and His blood counts for more than my sins." But to believe and hold fast to the Word of God in the times when everything in me, my conscience, my reason and my feelings, exclaim: "No, no. It is impossible that I am a child of God, unworthy as I am"—that is faith.

In order to attain to such faith, it is necessary that we constantly make progress in the doctrine and knowledge of the Gospel. Year by year we must read, hear, study and meditate upon the Word of God, as long as we live on earth and until the final struggle is ended. Therefore the apostle says: "To write the same thing to me indeed is not grievous, but for you it is safe" (Philippians 3:1). It is also in such times of the trial of faith, when our sins threaten to quench our trust in the mercy of God, that the glorious Scripture passage will serve us, which we now proceed to consider.

"HE IS FAITHFUL AND JUST TO FORGIVE US OUR SINS"
(*Continued*)

> *If we confess our sins, He is faithful and just to forgive us our sins, and to cleanse us from all unrighteousness* (1 JOHN 1: 9).

THE THIRTEENTH DAY

IS not this a short summary of the whole doctrine of the Scriptures concerning the acceptance of a poor sinner by God? Both with express words and with innumerable examples God has from the beginning of the world explained that the children of Adam are in this way to come to the grace of God. Let us therefore meditate upon these words of the Beloved Apostle. He says: "If we confess our sins". We understand readily from the context what is meant by the term "the confession of sin." The apostle has in the preceding verses spoken of them who "walk in darkness," who say that they "have no sin," but who "deceive" themselves (1 John 1:6-8). By way of contrast he adds: "But if we confess our sins, He is faithful and just to forgive us our sins and to cleanse us from all unrighteousness."

In the first place, we learn from the passage cited that the apostle is not speaking of an external, accidental or prescribed confession, but rather of the confession made by a poor, troubled sinner. A distinction must be made, however, between contrition and contrition. There are many who confess their sins with a certain kind of contrition, who yet continue in sin. We find this contrition in King Saul, who made this confession: "I have sinned: for I have transgressed the commandments of the Lord, and Thy words" (1 Samuel 15:24). But he never gained reconciliation and peace with God. Furthermore, King Pharaoh, who said: "I have sinned against the Lord your God and against you" (Exodus 10:16). But his confession was impelled by the fact that the Eighth Plague was already terrifying him. It was not actuated by a contrite heart and a repentant purpose to become reconciled with the God of Israel. Even Cain confessed: "My iniquity is greater than may be forgiven" (Genesis 4: 13); but he went away "from the presence of the Lord" and did not seek His forgiving grace. Judas exclaimed in the bitterness of his soul: "I have sinned in that I have betrayed innocent blood" (Matthew 27:4).

From all these examples we see that a true confession of sin can result only from a complete conversion produced by the Holy Spirit in the heart. Sin, as a crime against God, then causes sorrow and compels the heart to pour out its anguish before God, confess the sin and pray for forgiveness. Many an impenitent slave of sin may at times confess his sins with bitter regret. But he confesses from sheer dread of the consequences of his sin. It is not sin itself as a crime against God that worries him. Neither has he any special desire to be wholly reconciled and united with God. The thing that troubles him is nothing more than an incidental taste of the bitter fruit of sin. Therefore he remains a slave of sin.

A true confession of sin presupposes first of all the awakening of the conscience by the voice of God and the realization that sin has brought the soul under the condemnation of God. Then, secondly, true confession premises that the sinner, thanks to the gracious call of God and the power of the Gospel, has some hope of compassion and therefore throws himself before the Mercy-seat and begs forgiveness. He who knows nothing of grace, but only of sin and damnation, will never come to God. As a prime condition of confession, a spark of faith is essential. As long as Adam and Eve knew nothing but their sin and the penalty, they fled from the face of the Lord. Thus it was for a time with King David. He kept away from God and would not confess his sin. "When I kept silence," he says, "my bones waxed old through my roaring all the day long. For day and night Thy hand was heavy upon me: my moisture is turned into the drought of

summer." But then he continues: "I said, I will confess my transgressions unto the Lord, and Thou
forgavest the iniquity of my sin" (Psalm 32: 3-5).

He who would learn what a true knowledge of
sin is, as also a true confession of sin, let him consider the Fifty-first Psalm. We would note two elements only in this outpouring of David's heart. Although King David by his notorious sin had caused
great offense to the people, and had committed a
grievous sin particularly against Uriah, God and his
sin seem uppermost in his mind, and he, as it were,
passes by his sin against men and says to the Lord:
"Against Thee, Thee only have I sinned and done
this evil in Thy sight" (Psalm 51:4). There you
have the picture of a truly contrite heart.

Then again it is not the coarse outbreakings of
sin alone which distress him. He sees with sorrow the evil in his very nature and goes to the deepest root of it, when he says: "Behold, I was shapen
in iniquity, and in sin did my mother conceive me"
(Psalm 51: 5). The most important thing is to recognize the evil in our nature and the deep depravity
of our essential being. As long as men look only to
the individual outbreaks of sin, and not to the sinfulness of the heart, it is always possible to construct
some false consolation. They never feel that they
are lost and condemned sinners. Consequently they
are never made free and happy in Christ. It is
therefore the most vital element in a true knowledge
of sin, that we recognize the deep depravity of the
heart, the shameless contempt of God, the carnal
security, unbelief, obduracy and hypocrisy, in order

that our knowledge of sin may articulate with God's own description of the heart as "deceitful above all things, and desperately wicked."

Look now and see if this is not precisely the thing that troubles the weak and trembling souls who constantly complain in this wise: "My heart is desperately wicked. It is hard, cold, hypocritical, deceitful, false, unstable, frivolous and inclined to evil, yea, even diabolical." Then you know your heart is as God portrays it. Does it now seem to you that the judgment of God's Word concerning your heart is too drastic? On the contrary, you will find no condemnation that is too strong to fit the case.

"But I do not know my sin," you say. "I am secure, hard-hearted, frivolous and hypocritical." *Reply*: It is a great wickedness to be thus carnally secure, hypocritical and worldly-minded. That spirit is the fountain of all sin. It is the natural depravity of the heart itself which you thereby recognize. Such acknowledgment is necessary. You have arrived at the stage where you sit in judgment upon yourself out of a clear conviction. You believe from a full heart that you are the meanest and most unworthy of God's creatures.

"Well, but it is true that I have not a broken, contrite and humbled heart. I am, as a matter of fact, worldly-minded, vain, obdurate and frivolous." *Reply*: It is indeed true that such are the characteristics of the natural mind. You must recognize this depravity. It must become a frightful reality to you.

They, however, who confess their unhappy state of sinfulness, should comfort themselves with the blessed assurance given in the Scripture under consideration: "God is faithful and just to forgive us our sins, and to cleanse us from all unrighteousness" (1 John 1:9). Know, then, that the Law can do no more than make you wretchedly conscious of your sins, that "sin might become exceeding sinful" (Romans 7:13). God desires only to impart to you the riches of His grace.

The resistance of your mind is now broken. You admit the justice of God's judgments. You no longer shun the light. You condemn yourself. You would be glad to accept Christ if only you dared. Hear what this same apostle says in another connection: "As many as received Him, to them gave He power to become the sons of God, even to them that believe on His name" (John 1:12). Who are fit recipients of grace and forgiveness if not these wretched souls who condemn themselves?

Untamed human nature defends itself. It rouses itself against the judgments of God and becomes embittered. But he who condemns himself is open to the grace of God. To such all mercy is shown and declared. We should realize that the punishments referred to in the Scriptures, the judgments and penalties, are not addressed to those who condemn themselves and long for grace and reconciliation with God through the Savior. They are aimed at the arrogant despisers and contemners, who either openly resist the Spirit and the Word of God or as hypocrites go about with Judas Ishkarioth among the disciples of Jesus, cherishing some pet sin, which they refuse to give up, and even defending it.

"If we confess our sins, He is faithful and just to forgive us our sins." Though you be not born again, and possess not the power of faith and a renewed life, but permit yourself to be admonished and led by the Word of God, and even condemn yourself as a violator of the Law of God, then are you already an object of all the grace and comfort of God. But hear and believe this blessed truth, in order that you may not lose yourself in unbelief. Come confidently to the Mercy-seat and confess to God all your sins and weaknesses, and you shall be born again of God and justified, even though you may not instantly feel the great rebirth of your heart.

"HE IS FAITHFUL AND JUST TO FORGIVE US OUR SINS"
(*Continued*)

THE FOURTEENTH DAY

CONSIDER, friend, what the apostle says: "God is faithful and just to forgive us our sins, and to cleanse us from all unrighteousness" (1 John 1: 9). It is easy enough to understand that God is "faithful," that He cannot go back on His word and promise, that everything that He promises will surely come to pass. It is easy to comprehend that God makes no distinction between persons, as we do; but that every one without any exception is equally welcome with all others, and receives the same grace. "If we believe not, yet He abideth faithful: He cannot deny Himself" (2 Timothy 2:13).

But that word "just, to forgive us our sins"—
that is a strange term. There surely seems to be a
sharp contradiction between the two words "just"
and "faithful." What is the meaning? Research
has been made to find out if the word "just" might
not be translated by some other term. First and
last, though, the original Greek word means "just."
How, then, are we to understand it? Note once
more how far our thoughts are from the glorious
relationship that God has revealed to us. The apostles believed that which had been declared to them.
Therefore they spake. For this reason the Apostle
John in the second verse of the following chapter
writes: "If any man sin, we have an Advocate with
the Father, Jesus Christ, the righteous. And He is
the propitiation for our sins, and not for ours only,
but also for the sins of the whole world" (1 John 2:
1-2). Thus John also thought when he wrote:
"God is faithful and just to forgive us our sins."
For no matter how we twist and turn this passage,
there is no other meaning to be gotten out of it than
this glorious one that God forgives sin on the basis
of the satisfaction of justice rendered by the fulfilling of the Law by Christ.

It is a great fact, as the Scriptures from the beginning attest, that God has given His Son as a ransom for our sins; that "the Lord hath laid all our
sins upon Him"; and that Christ is the Redeemer,
"whom God hath set forth to be a propitiation
through faith in His blood to declare His righteousness for the remission of sins that are past, through
the forbearance of God, to declare, I say, at this time

His righteousness: that He might be just, and the justifier of him which believeth in Jesus" (Romans 3:25-26). "And you," says the Apostle Paul, "being dead in your sins, hath He quickened together with Him, having forgiven you all trespasses, blotting out the handwriting of ordinances that was against us, which was contrary to us, and took it out of the way, nailing it to His cross" (Colossians 2:13-14). God, then, is just, since He does not demand that the same debt be paid twice. When we come to Him and confess our sins, He gives us that which is purchased so dearly—the entire forgiveness of all our sins.

Not only are we, as it were, forced to see this meaning in the cited passage from the Apostle John, but another apostle has spoken expressly about this matter. At Romans 3:25 we read that "God hath set forth Christ to be a propitiation through faith in His blood, to declare His righteousness for the remission of sins." The sense of this passage is, that if God had forgiven sin without having made Christ the sacrifice for sin, God would not have been just, since divine justice demanded that sin be punished. But now God has set His Son to be the propitiation for sin, to show His justice in forgiving our sins through faith in the satisfaction wrought by Christ. All men and angels, even our accuser Satan himself, are to know that the remission of sins does not come about by some accident, but upon an absolutely legal basis, both law and justice having been perfectly satisfied.

O that we might become well enlightened in the

great truth, that our acceptance with God is founded upon a perfectly legal ground, that both law and justice are completely satisfied. O that we might be well informed of the fact that our acceptance with God is based upon a perfectly legal act, which in the Scriptures is thus defined: "If one died for all, then were all dead" (2 Corinthians 5:14); and, "He who knew no sin, Him hath God made to be sin for us, that we might be made the righteousness of God in Him" (2 Corinthians 3:9). Since now all things are accomplished for us, and we present ourselves at the Throne of Grace and accept the atonement rendered by Christ, then justice requires that our sins no longer stand against us. They are no longer laid to our account. How should we dare to be safe and happy in the grace of God if grace were not founded upon justice? Otherwise I should always fear that God might weary of the constant forgiveness of my constant depravity.

But thanks be to God! He is fully satisfied with the atonement which is forever valid. Everything is based upon law and justice. We have grace and righteousness in Christ. Our salvation is founded upon a complete satisfaction of the indebtedness— a full ransom has been paid. God has accepted the purchase-price. God is just. He does not keep both the purchase-money and the ransomed prisoner. The prisoner goes scot-free. As Luther says: "When God seems angry, as though He were about to drive you from His presence, then say: Gracious God, then Thou must first reject the purchase-price, Thy beloved Son; but Him Thou wilt not reject."

What grace! What glory! Very well, all ye that are athirst, come to the waters. Come and buy, without money and without price, both wine and milk. If so be that you are in the first throes of repentance, or if you are an old Christian, fallen into sin and misery: Confess, as King David, all your wretchedness. God is faithful and just. He will forgive your sins. You still have a great privilege open to you, a privilege which is eternally valid. God is faithful, remember. His words are everlasting. His covenant of peace remains immovable, more fixed than the mountain-pillars. Not a jot or tittle of God's Word shall fail you. Do you imagine that there is anything uncertain or unreliable in the promises of God? Do you suppose that He deceives miserable sinners? Do you think that He gives them the most precious promises and then when they come to Him, trusting in His Word, that He turns aside from them and refuses to keep His promises? You know that He is faithful.

What has God said concerning sinners? He has said: "Ye have sold yourselves for nought, and ye shall be redeemed without money" (Isaiah 52:3). He has said: "Confess your iniquities, O sinner. Come, let us reason together. Though your sins be as scarlet, they shall be white as snow. Though they be red like crimson, they shall be as wool" (Isaiah 1:18). Christ says: "And the publican, standing afar off, would not lift up so much as his eyes unto heaven, but smote upon his breast, saying, God be merciful to me a sinner. I tell you, this man went down to his house justified rather than the other" (Luke 18:13). Thus Christ speaks of the prodigal son. Note that this is His portrayal of every lost sinner: "When he was yet a great way off, his father saw him, and had compassion, and ran, and fell on his neck, and kissed him", and hark ye, "put on him the best robe" (Luke 15:20-22). So says the Lord Himself.

Now, then, is not this message trustworthy and reliable? Or would the Savior of the world say, "Come unto me," and then when you come upon His invitation, shall He refuse you the word of welcome and the kiss of love? Never. "God is faithful and just, to forgive us our sins, and to cleanse us from all unrighteousness." Amen.

THE LAW, CONVERSION, AND THE RIGHTEOUSNESS THAT AVAILS BEFORE GOD

THE FIFTEENTH DAY

IT is most deplorable and cause for tears that awakened souls, who strive to enter through the strait gate (Luke 18: 25), shall not be able to enter, for the simple reason that they have been led astray by the misleadings of their own heart, or by immature teachers and books. True conversion, the thorough and comprehensive work of the Law in the sinner's heart, is so necessary that without it every spiritual effort is utterly in vain. All faith,

all godliness, yea, Christ and His merits, are useless to that soul. He who only knows his concrete
sins in thought, words and deeds, who only regards
them, labors and wars on them, without realizing
the demands of the Law upon the heart, and without sinking into the mire of spiritual distress on account of his sinful nature, goes through an abbre-
viated hypocrite-conversion. He is converted, it is
true, but converted from unchecked worldliness to
self-righteousness, making of himself a first-class
Pharisee.

Even he who feels his evil nature, the corruption
and depravity of his heart, but takes refuge in
watchfulness, prayer, self-denial and godliness, not
losing confidence in the validity of his own righteousness by these methods, but hoping for victory
by these practises and looking to them for comfort
—he is in the same case. If he does not come to
Christ while he is yet in this spiritual misery, while
he has not yet attained the hoped-for victory, he will
never become a true Christian. He will either develop into a deluded work-saint, finding consolation in his pseudo-conversion and holiness or he will
become a worn-out slave, who gives up in despair,
sinking into a state of carnal security and indifference. We do not here speak of those who deliberately practise certain pet sins. We speak of those
who try to pass through the strait gate of repentance
but "are not able."

The fault with all these people is that they will
not heed instruction. Or they may not have been

told what true conversion is, what the real work of the Law is, what is its real purpose and intention. O that men would heed the Word of God; for example, the following Scripture passages, and take them to heart, so that their own opinions or the opinions of work-righteous saints may not divert them from the truth of God. Hear then what the Scriptures expressly teach:

"Now we know that what things soever the Law saith, it saith to them who are under the Law: that every mouth may be stopped, and all the world may become guilty before God" (Romans 3:19).

"Moreover the Law entered, that the offense might abound. But where sin abounded, grace did much more abound" (Romans 5:20).

"What shall we say then? Is the Law sin? God forbid. Nay, I had not known sin, but by the Law: for I had not known lust, except the Law had said, Thou shalt not covet. But sin, taking occasion by the commandment, wrought in me all manner of concupiscence. For without the Law sin was dead. For I was alive without the Law once: but when the commandment came sin revived, and I died. And the commandment, which was ordained to life, I found to be unto death" (Romans 7:7-10).

"Sin, that it might appear sin, working death in me by that which is good; that sin by the commandment might become exceeding sinful" (Romans 7: 13).

Note carefully the words. At Romans 3:13 we hear that the purpose of the Law is that "every mouth may be stopped, and all the world may be-

come guilty before God." The world is not to become pure and holy, but guilty. The reason why the
Law has no other aim and effect is given in verse
20: "Therefore by the deeds of the Law shall no
flesh be justified in His sight: for by the Law is the
knowledge of sin" (Romans 7:20). In chapter 5
we read that "the Law entered, that the offense
might abound"—"abound," not be overcome.
Where sin becomes abundant, grace becomes the
more abundant. In chapter 7 we read that this
abounding is not only that of the knowledge of sin
and the sorrow for sin, but that sin, sin itself,
abounded by the commandment. For we read that
sin took occasion by the commandment and wrought
in me all manner of concupiscence, that sin by that
which is good works death in me, in order that sin
might become exceeding sinful by the commandment. Yea, in the same chapter 7 we read, verses
4-6, that we must "become dead to the Law," if
we would "bring forth fruit unto God." We must
become dead to the Law "by the body of Christ,"
which is the sacrifice for sin, that we may serve God
in the new life.

So speak the Scriptures of the work of the Law
in conversion. Luther says on this topic: "What,
then, is the effect of the Law? By reason of the
depravity of our nature the Law becomes the occasion for sin, yea, it is the strength of sin, says the
Apostle Paul. It works wrath. It does not make
the heart godly, as the Papists chatter and as the
worldly-minded pretend. Externally it may hinder
the hand, but that only creates hypocrites before

God. But in the heart it produces such havoc that a man is not only not made godly, but he becomes worse than he was formerly."

The Law must perform this natural work in your heart if your conversion is to be a genuine conversion. You are not to become more pious and holy by the Law—that you are to become through another, who will baptize you with the Spirit and with fire. But by the Law you shall learn that you are guilty, sinful, "exceeding sinful." Otherwise you shall not rightly know the need of accepting Christ unto the creation of a new life in your heart. "If there had been a law given which could have given life, verily righteousness should have been by the Law" (Galatians 3:21). Then were "Christ dead in vain" (Galatians 2:21).

The Law will do its perfect work if only it gets into the heart. But if it merely reforms your external conduct, you may become godly in your own works and notions, to be sure; but that is the righteousness of the Pharisees. Such a self-righteous Pharisee was Saul of Tarsus before the "commandment" came, and the spiritual requirements of the Law had penetrated into his heart. Such are numerous religious persons in our day, who use the Law with the idea that by observing its outward prescriptions they will become godlier and better. They only need to go about the business in all earnestness and with a firm purpose to succeed, to continue courageously, and fight on in prayer and hope.

Genuine conversion goes far deeper. It stirs up the wickedness of the heart to resistance. It does not make me better and better. It makes me sinful, "exceeding sinful by the commandment." I become ashamed of myself and of all my self-righteous undertakings. I think very poorly of myself and of my conversion. I find no comfort in myself and my work-righteousness.

THE LAW, CONVERSION, AND THE RIGHTEOUSNESS THAT AVAILS BEFORE GOD
(*Continued*)

THE SIXTEENTH DAY

WILL you please note that when Christ began His public ministry, His very first service was to explain the spiritual character of the Law, showing that no human being can fulfil the Law of God (Matthew 5:21-28)? When a certain individual thought that he had kept the Law, Christ was not satisfied as to the correctness of the young man's claims. Christ instantly gave him a commandment which proved too onerous to him: "If thou wilt be perfect, go and sell that thou hast, and give to the poor, and thou shalt have treasure in heaven: and come and follow me." Christ did not help the young man to find comfort in his godliness. When therefore a person says that he is going to repent, and become righteous and holy, he should be told: Yes, when you realize that you are a sinner and an ungodly person; when you have learned that you are a lost and condemned sinner, naturally depraved and wicked, you are in a position to believe on Him who "justifieth the ungodly" (Romans 4:5). In this way only may you be saved.

Here let me quote a remarkable statement from Luther. Commenting upon the Fifth Psalm of David, he says: "It is an absolute certainty that he who would become righteous and godly must first become a sinner and an unrighteous person. He who would be healed, must first become ill. He who would become godly and righteous must first become unrighteous, unholy, foolish, depraved, devilish, a heretic, an unbeliever, a Turk. In other words, he must recognize that by nature he has a heart as despicable, as unfaithful, as full of sin and devilishness, as any Turk or heretic in the world. The Apostle Paul says: 'If any man among you seemeth to be wise in this world, let him become a fool, that he may be wise' (1 Corinthians 3:18).

"This doctrine, I repeat, stands absolutely immovable. It is the unchangeable will of God in heaven, that of the foolish He will make the wise, of the wicked He will make the pious, of sinners the just, of the perverted the upright, of lunatics rational people, of heretics believers, and of human demons will He make saints. This is to be understood to mean, as I have said before, that man must first of all recognize the work and character of the devil in his own life and heart before he comes to Christ and seeks redemption of Him who was manifested, that He might destroy the works of the devil, the Son of God (1 John 3:18).

"Now, if you ask how this miracle is to take place, the answer is, in a word, as follows: You can not become what you would be in God and in Christ unless you first become in yourself and before all men that which God would have you to be. But God wants you to be in yourself and before all men what you really are, a sinner, wicked, perverted, diabolical and unbelieving. Your correct name, title and dignity, is 'a child of wrath' (Ephesians 2: 3). This is true humility and the way to proceed in conversion. If you have had this experience, you are what you wish to be in the eyes of God, holy, godly, upright, believing, and a child of God." Thus far Luther.

But how does it happen, as Luther says, that he who is become ungodly in himself, sinful, perverted, devilish, now in the eyes of God is become holy, upright, godly and lovable? That has come about in the way described by the holy Apostle Paul: "Wherefore the Law was our schoolmaster to bring us unto Christ, that we might be justified by faith" (Galatians 3: 24). Now the sinner falls at the feet of Christ and seeks sanctuary under His righteousness. Now he no longer despises Christ, but trusts Him as his precious Redeemer. Now he is grateful for the crumbs that fall from the Master's table. He is content to be regarded as a dog, so long as he receives grace and the remission of his sins. It seems to him an overwhelming surprise that he who is so utterly unworthy should be the recipient of the entire merit of Christ. Behold, this was exactly God's purpose with the Law! No longer does God desire to cause the sinner grief and shame. The aim is reached. Now God grants the sinner all things, all for nothing—the entire Christ with all His merits. Now is the poor sinner a rich and glorious saint. Such is the order of grace. Now he is entitled to boast of the perfect fulfilment of the Law. Hear what the Scriptures say: "For what the Law could not do, in that it was weak through the flesh, God sending His own Son in the likeness of sinful flesh, and for sin, condemned sin in the flesh, that the righteousness of the Law might be fulfilled in us" (Romans 8:3-4). And again: "When the fulness of time was come, God sent forth His Son, made of a woman, made under the Law, to redeem them that were under the Law, that we might receive the adoption of sons" (Galatians 4:4-5). "Wherefore when He cometh into the world, He saith, Sacrifice and offering Thou wouldest not, but a body hast Thou prepared me: In burnt offerings and sacrifices for sin Thou hast had no pleasure. Then said I, Lo, I come (in the volume of the book it is written of me), to do Thy will, O God. Above when He said, Sacrifice and offering and burnt offerings and offering for sin Thou wouldest not, neither hadst Thou pleasure therein; which are offered by the Law; then said He, Lo, I come to do Thy will, O God. He taketh away the first, that He may establish the second. By the which will we are sanctified through the offering of the body of Jesus Christ once for all" (Hebrews 10:5-10).

Here the depressed sinner again lifts up his head. He has been put to shame by his external conformity to the Law. Now he has an obedience to the Law of which he may boast. What do you think of the statement of the Apostle Paul, who says that what the Law demanded of us, but which we could not produce on account of the weakness of the flesh, God has done when He sent His Son in the likeness of sinful flesh? The Son of God was "made under the Law," that He might in His own body fulfil the Law in our stead, and thus redeem us "who were under the Law."

When He came to the world, He declared that it was He who should fulfil the perfect will of God: "Lo, I come to do Thy will, O God." In Christ's perfect obedience to the holy will of God are we sanctified, once for all, by the sacrifice of the body of Jesus Christ. O the marvellous counsel of God's love. Ought we not, as Luther says, scorn our own poor righteousness and with Paul count it "but dung" (Philippians 3:8), since it has pleased God in this way to grant us the complete fulfilment of the Law for nothing? This He has done alone through His Son, who took upon Himself to do what we should have done but could not do. He suffered for us that which we alone should have suffered.

To summarize: To be saved, we must be righteous. We must fulfil the Law perfectly. But we are not capable of doing that. Christ only has perfectly kept the Law; not, however, for Himself—He had no need of that—but for us and in our place. As He most graciously says: "I sanctify myself, that they also might be sanctified through the truth" (John 17:19). Christ sanctified Himself "for our sakes" by suffering and obedience. He kept the Law perfectly. He loved God above all things. He had a holy heart, holy thoughts, holy life and holy speech. He loved also His neighbor as Himself. His love was so great that He died for His enemies. He suffered what we should have endured. When He was reviled, He reviled not again. When He suffered, He cursed not. His fulfilling of the Law thus through faith becomes my fulfilling of the Law. His righteousness is transferred to me and becomes my righteousness.

When the Apostle Paul says: "If one died for all, then were all dead," it may likewise be said: If one has fulfilled the Law, then all have fulfilled the Law. The apostle says expressly that Christ "was made under the Law, that He might redeem them that were under the Law." One person has fulfilled the Law for all. If, then, I would be a Christian, rightly believe and honor the Son, I am bound to say: I have completely kept the Law and am without guilt. To be sure, not in my own strength or in my own person, but by my mediator, my substitute Christ. I would deserve to be cast out into the outer darkness if I did not honor Him by regarding myself as just and righteous in Him. For if I did not believe and confess that, it would be the same as if I said that Christ had not perfected the work for which He was sent of God, had not fulfilled the Law perfectly, had not suffered the penalty for the sin of the world. It would be the same as saying that His sufferings and death on the cross were not for us and in our stead, but that He needed this fulfilment for Himself. What an awful confession that would be for a Christian to make!

THE LAW, CONVERSION, AND THE RIGHTEOUSNESS THAT AVAILS BEFORE GOD

(*Continued*)

THE SEVENTEENTH DAY

IF a king's son from sheer compassion and out of pure sympathy for an unfortunate servant, who has destroyed the king's property and is in prison on account of his guilt, pays the indebtedness and even suffers the imprisonment to which the guilty servant had been sentenced, and the king approved of the substitute payment and imprisonment, how could that payment and imprisonment ever be exacted from the servant? What should the guilty servant do in case of such release? Ought he not with joy and gratefulness fall down before the king's son and say: "Thou hast accomplished my release completely. I am freed from my guilt through all eternity." Would it not be the sin above all sin if the servant still said: "But I have not personally suffered the penalty for my sins, nor have I paid the indebtedness with my own means. How, then, can I be sure that I may not have to languish in prison?" Would not that be equivalent to saying: "How can anyone rely upon what the king has said and done?"

The Word of God says expressly: "For what the Law could not do, in that it was weak through the flesh, God sending His own Son in the likeness of sinful flesh, and for sin, condemned sin in the flesh" (Romans 8:3). And again: "God sent forth His Son, made of a woman, made under the Law, to redeem them that were under the Law, that we might receive the adoption of sons" (Galatians 4:4-5). We read here very definitely that God sent His Son for the express purpose of doing that which the Law could not do. He "was made under the Law." He endured the imprisonment that we had deserved, "that He might redeem them that were under the Law."

It is no dream, no hallucination. It is the eternal, divine truth, which the Scriptures from the beginning have revealed as the summary of all: God has given His Son to be our Mediator and Savior. He Himself says of the Law: "I am come to fulfil the Law." "I sanctify myself for them, that they may be sanctified in the truth." "Lo, I come, (in the volume of the book it is written of me), to do Thy will, O God." By which will we are sanctified, once for all, by the sacrifice of the body of Jesus Christ.

What should be our response to this revelation? It would seem to be too much, that God should grant us as a pure gift of mercy the entire fulfilment of the Law. But God is in every way too great and wonderful for us to comprehend. What else ought we do than to accept His gift of grace, thank Him with joy and love, make use of the liberty Christ has purchased for us by His sufferings and death and willingly as children love and serve our heavenly Father? We should do that which is good as God gives us grace. But above and beyond all remember that our righteousness before God consists of the righteousness of Another, which righteousness remains intact and unabridged even when we feel most unworthy. In Christ we have the remission of our sins. If this grace of God does not move us to love and serve God, then everything we do is equally without any value whatever. It is of no value to us personally to do that which is good simply in obedience to the Law or from fear of punishment. "For whatsoever is not of faith is sin" (Romans 14:24). "As many as are of the works of the Law are under the curse" (Galatians 3:10).

Christians ought to consider all this and apply it to their daily lives. For it is not only in the first great conversion that God humiliates us by the Law, revealing to us our sinful condition. As long as we live upon earth we need to practice trust and confidence in God and His Word in a daily conversion. The nearer we come to God, the better we shall know His holiness. The more grace He vouchsafes us, the greater become our duties and responsibilities.

Everything which requires something of us, however, is Law. As a result of this fact, no one has a deeper understanding of the Law and a keener recognition of his defects and weaknesses than has an enlightened Christian. On this point Luther says: "The greater light in the Law, the greater knowledge of sin." The Law, to be sure, is our delight and rule of life and conduct. But it never leaves us just and righteous. For then we would have to be as holy in ourselves as God is. When we thus feel our defects and feel them more and more as time passes, we must "stand fast in the liberty wherewith Christ hath made us free, and be not entangled again with the yoke of bondage." In the same degree that we are again entangled in the spirit of bondage, the Law will exert its old influence upon us, arouse sin to renewed energy and rob us of our ·joy in the Lord.

When the Law chastises us for our sins, what are we to do? We are to admit that in our flesh dwelleth no good thing, but simultaneously point to Christ as our only righteousness and say: "There is the Man who has in my stead performed all that I should have done. Go to Him. He is my ransom. He was made under the Law and has committed no sin." If the objection is made: But you yourself should be holy and do good, then answer: All that is true.   When the question is as to my life and conduct, and I am at fault, then admonish me, and I shall hear you. But when the question is as to my righteousness before God, my life and works do not count. Only the righteousness of another avails for me. Neither my godliness nor my sins are taken into account. I should be utterly lost if I were to be judged by my life and conduct, my piety or my sins. But I possess the righteousness, holiness and purity of Another, the love and good works of the Son of God, who was made under the Law for my sake. I am entirely willing to be a sinner in myself and bear no other name, in order that Christ alone may be my righteousness. Here I say with the Apostle Paul: "Not having my own righteousness, which is of the Law, but that which is through the faith of Christ, the righteousness which is of God by faith" (Philippians 3: 9).

Though my sins were a thousand times more heinous, and my heart condemned me a thousand times more severely, God is yet greater than my heart. The blood of Christ and His obedience are a thousand times more efficacious than my sin. The work of Christ, the heart of Christ, the perfectness of Christ—this is my comfort, my righteousness, and my boast forever. Amen.

THE GOSPEL FOR THE UNGODLY

THE EIGHTEENTH DAY

THE first thing to be noted about the Gospel is that it is a subject which most people seem to think they have learned to perfection. Everybody seems to know all about it. The truth is that the Gospel is a matter which no human being on earth has fully understood and comprehended. Even Saint Paul confesses: "Not as though I had already attained, either were already perfect, but I follow after, if that I may apprehend that for which also I am apprehended of Christ Jesus" (Philippians 3: 12). Dr. Swebelius says: "The Law is fairly well known by nature, but the Gospel is a mystery, hidden from reason." Dr. Luther says: "The Gospel is the Christian's greatest science and highest wisdom, in the study of which he remains a humble student all the days of his life. But," he continues, "there is this peculiarity about the Gospel, that nothing seems easier to learn. The result is, that as soon as a person has heard or read something of it, he imagines that he is master of the subject, and is quite ready for something new."

People who thus fancy themselves expert in the Gospel should realize their ignorance by the circumstance that they think very little upon the Gospel and are not much concerned to know more of God and Jesus Christ whom He hath sent, and to know the unsearchable mysteries of the Atonement. They should realize their obtuseness by the fact that they do not care to hear or read about the subject, nor to pray for the enlightenment of the Holy Spirit. On the contrary, whenever anything of an evangelical character is heard in a sermon, they impatiently wait to hear something new and more interesting. Such people usually reason in this way: "I know very well what I am to believe. I know all about the grace and forgiving love of God in Christ. That has been given once for all. That matter is clear as daylight. I am satisfied on that subject. But what am I to do? How am I to live? Those are questions worth while. Give us the answers to these questions."

Thus they never arrive at the right way of life, the right principle of daily conduct. They have never learned their chief spiritual lack, which is life itself, genuine repentance and a living faith in

Christ. They do not realize the utter futility of their own works in the matter of justification before God. They have never despaired of themselves, nor have they experienced the meaning and the power of true faith. For in that case they would not say that they have had enough of the Gospel. They would rather say, as God's Word and experience abundantly verify, that only in the knowledge of God and His unbounded grace lies the power and joy of leading a truly God-pleasing life. As the Apostle John says: "He that loveth not, knoweth not God; for God is love" (1 John 4: 8). If they knew God, they would love Him and delight to walk in His statutes and do His will. They would be burning and shining lights in the world, as John was. For God is a great and burning light of love. No one can know Him without being enkindled by His love. Now, love is the mother of good works. "Love is the fulfilling of the Law" (Romans 13: 10).

The conclusion, then, of this matter is, that they who imagine that they possess a sufficient knowledge of the Gospel, have not learned the A B C's of it. Paul says: "If any man think that he knoweth anything, he knoweth nothing yet as he ought to know" (1 Corinthians 2: 2). It is true that a believer may be so confused in the darkness of temptation that he forgets what experience has taught him, and once more begins to seek in the Law that which is nowhere found in the Law. But he does not remain in soul-confusion. He permits the Holy Ghost to guide him out of the darkness. He holds fast to the Gospel. He remains a suckling infant at "the breasts of her consolations" (Isaiah 66: 11).

The apostle wrote: "If any man think that he knoweth anything, he knoweth nothing yet as he ought to know" (1 Corinthians 2: 2). This truth is especially applicable to the knowledge of the Gospel. The Gospel contains such facts that he who sees what it conveys, is unable to believe it. He who readily believes the Gospel scarcely realizes what it contains. He may think that he has grasped the content of the Gospel. He is so sure of this that he is ready to take a thousand oaths to that effect. But his whole personality denies his assertion. Luther truly says that he who could rightly comprehend and believe what the Gospel implies, could "no longer live upon earth—he would perish from sheer joy." He certainly would not be as cold and insensate and unspiritual as are these satiated and conceited souls who imagine that they have learned all there is to know about the Gospel. It would not be so hard to follow Christ, to love, serve and obey Him, to suffer for His name's sake, and to deny oneself, if one believed what the Gospel contains.

Observe here a principal reason why many who are constantly learning never arrive at the knowledge of the truth. Jesus said: "No man knoweth the Father, save the Son, and he to whomsoever the Son will reveal Him" (Matthew 11: 27). So long as the Son does not reveal the Father and the Father's heart to a man, he will never understand or know God and the Gospel. All learning is vain. Shortly before (verse 25), Jesus had said: "Thou hast hid these things from the wise and prudent and hast revealed them unto babes." That is, the Father has not revealed the glories of the Gospel to those who do not regard themselves as ignorant, who imagine that by their own unaided study they will be able to comprehend the Gospel. Many hear and read the Gospel as they would any secular science, without submitting to the guidance and direction of God. God hides the meaning from their sight. "Even so, Father," says Jesus, "for so it seemed good in Thy sight" (verse 26).

Saint Paul was certainly a master in clearly and correctly expounding the Gospel. But he did not consider it sufficient that the people heard his sermons and read his epistles. He still regarded a true knowledge of the Gospel to be dependent upon the "revelation of God," upon the impartation of "the Spirit of wisdom and revelation in the knowledge of Christ, the eyes of the understanding being enlightened" (Ephesians 1: 17-18). He constantly implored God to grant this Spirit of revelation to his congregations. Twice in the epistle to the Ephesians alone he prays God that "the God of our Lord Jesus Christ, the Father of Glory, may give unto you the Spirit of wisdom and revelation in the knowledge of Him: the eyes of your understanding being enlightened, that ye may know what is the hope of His calling, and what the riches of the glory of His inheritance in the saints" (Ephesians 1: 16, 23). According to chapter 3: 14-19, he prays God that they might be "strengthened with might by His Spirit in the inner man, that Christ may dwell in your hearts by faith; that ye, being rooted and grounded in love, may be able to comprehend with all saints what is the breadth, and length, and depth, and height; and to know the love of Christ, which passeth knowledge, that ye might be filled with all the fulness of God."

Since there are people who never feel the need of bending the knee before God, nor of searching in the Word of God with diligence after the knowledge of the Gospel, who know enough already, while the greatest saints and heroes of faith confessed, despite all their study and prayer, that they had not fully apprehended the Gospel but reached after it in larger comprehension—what are we to think? Nothing else than that these people who understand well enough, who have learned all there is to know of the Gospel, are deluded by the devil. They need to learn the first letters of the alphabet of God's wonderful love. God grant that they may learn before it is too late!

THE GOSPEL FOR THE UNGODLY
(*Continued*)

THE NINETEENTH DAY

WHAT, then, is the Gospel? What is the essential content of the Gospel? We shall see presently what the Scriptures say upon the subject. But first we shall quote a short explanation of the Gospel which Luther gives in his preface to the New Testament:

"The word *evangelion* is a Greek word and means good tidings, good news, a good announcement, which people report far and wide, sing about, and which creates much joy and happiness. Thus, when David conquered the great Goliath, it created a good piece of news, glad tidings to the Jewish people. Their terrible enemy was slain. As a redeemed nation, they were filled with joy and peace. They sang songs of deliverance. They rejoiced exceedingly. So also the Gospel is good news, a glad announcement gone forth to the whole world by the apostles. It tells the story of the true David, who has fought with sin, death and the devil and conquered them, thus redeeming all who were held in captivity by sin, tormented by death and in the power of the devil. By His victory He has saved them without any merit or assistance on their part, and made them just and holy and blessed. He has brought them peace. He has brought them back to God. Why should they not sing, thank and praise God and be eternally happy, providing they firmly believe this Gospel and remain steadfast in the faith?

"These tidings, this comforting, evangelical and divine news, is also called the 'New Testament,' because, as a person makes his last will and testament, in which he bequeaths all his property, stating who the beneficiaries are to be after his death, so Christ has commanded that after His death and resurrection, the Gospel or the news of it, shall be proclaimed to all the world. By this Gospel He has bequeathed and devised all that is His to all who believe on Him. He has bequeathed to them

His life, by which death has been swallowed up; His righteousness, by which He has blotted out their sins; His redemption, by which He has conquered eternal damnation. A poor soul, dead in trespasses and sins, chained to the portals of hell, can not possibly hear a more comforting message than the precious news of what Christ has done for him. His heart leaps for joy and gratefulness, that is, if he believes the good news."—Thus far Luther.

The Scriptures speak instructively and comfortingly in many places concerning this consolatory message from heaven. Among the passages which deal primarily with the Gospel, is 2 Corinthians 5: 18-20, reading as follows:

"All things are of God, who hath reconciled us to Himself by Jesus Christ and hath given to us the ministry of reconciliation, to wit, that God was in Christ, reconciling the world unto Himself, not imputing their trespasses unto them; and hath committed unto us the word of reconciliation. Now then we are ambassadors for Christ, as though God did beseech you by us: we pray you in Christ's stead, Be ye reconciled to God."

Here are the great essentials to be noted in the Gospel. But already from the meditation upon these words just cited, we see the truth of the statement of Jesus, that He has "revealed it to whomsoever He will" and hidden it from the others. O that we may be among those to whom the Lord will reveal the Gospel—needy souls, who recognize their own spiritual darkness.

The first great essential of the Gospel, which

needs to be indelibly impressed upon our hearts, is
that the Gospel "is not of man" (Galatians 1: 11).
It has not arisen in the thought of any man. The
Gospel is a message from heaven. It is a message
from the great eternal God to the fallen children
of Adam on earth, a message to the effect that the
same great and almighty God who has created all
things, heaven and earth, mountains and seas, and
all that in them is; who made man in His own image,
has had the Gospel proclaimed to the world, first
by angels and prophets, then by His only-begotten
Son, then by "a host of evangelists." "And all
things are of God, who hath reconciled us to Himself by Jesus Christ, and hath given to us the ministry of reconciliation—and hath committed unto us
the word of reconciliation—. We are ambassadors
for Christ—. God beseecheth you by us: Be ye reconciled to God."

We recall the sacred incident when Christ, having
completed the work of redemption, risen from the
dead, transfigured, and was ready to ascend to the
Father in heaven, called His disciples together "into
a mountain" in Galilee, who, "when they saw Him,
they worshipped Him." Then we read: "And Jesus
came and spake unto them, saying, All power is
given unto me in heaven and in earth. Go ye therefore, and teach all nations, baptizing them in the
name of the Father, and of the Son, and of the
Holy Ghost: teaching them to observe all things
whatsoever I have commanded you: and, lo, I am
with you alway, even unto the end of the world"
(Matthew 28: 17-20). Saint Mark records the

Great Commission in these words: "Go ye into all the world, and preach the Gospel to every creature. He that believeth and is baptized shall be saved; but he that believeth not shall be damned" (Mark 16: 16-17).

Here, then, we have the Great Command of our Lord, whose Word shall judge us on the Last Day, the Word of Him who has the keys of life and death, who "openeth, and no man shutteth; who shutteth, and no man openeth" (Revelation 3: 7). We do not need to beg or beseech any man for the Gospel. It is the gift of God. It is the last will and testament of Christ to the world. It is "the Gospel of Christ," the Great Commission of Christ, "the everlasting Gospel" (Revelation 14: 6). Thank God, I have a sure foundation upon which to build my faith. I know how to live and die happily, if only I believe His last word and testament. Christ has said: "All power is given unto me in heaven and in earth. Go ye, therefore, and preach the Gospel to every creature."

"Who is he that condemneth? It is Christ that died, yea, rather, that is risen again, who is even at the right hand of God, who also maketh intercession for us" (Romans 8: 34). Whatever He has said remains valid in heaven and in earth, in time, in eternity, and in the judgment. He it is who has sent forth the glad tidings to be proclaimed to the ends of the earth, hence also to me. He said: "Go ye into all the world." I, too, am in the world. He said: "Preach the Gospel to every creature." I, too, am one of God's creatures.

The word "Gospel," which He Himself chose, means, as we have seen, good news, glad tidings, a joyful announcement. "Preach the Gospel," then means: Proclaim the glad message. Spread the comforting news. What was the comforting message? What was the glad news? What was it that Christ was sent to accomplish in the world? What was it that He had accomplished? What was the great work that He had finished, the proclamation of which became the best of tidings to lost and condemned sinners? The apostle explains the Gospel to us: "And all things are of God, who hath reconciled us to Himself by Jesus Christ, and hath given to us the ministry of reconciliation, to wit, that God was in Christ, reconciling the world unto Himself, not imputing their trespasses unto them; and hath committed unto us the word of reconciliation."

———

THE GOSPEL FOR THE UNGODLY
(*Continued*)

THE TWENTIETH DAY

THIS glad message, this comforting news, which Christ commanded His disciples to preach to every creature, this word of reconciliation, that "God was in Christ and reconciled the world to Himself," Christ designates by the word "Gospel." This message was proclaimed by men of God, filled with the Holy Ghost and with power, who with "open mouth" spake "comfortably" to anxious and troubled sinners, as we see recorded at many places in the Acts of the Apostles, for example, Acts 15. Paul, preaching in the city of Antioch on a Sabbath day, cried out and said: "Be it known unto you, therefore, men and brethren, that through this Man is preached unto you the forgiveness of sins, and by Him all that believe are justified from all things, from which ye could not be justified by the Law of Moses" (Acts 15: 38-39).

This same Gospel they wrote in their epistles, in order that it might be bruited in all the world and preserved to the end of time. In Romans 8: 3, for instance, we read: "For what the Law could not do, in that it was weak through the flesh, God sending His own Son in the likeness of sinful flesh, and for sin, condemned sin in the flesh." At 2 Corinthians 5: 21, we read: "For He hath made Him to be sin for us, who knew no sin; that we might be made the righteousness of God in Him." Again, Romans 5: 18-19: "Therefore as by the offense of one, judgment came upon all men to condemnation; even so, by the righteousness of One, the free gift came upon all men unto justification of life. For as by one man's disobedience many were made sinners, so by the obedience of One shall many be made righteous."

From these and innumerable similar Scripture passages we clearly see what the Gospel really is, what it contains and brings. We see, going back to the passage which we had begun to contemplate (2 Corinthians 5: 18-19), that the event, the news, the message, which the Gospel of God proclaims, may be comprised in the short sentence: "God was in Christ, reconciling the world unto Himself."

"The world" is the fallen race of Adam on earth. The world, together with its original ancestor, had fallen into sin and was under sentence of eternal death. The sentence was irrevocable: "The soul that sinneth, it shall die." Again: "Cursed is every one that continueth not in all things which are written in the book of the Law to do them" (Galatians 3: 10). There was no one to save himself, no one without sin. "The wages of sin is death." Thus "death came upon all men, for that all have sinned." The eternal Kingdom of Death was hell. Its king, the devil, had all men in his power. The great merciful God, who had created men to be His children, could not endure their eternal destruction. Hence He devised a means by which they might be saved.

"The Word was made flesh." "God was in Christ." "In Christ dwelleth all the fulness of the Godhead bodily." In this assumed human nature, God reconciled the world unto Himself. Christ became humanity's Second Adam. He agreed to assume the responsibility for the sins of the world. He stood in the place of mankind before the Law and judgment of God. He did what we should have done. He suffered what we should have endured. He died for all. "He redeemed for the world the grace, the heart which God had for humanity before the Fall. He fulfilled the Law, suffered the penalty, atoned for the crime, conquered death, the devil and hell. He purchased eternal redemption for men."

"Not imputing their trespasses unto them." As before the Fall, God saw humanity in Adam and it was "very good," so He now saw humanity reconciled unto Himself in the Second Adam, Christ. "For, when we were enemies, we were reconciled to God by the death of His Son" (Romans 5: 10).

"God hath committed unto us the word of reconciliation," that is, the word of the redemption which is in Christ Jesus. Now God beseeches us: "Be ye reconciled unto God." God is already reconciled unto you. Be ye now reconciled unto God, and all will be well. Return to God, ye runaway, lost sons! The Father's heart and arms have long been open to you. The Father's house and the best robe have long been prepared for you. You have no need of doing the least to appease the Father. He was Himself in Christ and has reconciled the world unto Himself. Only come ye now, and be reconciled with God!

This is the Gospel message. Let us note a fact of which many are in ignorance, namely, that the Gospel it not a promise, but the announcement of a message that the promise is already fulfilled. The Gospel does not tell us of something that is to transpire in the future, but, as Luther says, it is an information, an announcement of something that has already taken place, something actually present, whether we accept it or not, something that has existence whether we believe it or not. This is a subject covered with Cimmerian darkness to many to whom the Gospel has never been the glad message of hope and redemption. They always reason that God must be appeased, that sin must be atoned for, that somehow we must blot out our own iniquities by our good works—not that God is already reconciled, that sin is already blotted out.

In this way there would be no Gospel. In this way the Word of God does not speak. The Gospel is the blessed announcement of something that has already taken place, of something that occurred outside the gates of Jerusalem on the great Day of Atonement. That event spells: "God was in Christ, reconciling the world unto Himself." It announces: "We are reconciled to God by the death of His Son while we were yet enemies." "Comfort ye, comfort ye my people, saith the Lord: Speak ye comfortably to Jerusalem, and say that her warfare is accomplished, that her iniquity is pardoned: for she hath received of the Lord's hand double for her sins" (Isaiah 40: 1-2).

All these precious passages tell us of something that has taken place: that God is reconciled, that we are redeemed, that our iniquities are forgiven. It all transpired in the fulness of time, in God's own time, as foretold in the Old Testament: "Seventy weeks are determined upon Thy people and upon Thy holy city, to finish the transgression, and to make an end of sins, and to make reconciliation for iniquity, and to bring everlasting righteousness, and to seal up the vision and prophecy, and to anoint the Most Holy" (Daniel 9: 24).

O that we might believe that all the sin of the

world, also the sin which now burdens us, was blotted out, covered, sunk in the depth of the sea, eighteen hundred years ago, by the death of Christ; that God is a reconciled God, and that eternal righteousness is come to us! That would make a Gospel indeed for us.

THE GOSPEL FOR THE UNGODLY
(*Continued*)

THE TWENTY-FIRST DAY

INTENSIFYING the spiritual darkness which rests upon many hearts in regard to the nature of the Gospel, who imagine that God is not reconciled, but that He must be reconciled, not believing that "God was in Christ, reconciling the world unto Himself," comes also the error that even if one believes that some sort of reconciliation took place in the death of Christ, yet when the question arises as to the application of Christ's redemption to one's own soul, men do not comprehend what the atonement made by Christ really involves. Or, such a lot of hard conditions are attached to the appropriation of Christ's atonement, as they think even the Word of God makes, that there is the same misery about becoming a partaker in the atonement of Christ as there is in attaining righteousness by the Law. They act as if Christ had not made full atonement for sin.

The chief trouble in this confusion of thought is that men refuse to accept what the Word says concerning the atonement. They refuse to accept the essential contents of the Gospel, namely, that "we were reconciled to God by the death of His Son, while we were yet enemies." Men will not believe that "God reconciled the world unto Himself, not imputing their trespasses unto them." Even though they may confess this truth with their lips, their heart still says: But only the godly, the repentant and believing, the pious and good, ever become reconciled with God. When, therefore, the messengers of the Gospel come and invite sinners to the wedding-feast of God's grace in the very words of Christ, "Come, for all things are now ready" (Luke 14:17), their unbelief alters the invitation to read: Wait. Wait a while until all things are made ready.

"But, you say, "surely one must be rightly prepared, rightly repentant, rightly believing, before one may dare to come." But the Scriptures say: "Come. And let him that is athirst come. And whosoever will, let him take of the water of life freely" (Revelation 22: 17). If you had said: They would not come before they were rightly prepared in the sense of being of a contrite heart, of being willing and desirous of accepting the royal invitation, the only correct preparation spoken of in the Gospel, then had you spoken the truth. But the notion that any one in the world is prohibited from coming to Christ, is a pernicious error. For whosoever will, may come to Christ. "Whosoever will, let him take of the water of life freely."

The reason why all men are not saved is the one given by Christ concerning those who had been bidden to the wedding-feast and did not come: "They would not come" (Matthew 22:3). When the invitation comes, men begin by staying away on account of their fields, their merchandise, their wife, their family, their domestic demands upon them. When a man is awakened from his carnal security, he first tries by every method to save himself. He remains unwilling to accept the grace of God in Christ, grace for grace. All the betterment, contrition, anguish of soul, in a word, all the preparation spoken of in the Scriptures has but one purpose— to drive men to Christ (Galatians 3:54), to persuade them to come. When a man has arrived at the stage when he prays: "O that I, too, might come to Jesus! O that God, for Jesus' sake, through grace, would forgive me all my sins! O that I, too, had the grace of God in my heart, and a living faith in the Savior!"—then it is high time for you to come, to believe, to quit all your preparations, and all your works. "All things are ready. Come." The Lord said concerning that same invitation: "Go ye therefore into the highways, and as many as ye shall find, bid to the marriage" (Matthew 22:9).

At this point, let me quote a few lines from Mr. J. A. James: "Seeking souls frequently forget that it is their inexorable duty instantly to believe, instantly to go to the Savior. They want to wait until they feel more needy, and until they feel an inner call to believe. They try to pray, and do not understand that their duty is to surrender immediately to Christ. They wait for some remarkable impression upon the soul, some suggestion as to the time when they are to believe, which suggestion, they think, also will grant them the power to believe."

Where do we read in the Bible that sinners are to wait for the time when they are to be enabled to believe? Where do we read, Believe, but not now? Come, but not now? Wait until you are prepared? Wait for a special impulse? On the contrary we read: "Behold, now is the accepted time; behold, now is the day of salvation" (2 Corinthians 6:2). "Wherefore, as the Holy Ghost saith, Today if ye will hear His voice, harden not your hearts, as in the provocation" (Hebrews 8:7-8). Is not God ready to forgive your sin now, at this moment? Is not Christ ready? Is not God reconciled? Are not your sins already blotted out? Did not Christ die for you now as well as at any other time? Was not the heart of the father of the prodigal son full of mercy and longing even before the son came home? Was not the best robe ready for the young man before he returned to the father's house? "But when he was yet a great way off, his father saw him, and had compassion, and ran, and fell on his neck, and kissed him" (Luke 15:20). Are not all the treasures of His grace ready to be received by you? What are you waiting for? Would you rely more upon a voice from heaven or an emotion in your heart than upon the Word of God, which says that "all things are now ready"?

Look steadfastly upon the promise of Christ: "Come unto me, all ye that labor and are heavy laden, and I will give you rest. Take my yoke upon you, and learn of me: for I am meek and lowly in heart: and ye shall find rest unto your souls" (Matthew 11:28-29). Are not these the words of Christ? Yes. Does Jesus speak the truth? Yes. Do you read anything about waiting for an invitation? No. Why then do you hesitate?

Once more let me cite a few words from Mr. James: "Note the episode of the jailer at Philippi (Acts 16:25-34). The same night in which he was awakened to a knowledge of his sins, he believed in Christ, was baptized, and rejoiced, believing in God with all his house. When, in the agony of his soul, he cried: 'Sirs, what must I do to be saved?', the apostle answered, 'Believe on the Lord Jesus Christ, and thou shalt be saved, thou and thy house.' The apostle speaks of no manner of preparation, no long list of prescribed duties, but says simply, 'Believe,' meaning, of course, now. And thus the terrified man understood him, for he believed instantly and had peace."

It has been demonstrated that not all come equally soon to faith, but that all may come equally soon; that there is nothing to hinder on God's part, but that "all things are ready"; that the Gospel proclaims a complete and present grace, so that nothing remains but to accept the grace of God; that you may come and ought to come as you are, wretched and halt, sinful and unworthy, young or old, hard-hearted or emotional. The Gospel invites you to come and accept the grace given in Christ unto justification and sanctification.

THE GOSPEL FOR THE UNGODLY
(*Continued*)

THE TWENTY-SECOND DAY

THIS must be all wrong. The believers, the good people, the godly people, the sincere and upright Christians who really walk in the Spirit and in newness of life—these are the people whom God can love. Not me, an ungodly wretch, frivolous, unstable, disobedient, a vile sinner against the Law of God, who knows to do good, but does the evil, insincere, unable even to repent of my sins, unable earnestly to watch and pray. God, is it possible that the Gospel is also for me? Can God love sinners such as I am? No, no. That is not possible." Such thoughts lie deep in the hearts of men. In fact, they cannot be entirely banished from any heart. When anyone speaks of "the Gospel for the ungodly," it sounds like a strange and dangerous Gospel.

Hark, then, ye poor sinners, ye despised ones! Hear what the Lord God Himself has to say to you. For "the foolishness of God is wiser than men" (1 Corinthians 1:25). God still speaks the Gospel of grace to all His fallen and lost children. "As I live, saith the Lord God, I have no pleasure in the death of the wicked; but that the wicked turn from his way and live: Turn ye, turn ye from your evil ways, for why will ye die, O house of Israel?" (Ezekiel 33: 11). "Speak ye comfortably to Jerusalem"—the most sin-stained spot on earth—"thou that killest the prophets, and stonest them which are sent unto thee. How often would I have gathered thy children together, even as a hen gathereth her chickens under her wings, and ye would not" (Matthew 23:37). "I, even I, am He that blotteth out thy transgressions for mine own sake, and will not remember thy sins" (Isaiah 43:25). "Speak ye comfortably to Jerusalem, and cry unto her, that her warfare is accomplished, that her iniquity is pardoned: for she hath received of the Lord's hand double for all her sins" (Isaiah 40:2).

When God announced the first Gospel to the first sinners on earth, they were filled with excuses and bitterness against God, and yet He came to them with the word of reconciliation (Leviticus 3:12-15). Hear what the apostle says: "Now to him that worketh is the reward not reckoned of grace, but of debt. But to him that worketh not, but believeth on Him that justifieth the ungodly, his faith is counted for righteousness. Even as David also describeth the blessedness of the man unto whom God imputeth righteousness without works" (Romans 4: 4-6). Come now and hear that which follows. Receive it as a brand new message from your God in heaven. Note carefully how this Gospel came about, and whereon it is founded.

The blessed mystery, the remarkable message is based upon the following strange occurrences:

When we poor human beings had fallen in sin, and were as a result lost and condemned creatures, God had compassion upon us, and humbled Himself and took upon Himself the likeness of sinful flesh.

He became as truly man as He was God, like us in all things except in sin.

The reason was that His eternal Father-love for His children could not change by their fall into sin. It burned as mightily as before in His heart. He could not let us remain lost, when separated from Him by the wiles of Satan. He would wage war with the enemy of mankind in order to bring us back to Himself. This is indicated in His threatening words to the serpent about "the seed of the woman" which was to "bruise the serpent's head". So "when the time was fulfilled, God sent forth His Son, made of a woman." He became man, such as we are, yea, He became the most despised and forsaken of men, full of our diseases. He was "a worm, and not a man," ridiculed by men, the contempt of the nations. He was a servant, a slave. "He came to minister, not to be ministered unto." He gave His life as a ransom for us. For this purpose He descended to such ignominy.

This despised man, who yet was God and man, Jesus Christ, "in whom dwelt the fulness of the Godhead bodily," nineteen hundred years ago, in Jerusalem, was suspended on a shameful cross, and there, in the place of all ungodly men in the world, He suffered death. You have heard and you know that it was in the room and stead of mankind that He tasted death. But first He was crowned with thorns, smitten and scourged. His hands were pierced with cruel nails, His feet likewise. A spear was thrust through His side. Thus He shed His blood for us poor men. Where could greater love be found on earth?

Through this Redeemer, who died the death of a criminal upon the cross, grace and salvation has been secured for all the ungodly that have ever lived and that now live and that will live, until the Judgment Day. Death, in the bonds of which we lay, has been deprived of its power. The right of Satan to the souls and bodies of men has been wrenched from him. The portals of heaven are again open. Life has been reconquered. God has now reconciled all things to Himself, in order that He might make peace by the power of the blood shed upon the cross. The pleasure of the Triune God in again dwelling among men upon earth is a result of the atonement made by Christ, an atonement passing all knowledge.

These truths are so clearly presented in the Bible that whoever will may read them. The crucified Christ has atoned for the sin of the world, suffered the penalty for man's sin in His body on the tree, the sin of every human being who has lived, or now lives, or shall live on earth. Christ has borne them all. He has blotted out all our transgressions. This fact remains through all eternity.

"Neither is there salvation in any other: for there is none other name under heaven given among men whereby we must be saved" (Acts 4:12). The atonement made by Christ is the only foundation for our salvation.

Whoever believes in Christ shall be saved. He never needs to be uncomforted. He never needs to have any doubt as to the forgiveness of his sins, though they be as multitudinous as the sands of the seashore. But he who does not believe is already condemned because "he hath not believed in the name of the only begotten Son of God" (John 3: 18). He who cherishes any other method of salvation is radically wrong. Even if any man might say: My conscience does not condemn me for one single sin in all my life, considering himself at least a step nearer heaven than the thief, the harlot and the publican, he would by such argumentation only prove the deceitfulness of his own heart. Our own righteousness is an idle dream. Amid all the Babel of the world, we gratefully hold to the supreme truth. Jesus alone is our righteousness. That blessed fact, and nothing else, assures us of salvation and the hope of heaven.

THE GOSPEL FOR THE UNGODLY
(*Continued*)

THE TWENTY-THIRD DAY

WHO are they whom the Savior has redeemed from their sin and guilt, and granted the right to eternal life, providing only that they believe on Him? The apostle answers the question thus: They are the ungodly (Romans 4:5). Reason would say: God must have found something quite extraordinary in these people, since He did not even spare His only begotten Son, but gave Him into death for them. But the Bible says: "We were reconciled with

God by the death of His Son, while we were yet His enemies" (Romans 5:10). The men whom God reconciled unto Himself by the death of His Son, a death which even to Him was so terrible that He writhed in anguish as a woman in travail, so awful that He "sweat, as it were, great drops of blood," were "the ungodly," enemies of God, who would have surrendered to the devil for time and eternity if God had not taken pity on them. We are redeemed as the enemies of God. The Savior died for slaves. Our redemption was not the product of our will, but of the mercy of God.

This Gospel proves itself in the hearts of men as "the power of God," leading them to faith. The preaching of the cross, the Lamb of God slain for our sins, who had compassion upon us when otherwise we must have despaired, is not the dry, mechanical doctrine which some people imagine. The faith by which we are justified and saved is the result of the preaching of the crucified Christ, painted before our eyes in His blood and wounds, who calls to every sinner: Believe in me, and thou shalt be saved. I know of no other way by which a soul may come to faith in Christ.

The spiritual process by which the soul comes to faith cannot be made entirely clear and intelligible to anyone. The believer himself cannot define it in its mysterious development. He says with the man born blind, whose eyes Jesus had opened: "One thing I know, that, whereas I was blind, now I see" (John 9:25). The creation of faith in the heart of a sinner cannot be defined—it is only experienced.

Meantime we shall express ourselves on this abstruse subject as well as we can: "The dead shall hear the voice of the Son of God: and they that hear shall live" (John 5:25). As soon as the Spirit of God by the Word has opened the spiritual eyes of a man, he sees his essential ungodliness, his natural depravity, his estrangement from God. Even if he has been as correct as Paul in his Phariseeism, blameless before the Law, even zealous for the Law, his enlightened conscience now cries out: "I am the chief of sinners. What must I do to be saved?"

Pleasure in the commission of sin sometimes evaporates, sometimes as the result of a nameless dread. A man in the midst of a merry feast will blanch, and his heart will quail within him if some dread news is presented to him; if, for instance, a threat of certain death is hissed into his ear. The sinner sees his wretchedness. He knows that the sentence of death has been pronounced upon him. He has heard that Christ, the "Man of Sorrows," has paid the ransom for his soul. But he has had no experience of the power of the Gospel in his heart. He knows that he possesses no true faith in the Savior. As a consequence, he knows that he is sentenced and condemned; for "the soul that sinneth, it shall die" (Ezekiel 18:20).

This soul-experience is called "melancholy" by the world. But the Bible calls it "godly sorrow" which "worketh repentance to salvation" (2 Corinthians 7:10), that is, a sorrow after God's heart and pleasing to God. He who no longer trusts to his good works, no longer promises that which he cannot perform; no longer tries to help himself;

no longer indulges in cant; no longer makes himself out to be better than he really is, but goes to the great Friend of Sinners just as he is, ungodly, unbelieving, an enemy of the cross, but oppressed by sin, casts himself at the feet of the Savior, trusts to His grace and is willing to be saved, to him is granted faith in Christ who "justifieth the ungodly." He says to the humbled sinner: "Thy sins are forgiven. Go, and sin no more." The Holy Ghost applies the "word of reconciliation" to the heart of such an one, removes the veil from his eyes, takes him by the hand, and leads him to the Lamb of God, who was slain for his sins upon the cross. The Spirit by the Word assures him: Christ has died for you. He has purchased for you childhood with God and a place in the Father's house.

In this way the Holy Ghost by the Word brings the heart of a sinner to faith in Christ crucified. Though the heart be as stone, it becomes as wax as soon as it hears and believes that the Son of God died upon the cross as the propitiation for our sins. He who does not come to faith by the contemplation of the bleeding Son of God, whose heart remains obdurate, unchanged and unrepentant, will not be moved by outward calamities, war, famine and pestilence, to turn for help to God.

The order in which a sinner is led to faith is, that he gives up all trust in his own good works, his upright life, his fine character. For it is written: "But to him that worketh not, but believeth on Him that justifieth the ungodly, his faith is counted for righteousness" (Romans 4:5). Contrary to all faith and confidence in good works as the way of salvation, the Bible says: "As many as are of the works of the Law are under the curse: for it is written, Cursed is every one that continueth not in all things which are written in the book of the Law to do them" (Galatians 3:10). No sane man will contend that he is in thought, word and deed as holy and pure as God Himself. If he does, he is a liar. As long as the Bible discards works as the way of salvation, all externally godly men, however they may boast of their good works and fine character, are under the condemnation of the Law and sinners like the rest. Nay, publicans and sinners are nearer heaven than they are (Matthew 21:31). Consequently, it is a false order of salvation, the product of hatred to the cross of Christ, which says that by doing good works, leading a virtuous life and keeping the Law, a man will propitiate God, merit the forgiveness of his sins and be saved. This carnal idea is work-righteousness, a denial of the atonement of Christ.

But as soon as the soul has learned to realize its deep corruption and sinful misery, has heard the great, acceptable Gospel truth, that Jesus came to the world to save sinners, and no longer hesitates but in despair of its own righteousness throws itself at the feet of Jesus, crying out in its wretchedness, "Lord, have mercy on me, a poor, lost and condemned sinner," faith, a living, saving, comforting and sanctifying faith, is granted to him.

THE GOSPEL FOR THE UNGODLY
(*Continued*)

THE TWENTY-FOURTH DAY

WHEN God creates faith in a soul, He has no regard as to whether a man is a good man or a sinner, a fine character or a wretch who needs mercy and loves to hear the assuring words: "Thou shalt live." He who has no other recourse than to flee to the grace of God at the cross of Christ, soon experiences what is meant by faith in the merits of Christ, who has won for us eternal redemption. The exhortation, Believe in Him who "justifieth the ungodly," an utterly unintelligible word to the individual who preens himself with his "fine character," becomes a living word with the power of salvation. He thanks God, that salvation does not depend upon our running back and fro, upon our willing and doing, but solely and only upon the grace of God and His compassionate love in Christ. He experiences more ecstasy of soul, sees broader horizons of God's love, than ever his life will be able to express.

The Gospel brings joy to all who believe it, because faith is imputed to them for righteousness. He who receives grace and remission of sins, being buried with Christ in His death, is from that hour a happy man, who goes his way joyfully. The heart weeps for joy. The soul is filled with holy rapture. There are instances where souls have been literally "sick of love" for the Savior on realizing His love which caused Him to enter the jaws of hell to save

them. They have had the same experience as
Mary, " a sinner in the city," who bathed the feet
of the Lord and dried them with her beautiful
hair. Their heart has been set on fire with an ecstasy
of sacred affection. The Savior is all in all to a
child of grace. It rests nowhere as well as in the
bosom of His love. It boasts of nothing but of His
love.

This is the truest happiness. This is the possession of that serene bliss of which no one can deprive
us. We know that we have a Savior. We know
Him "in whom we believe." We know our Lord
by the wounds in His blessed hands, in His feet,
and in His side. The Bible is full of these truths,
truths which have been verified in the souls of millions, many of whom now stand before the throne
of God in heaven, hailing in ecstatic gratefulness
His wounds as everlasting marks of His love.
Others are still upon earth, rejoicing in God their
Savior.

These are matters which may be experienced by
anyone who seriously seeks the salvation of his soul.
Those who have experienced in their hearts what
has been gained for them by the death of the Lamb
of God, have from that moment become new creatures. Their hearts have learned to sing a new
song. They have begun to understand those Scripture passages which formerly were dark and incomprehensible to their unregenerate minds. Remember Thomas, Paul, and others. The blood of Christ
has today the same power and effect.

The mercy of Christ justifies us. The wounds of

the Lamb of God are our cities of refuge. To them we fly and escape the Avenger. The merits of Christ are to us the gates of heaven. We need nothing more and nothing else in the world in order to be saved. Even if an angel from heaven should use his eloquence to persuade us that something more is needed than the blood of Christ, we would say: Please keep your suggestions to yourself. And if he should attempt to show us another way of salvation, we would say: Get thee behind me, thou evil spirit. Jesus receives sinners. He dwells with them. He lives in their hearts by faith. Happy are we if we believe. We live by His grace. We rejoice in His redemption. We grow daily more assured of our salvation.

Friends, it now becomes a question for each one of you to answer before God and your own soul whether you believe this marvellous Gospel of God's love in Christ Jesus. For this phrase, "for you," requires truly believing hearts. O that you might be persuaded from the heart to accept the grace of God as sinners without any manner of excuse or self-justification! Then not one of you would pass out of this world as a lost and condemned soul. Should any one of you think: "That is all true. I am an ungodly person. I am the slave of sin. I do not know the Savior. I can not think of death without shuddering. Who knows how soon death may call me? What will be the judgment when I am required to stand before Him who gave His life for me?" Let him who thus travails in his soul, read carefully the Gospel for the wicked. Let him cast the burden of his sins at the foot of the cross of Christ and cry: "Have mercy upon me, Lord Jesus." Then shall he find comfort in the Gospel of God's love for sinners, and with joyful anticipation pass on to his heavenly home whenever death shall call him away from this world.

THE GREAT MYSTERY REVEALED

> *If there had been a law given which could have given life, verily righteousness should have been by the Law* (GALATIANS 3: 21).

THE TWENTY-FIFTH DAY

A SCHOOLMASTER in Sweden once wrote the following letter to some friends. Believing that it may be helpful to others, we shall insert it here:

"A still greater change has taken place in regard to my inner life. After many years of seeking, praying, hearing, reading, questioning and waiting, I came to the conclusion that the doctrine in most of the devotional books that I had read, consisted rather of Old Testament Judaism than of Christianity. That is to say: They dealt with sacrifices and of a coming Savior. They taught me that by prayer, tears, the daily betterment of my life, by self-denial and such like exercises, I was to wait and look forward to the salvation that I needed, while the Gospel says that this salvation was prepared before the foundation of the world. It tells me that this salvation was purchased eighteen hundred years ago on

Mount Calvary by the bloody sacrifice of the Lamb of God, Jesus Christ, who thus atoned for the sin of the world 'in one day' (Zechariah 3: 9).

"I then thought that the reason for my misery, the reason why I did not secure peace in my heart, was that I was lacking in faithfulness to the work of grace in my soul, that I was lacking in earnestness, sincerity, and so on, in other words, that I was deficient in good works. My life, conduct and good works were to bring peace to my heart. I failed to understand the meaning and purpose of the Law. I did not realize the spiritual character of the Law. While struggling thus to produce the good works of the Law, I failed to see the real object of the Law.

"Neither did I understand that it was precisely the purpose of the Law to wear me out, to slay and condemn me. I thought that the more I indulged in prayer, renunciation, and all virtues, the more spiritual life, power, love and peace would be the logical result. I never really believed that man is and remains dead in trespasses and sins in despite of his good works and his fine character, so long as he has not found the Son of God, in whom alone all life is to be found. 'And this is the record, that God has given to us eternal life, and this life is in His Son. He that hath the Son hath life; and he that hath not the Son of God hath not life' (1 John 5: 11-12). My reason could of course admit all this. But all my effort, nevertheless, was based upon the delusion that there were powers in me of intelligence and will and purpose which only needed to be developed by the Law. Surely, he is not dead who is able to move, to pray, to watch, to wage war, to renounce evil inclinations, to love, or at least to cherish kindly feelings toward everybody, and so forth, all of which are powers inherent in the life of such only as are born of God.

"Such a person has not had the experience of the Apostle Paul, as he explains it: 'For I was alive without the Law once: but when the commandment came, sin revived, and I died. And the commandment, which was ordained to life, I found to be unto death' (Romans 7: 9-10). Nor has he understood the purpose of the Law as explained by the Spirit. We read: 'Now we know that what things soever the Law saith, it saith to them who are under the Law: that every mouth may be stopped, and all the world may become guilty before God. Therefore, by the deeds of the Law there shall no flesh be justified in His sight: for by the Law is the knowledge of sin' (Romans 3: 19-20). 'Moreover the Law entered, that the offense might abound. But where sin abounded, grace did much more abound: That as sin hath reigned unto death, even so might grace reign through righteousness unto eternal life by Jesus Christ our Lord' (Romans 5: 20-21). 'Knowing that a man is not justified by the works of the Law, but by the faith of Jesus Christ, even we have believed in Jesus Christ, that we might be justified by the faith of Christ and not by the works of the Law: for by the works of the Law shall no flesh be justified' (Galatians 2: 16). 'Wherefore the Law was our schoolmaster to bring us unto Christ, that we might be justified by faith' (Galatians 3: 24).

"Nor has he who trusts in good works, the development of character, believed the obvious truth, that 'that which is born of the flesh is flesh and cannot see the Kingdom of God,' that the unregenerate soul is 'dead in trespasses and sins.' The self-righteous person does not believe the life-giving truth expressed by the Apostle Paul in the following words: 'For if by one man's offense death reigned by one, much more they which receive abundance of grace and of the gift of righteousness shall reign in life by one, Jesus Christ. Therefore, as by the offense of one, judgment came upon all men to condemnation, even so by the righteousness of one the free gift came upon all men unto justification of life. For as by one man's disobedience many were made sinners, so by the obedience of one shall many be made righteous' (Romans 5: 17, 18, 19). 'If one died for all, then were all dead' (2 Corinthians 5: 14), and are revived by Him.

"I begin to see more and more clearly that the Gospel in its true nature and essence was utterly foreign to me. For I believed that repentance was a betterment of the heart, the mind and conduct, which I should attain with the help of the grace of God. I did not understand that it was nothing more thàn the conviction of sin, condemnation and death, as the Scriptures teach. 'Sin, that it might appear sin, working death in me by that which is good, that is, the Law of God, that sin by the commandment might become exceeding sinful. For we know that the Law is spiritual: but I am carnal, sold under sin' (Romans 7: 13-14). 'Behold, I was shapen in iniquity, and in sin did my mother conceive me. Purge me with hyssop, and I shall be clean: wash me, and I shall be whiter than snow' (Psalm 51: 5, 7).

"I did not realize that grace can not, nay, will not save a sinner who still trusts in himself, who is not spiritually naked (2 Corinthians 5: 3), who has not found life in Christ alone, but covers himself with the ragged garments of his own righteousness. Grace can not build up the self-righteous. On the contrary, it would break him down, crush and annihilate that individual's pride, his trust in himself, his character and good works. When that process is accomplished, grace could restore, forgive, and impart life. Jesus says: 'Every plant which my heavenly Father hath not planted shall be rooted up' (Matthew 15: 13). I could not comprehend why this should be called self-righteousness, so long as I tried to better myself with the aid of the impulses of God's grace and the determination of my strong will. I now see that in this way I would have to become my own savior.

"The idea was, that the more I labored at my self-improvement, the more certainly I should succeed. I would be the masterbuilder of my salvation. God was to furnish the materials that I needed. Who does not see that such labor under the Law simply means that a man desires at all odds to save his own pride, thus avoiding the acceptance of God's free gift of grace? Who does not see that it means the soul's refusal of the sacrificial death of our divine-human Mediator Jesus Christ? Who does not in this connection see the force of the words of the apostle: 'If righteousness came by the Law, then Christ is dead in vain' (Galatians 2: 21). The self-righteous Pharisee, or, in modern terms, the man who trusts for salvation in the development of 'character,' as he terms the process, is an abomination to the Lord. (See Luther's *Sermons*, Sunday after Christmas.)

"Equally erroneous was my idea of the aim and benefit of repentance. I thought that God would be moved by the contrition of my heart, my prayers, my anguish and my tears, to become gracious to me. I thought that all this would make me more worthy of grace and forgiveness. I did not understand that God is already moved; that His heart is already full of mercy in Christ; that God for His sake has grace for all men; that He is reconciled to the world; that all things are ready; that He only waits for all to come to His loving arms and receive His pardoning grace. 'God hath reconciled us to Himself by Jesus Christ; we pray you in Christ's stead, Be ye reconciled to God' (2 Corinthians 5: 19, 20). 'He is the propitiation for our sins: and not for ours only, but for the sins of the whole world' (1 John 2: 2). 'He hath not dealt with us after our sins, nor rewarded us according to our iniquities. For as the heaven is high above the earth, so great is His lovingkindness toward them that fear Him. As far as the east is from the west, so far hath He removed our transgressions from us' (Psalm 103: 10-12). There are numberless passages in the Bible to prove that God by the atonement of Christ is ready to receive and pardon any sinner who comes to Him. I did not see that repentance was necessary for myself alone, in order that I might be induced to come to Christ and through Him receive grace for grace. I still desired to avoid the humiliation of my natural pride.

"At that period of my life, I was in a manner converted. But my state was that of a stone—dead. In turning it over, possibly the stone might show a cleaner surface; but it was the same stone, nevertheless, and—dead. The Law could not give life. It was powerless to cleanse my heart, purify and sanctify my soul. This remains God's own work through His abundant grace accepted in faith.

"After I had worn myself out by many vain efforts to produce righteousness before God, the mystery of the Gospel finally opened up before my soul. I saw that the redemption and righteousness that I needed was already purchased and won for me and for all the world beside. I saw that the fetters in which my soul was bound were but spiritual blindness, unbelief, error and ignorance. I had looked in my heart for light, life and righteousness, instead of looking to Christ. Instead of believing the grace in the heart of God, I had sought grace in my own heart, wherewith to comfort myself. Instead of hearing and accepting the promises of God in the Gospel, I looked for emotions and testimonials in my inner personality. The peace in my heart was therefore a fragile, uncertain thing, imaginary and unreliable, proportioned to the degree of pleasureable feelings that I had. I thus made God a liar. I could not surrender to His mercy nor trust in His promises alone.

"This, then, was the real reason of my continued and suffocating unbelief. But blessed be the name of the Lord. The mystery of the Gospel was revealed to me. I learned that I might come as I was to a table already prepared, yes, just as I was, without any attempt at dressing up for the occasion. My dear Lord and Savior by His life of obedience and His sacrificial death had purchased for me and every sinner the wedding garment of His righteousness, in which I might stand before God without the addition of a single patch of my own righteousness.

"When I realized this, it seemed to me the greatest sin in the world was to try to sew new patches of my own upon the precious garment of Christ's righteousness, a garment of shining silk, without spot or wrinkle. I was horrified and ashamed to recall that I had hitherto robbed Him of His honor, made myself so important and Christ so insignificant. No intelligence can fathom the depth of unbelief which underlies such effort at self-justification before God. It is the deepest and blackest cavern of human arrogance. No soul understands that fact before he has received mercy, life and peace for nothing, for nothing absolutely. Then only are we ready to give all honor, praise and glory to the Lamb of God, which was slain for our sins as the ransom of our souls. The Prophet Isaiah says: 'Ho, every one that thirsteth, come ye to the waters, and he that hath no money; come ye, buy, and eat. Yea, come, buy

wine and milk without money and without price'
(Isaiah 55: 1). 'For if by grace, then is it no more
of works; otherwise grace is no more grace'"
(Romans 11: 6).

THE GREAT MYSTERY REVEALED
(*Continued*)

THE TWENTY-SIXTH DAY

WITHOUT any self-improvement, without faith
or even hatred of sin, I ought to come to Christ
and buy all this of Him for nothing. For He says
in wonderfully beautiful language: "I counsel thee
to buy of me gold tried in the fire, that thou mayest
be rich; and white raiment, that thou mayest be
clothed, and that the shame of thy nakedness do not
appear; and anoint thine eyes with eyesalve, that
thou mayest see" (Revelation 3: 18). In a true
conversion I realize that I ought to possess this or
that good, and also, that I lack everything. To me
as a lost and condemned sinner, Christ has granted
all things. He now expects me to accept the entire
gift. For this purpose He came to the earth. "The
Spirit of the Lord God is upon me, because the
Lord hath anointed me to preach good tidings unto
the meek. He hath sent me to bind up the broken-
hearted, to proclaim liberty to the captives, and the
opening of the prison to them that are bound; to
proclaim the acceptable year of the Lord, and the
day of the vengeance of our God; to comfort all
that mourn; to appoint unto them that mourn in Zion,

to give unto them beauty for ashes, the oil of joy for mourning, the garment of praise for the spirit of heaviness; and that they might be called trees of righteousness, the planting of the Lord, that He might be glorified" (Isaiah 61: 1-3).

Our blessed Lord preaches free and unconditional grace to all sinners, without the help of the Law. Whosoever will may come and receive the pardoning grace of God without the works of the Law. Praise to the Eternal Father, who sent His Son to be our Savior. "Who is a God like unto Thee, that pardoneth iniquity, and passeth by the transgression of the remnant of His heritage? He retaineth not His anger for ever, because He delighteth in mercy. He will turn again. He will have compassion upon us. He will subdue our iniquities, and Thou wilt cast all their sins into the depths of the sea" (Micah 7: 18-19). Our sins are so effectively hidden and forgotten of God, that even if we "sought for them, they shall not be found" (Jeremiah 50: 20).

Why, then, do we remain under the Law, since the Law can do nothing but make us sinners, condemned sinners? If God has not made a new covenant with us in Christ, "a new and living way, which He hath consecrated for us, through the vail, that is, His flesh" (Hebrews 10: 20), then we must look about and see whether we can be justified by the Law. In that case, no flesh shall be saved. Then are all sinners irretrievably lost forever. But confessing the new covenant with Christ and at the same time looking and trusting to one's self, that is equivalent to unbelief and resultant misery. That is making God a liar by disbelieving His Word. Acting thus, we might as well say: We do not believe a word about Christ and the atonement on the cross. Or: True, Christ was given as a sacrifice for sin. But He has not accomplished the atonement. He died in vain. What Turk or Jew could speak more contemptibly of Christ?

But thanks be to God! Christ has fulfilled every jot and tittle of the Law. He has kept the Law perfectly. For this reason, they who accept His redemption are called "the redeemed of the Lord" (Psalm 107: 2). He has purchased an eternal redemption and perfected His saints with an offering. "He hath put away their sin by the sacrifice of Himself" (Hebrews 2: 26). All men are now redeemed. For this reason, every unhappy slave of sin when he hears the good news of salvation, should receive it with joy, because it is proclaimed to the whole world without any exception: "For there is no difference: for all have sinned and come short of the glory of God; being justified freely by His grace through the redemption that is in Christ Jesus" (Romans 3: 22-24). Note the expression: "the redemption that is," not: that is to be.

Now, if this be truth, we all should rejoice and be glad. Here is reason for rejoicing. What reason is there? Listen: God has been merciful to us, who deserved death.

> *"For Christ has said it by His blood,*
> *That God is merciful and good."*

When the mystery of the Gospel arose on my sight as does the beautiful sun of the morning, my heart was filled with gladness. Peace came to my soul. The prison-doors flew open. The chains fell off my feet. I was loosed "from the bands of my neck," by which I had been decorated in my captivity. I refer to my good resolutions, my enforced godliness, my artificial worship. Instead, the ways of the Lord became the delight of my heart. To me the transformation in my life and in my soul is the fulfilment of the words of the apostle: "But now we are delivered from the Law, that being dead wherein we were held, that we should serve in newness of the spirit, and not in the oldness of the letter" (Romans 7: 6).

Do not think, friends, that as a result of my soul's deliverance from the bands of sin, I now lead a free and lawless life, without prayer, without fear, without renunciation, without war against the evil desires of the flesh. I have not so learned Christ. "If so be that ye have heard Him, and have been taught by Him, as the truth is in Jesus: that ye put off concerning the former conversation the old man, which is corrupt according to the deceitful lusts, and be renewed in the spirit of your mind, and that ye put on the new man, which after God is created in righteousness and true holiness" (Ephesians 4: 20-24). The cohorts of sin, the Law, my own flesh, the world, death and the devil, pursue me relentlessly by day and night. I am constantly constrained to fight for my faith, to be strong and courageous, not in my own strength, but in the Lord.

There is a Scripture passage which frequently is misapplied by inculcators of work-righteousness and by souls that are in captivity under the Law. They use it as a support for their unbelief and uncertainty as to their state of grace. As if such a spirit of doubt and vacillation were pleasing to the Lord. They call that state of mind the true spiritual condition of a believer. They speak of this timidity, fearsomeness, and uncertainty as a sure sign of "poverty of spirit," and commend it most highly. But God says something quite different concerning these people when He registers "the fearful and unbelieving" together with murderers, idolaters and liars (Revelation 21:8).

"But," some one asks, "are not Christians to work out their salvation with fear and trembling?" Most certainly. But observe that the apostle writes to such as are already believers, pardoned and saved. He admonishes these to work out their salvation with fear and trembling, in order that they may reach the goal—the crown of life. That does not mean that they are admonished to be in constant doubt and uncertainty regarding their state of grace, or as to whether they are God's children or not. On the contrary, the same apostle says also: "For ye have not received the spirit of bondage again to fear, but ye have received the Spirit of adoption, whereby we cry Abba, Father. The Spirit itself beareth witness with our spirit, that we are the children of God" (Romans 8:15-16).

The "fear and trembling" of which the apostle speaks, is that which a man feels who has received a great treasure which he must carry with him through a land filled with enemies and robbers. In such circumstances, we are not to feel secure and careless. We ought to be well armed and move forward circumspectly. However, we do not believe that a Christian is always able to be secure and happy in his faith. That faith which is never assaulted is not the true faith. Still we ought to strive after the perfecting of our faith with all diligence.

Finally, I believe very simply that everything flowing from faith in Christ is and is called sanctification, even though my reason would not thus designate it. For it sees nothing but sin and shortcoming in all my life and conduct. However, the Bible says: "And God which knoweth the hearts, bare them witness, ... purifying their hearts by faith" (Acts 15:8-9). And again: "Received ye the Spirit by the works of the Law, or by the hearing of faith?" (Galatians 3:2). Hence we ask the same question as does the apostle: "Do we then make void the Law through faith? God forbid: yea, we establish it" (Romans 3:31).

INFANT BAPTISM

THE TWENTY-SEVENTH DAY

"AND they brought young children to Him, that He should touch them; and His disciples rebuked those that brought them. But when Jesus saw it, He was much displeased, and said unto them, 'Suffer the little children to come unto me, and forbid them not: for of such is the Kingdom of God. Verily I say unto you, Whosoever shall not receive the Kingdom of God as a little child, he shall not enter therein.' And He took them up in His arms, put His hands upon them, and blessed them" (Mark 10: 13-16).

In these words Our Lord makes four important statements:

I. Little children need to receive the Kingdom of God.

II. Little children alone are prepared to receive the Kingdom of God.

III. The Kingdom of God belongs to them.

IV. Jesus would have the little children come to Him, in order that He may bless them.

I. *The little children need to receive the Kingdom of God.*

That the children who upon this occasion were brought to Jesus were little children, is evident from the fact that they "were brought to Him," or as Saint Luke says: "And they brought (carried) unto Him also infants, that He would touch them" (Luke 18: 15). That these children, and thus all children, are in need of receiving the Kingdom of God, is patent from the fact that Jesus says: "Whosoever shall not receive the Kingdom of God as a little child, he shall not enter therein."

Why do the little children need to receive the Kingdom of God? Because they are born of sinful parents, and therefore conceived in sin. "Behold, I was shapen in iniquity, and in sin did my mother conceive me" (Psalm 51: 5). Consequently all children are born outside the Kingdom of God and are the children of wrath. They are not the children of God. But none but the children of God belong to the Kingdom of God. None are the children of God but those that are born of God. For the children of God are born, "not of blood, nor of the will of the flesh, nor of the will of man, but of God" (John 1:13).

A child, as it is born into the world, is as Adam was after the Fall. For we do not read that the son of Adam became like Adam during the period of his growth and development, but that "Adam begat a son in his own likeness, after his own image." What was the state of Adam after he had fallen into sin? He was afraid and "hid from the presence of the Lord amongst the trees of the garden." Adam would not humble himself before God and honestly confess his sin. He put the blame for his sin upon his wife Eve, and she blamed the serpent (Genesis 3).

The fact that Adam begat a son in the likeness of himself as a fallen sinner is clear from the Word of God. The Bible shows that we all are born in sin, that is, of sinful flesh. Experience proves all too abundantly that even believing parents, in whom the image of God has been restored, do not bear sinless children but sinful children. Sin was incarnate in our nature when we were born. A corrupt tree does not become corrupt after it has produced corrupt fruit—it was corrupt originally. It grew from corrupted roots, and was therefore corrupt. We are sinful by nature. Sin is not something that came to us after we were grown up. Sin has tainted both soul and body, because we are born of sinful seed. We did not become sinners when we began to think, speak and do evil—we are born sinners. We cannot help sinning. As surely as the fallen Adam needed the restoration of the image of God in his soul, just as surely all children born after the image of Adam need to have the image of God restored in their hearts, since nothing unclean may enter the Kingdom of God (Revelation 21: 27). Little children alone are prepared to receive the Kingdom of God.

II. *That little children, and none but little children, are prepared to receive the Kingdom of God,* is also clear from the word of the Lord, who says: "He that receiveth not the Kingdom of God as a little child, shall not enter therein."

In these words Jesus has shown that a child needs only to be a child in order to be prepared to receive the Kingdom of God, but that all who have passed beyond the stage of childhood, no matter who they are or what they are, are unfit to receive the Kingdom of God. They must become as little children before they are fit and ready to receive the Kingdom of God. As surely as an infant at its birth has a nude body, and needs clothing, so surely has that same infant a naked soul which needs to be clothed. And just as surely as the mother has thought of clothing for the child before it was born, so surely has Christ prepared a garment of righteousness for the soul of that child. As surely as the mother cares for the infant's body, so surely does the Holy Ghost care for its soul. As little as an infant can run away from its mother so that she cannot care for it, so little can the same child resist the Holy Ghost and prevent Him from taking possession of the child's heart. We read of John the Baptist: "He shall be filled with the Holy Ghost, even from his mother's womb" (Luke 1: 15). Who had preached a sermon to him in order that he might receive the Holy Ghost? The preaching of the Word of God is necessary to make fit and receptive all those who have passed beyond the stage of childhood. Grown-up people need to become as little children if they would receive the Kingdom of God. But children, precisely as children, are fit and prepared to receive the Kingdom of God.

III. *The Kingdom of God belongs to them.*

The Kingdom of God belongs to the little children, but children as children do not belong to the Kingdom of God. They are outside of the Kingdom of God, because they are born in the likeness of Adam, that is, they are by nature sinful. But they have a right to the Kingdom of God. The kingdom belongs to them. Since the children have part in the sinful corruption of Adam, they are outside of the Kingdom of God. But since Christ is the propitiation for the sin of the world and thus also for the inherited sin of the children, their sins are paid and they have the right to the Kingdom of God. Jesus has paid for all sin. He has suffered the penalty for the sin of the world. Inherited sin, like any other sin, carries with it guilt and punishment. It is a corruption which has tainted every human being. As truly as Jesus has suffered death for our sins of thought, word and deed, that is, our active sins, just so truly has He paid the price of His death for all inherited sin.

It is necessary, however, for us to become partakers in the sufferings of Christ. We need to be born again. We need the new mind and the clean heart. We need to hate our carnal mind, our evil thoughts, words and works. We need to learn to "speak with new tongues," to walk in newness of life. For as truly as sin and death were in the world before we were born, even so truly were the grace of our Lord Jesus Christ and eternal life in the world before we were born. As no one has part in the sin of Adam and the guilt of that sin before he is born after the flesh, so no one has part in the grace of Christ and eternal life before he is born anew by the Spirit, that is, born of God. The atonement of Christ is greater than the sin of Adam. For this reason the atonement rendered by Christ belongs to every one that is born in sin, that is, to all men. God would that all men become partakers of this same atonement.

INFANT BAPTISM
(*Continued*)

THE TWENTY-EIGHTH DAY

IV. *Jesus wants the little children to come to Him, in order that He may bless them.*

NO one is a participant in the atonement of Christ but he who is a participant in Christ Himself. For this reason Jesus says not only to grown people, "Come unto me," but He says also to the children, "Suffer the little children to come unto me." No one is a member of the Kingdom of Christ but he who has entered through the door into this kingdom. Now Christ says: "I am the door; by me, if any man enter in, he shall be saved, and shall go in and out, and find pasture" (John 10:9). "I am the way, the truth, and the life: no man cometh unto the Father but by me" (John 10: 6). No one—hence not even a little child is saved except by the forgiveness of sin and the righteousness of Christ. No one is saved who is not a participant in Christ Himself. The little children must therefore come to Him, in order that they may be blessed of Him, in order that He may endow them with the white robe of His righteousness.

How, now, does an adult become a participant in Jesus and His atonement for the sin of the world? The Apostle Paul says: "For as many of you as have been baptized into Christ have put on Christ" (Galatians 3: 27). "Christ also loved the Church, and gave Himself for it, that He might sanctify and cleanse it with the washing of water by the Word" (Ephesians 5 : 25-30). They who are thus cleansed in Baptism become members of the body of Christ, flesh of His flesh, and bone of His bone. At Colossians 2 : 11-12, the apostle shows that Baptism is not only an external burial in water, but that it is a burial with Christ, a means by which the person baptized becomes a participant in the burial and resurrection of Christ. Being buried with Christ in Baptism, he has put off the body of sin in the flesh. He has been circumcised with the circumcision of Christ.

Baptism is thus not only a means by which we are sanctified in the spirit: we are also sanctified in the body. In Baptism, as in the Lord's Supper, there is not only a spiritual participation and communion with Christ, but also a physical incarnation in Christ. He who in Baptism is become a participant in Christ and His righteousness, is regarded by God not as he is here on earth in the body, with sin to harass him, but as he is to be when the body of this death has been put off and he has been clothed on the Last Day with a body like unto the glorified body of Christ. Here the believer feels that he is a partaker of Adam's nature; but before God the body of sin, which as a matter of actual experience he will put off at death, has already been put off in Baptism: before God he is already a member of the body of Christ, flesh of His flesh, bone of His bone. Experimentally, however, he is not clothed upon with this holy body before the Last Day.

Baptism is, therefore, the means by which we

rightly become participants in Jesus, His merits and righteousness. By Baptism we are taken out of the stock of Adam and grafted into a new stock, the True Vine, by which divine operation we become partakers of the same nature as the stock, but do not become the stock itself. Baptism is Baptism, not because the person baptized is in himself fit for Baptism, but because Baptism is a divine ordinance instituted by Christ in the name of the Triune God, in whose name the person is baptized. Only he who is a child, or is become as a little child, is fit and ready to receive Holy Baptism. He only is a branch who is capable of growing together with the stock, the True Vine. Infant Baptism is, consequently, the most certain Baptism, that is, incorporation in Christ, because the person baptized is not only rightly engrafted in the Vine, but also because he is fit and prepared not only for a sacramental union with Christ, but also for a permanent life-union with the Savior.

If a person has been baptized as an adult, and does not feel certain that he was fit and prepared to receive the sacred ordinance, let him not reason in this wise: "Possibly the Gardener did not graft me rightly into the Vine. Perhaps I ought to be baptized again." Since he has been engrafted, let him rejoice in the fact that he is in the stock of the Vine. But not only that: let him also draw sap and nourishment for his soul from the Vine. Else he will go dry and decay in spite of the fact that he has been rightly engrafted in the stock of the Vine.

But he who has been baptized as a child ought to

make certain not only that he has been rightly grafted in the stock, but also that he has grown together with it, since his Baptism took place at a period of his life in which alone, according to the words of Jesus, a person is fit and ready to receive the Kingdom of God. In Baptism, the grafting into Christ, nothing was lacking; for that was the work of God Himself. We must not make Baptism a work of our own. Let it remain what it is: a work of God by which He calls sinners to Christ.

Let us thank God that in childhood He set us in Christ Jesus. Let us accept grace and power from Him to live in Christ and for Christ, in order that we become not dry branches, fit only to be cast into the fire and burned (John 15: 6). But he who is and continues to be a withered branch shall receive a more severe judgment from the very fact that he has been baptized. "For unto whomsoever much is given, of him shall be much required: and to whom men have committed much, of him they will ask the more" (Luke 12: 28). He who has been made a branch on the True Vine which is Christ, but neglects to make use of the blessed privilege of drawing sap and spiritual nutrition from Him, remaining a withered branch, shall some day be all the more wretched for the very reason that he neglected to make use of the rich opportunity given him.

However, a withered branch, that is to say, a Christian fallen from grace, may still regain life. For even though the life-union with Christ has been lost, yet the sacramental union with Him has not been lost. Only return to your Savior and to the covenant relationship of your Baptism. The restoration to spiritual life is equally as necessary and possible to you as it was to the angels of the churches at Ephesus and Laodicea. (Read Revelation, Chapters 2 and 3.) What you have received of God in your Baptism is enough. Remember what you have received and heard. Treasure it in your heart and return to your Covenant God.

BRANCHES ON THE VINE

I am the true Vine, and my Father is the Husbandman. Every branch in me that beareth not fruit He taketh away: and every branch that beareth fruit, He purgeth it, that it may bring forth more fruit (JOHN 15: 1-2).

THE TWENTY-NINTH DAY

WHAT a blessing to hear the Lord Himself speak in a matter of such vital importance! It is matter of moment for all ages, and not least for our age. On the one hand, the age is glorious, because a Pentecostal wind passes over our beloved land, awakening souls to an interest in their eternal welfare. On the other hand, our age is an ominous age, because there are gales of false doctrine rushing all about us. There is much of indifference and worldliness among Christians, especially in localities where manners have become more polished and refined. It has become quite fashionable to be Christian, even to go to church. At the same time the tendency is toward an amalgamation of believers and unbelievers by compromises on doctrine and principle, as also in customs and indulgences. "Ye are the salt of the earth: but if the salt have lost its savor, wherewith shall it be salted? It is henceforth good for nothing, but to be cast out, and be trodden under foot of men" (Matthew 5:13). Little attention is given to those whose conversation is such as "becometh the Gospel" (Philippians 1:27).

It is, therefore, of the greater importance to hear how the Lord Jesus Himself explains "the true grace of God wherein ye stand" (1 Peter 5:12). To us who love the Word of God, this matter of genuine Christianity is always of the greatest importance. It is not necessary to inform us that "the world lieth in wickedness," that the brazen, ungodly crowd dance along the primrose way to damnation. We know that only too well. But that which may cause the downfall even of the elect is the sinister fact that not every conversion is a genuine conversion; not every faith a saving faith; not every communion with Christ a true and blessed union with Him. Among the godly are those who shall be condemned.

For this reason it is highly important that we understand the distinction between true Christianity and spurious Christianity. Christ tells us the difference. Why concern yourself at all about Christianity, if the Lord Himself did not press upon you its great importance? He is the judge who decides the matter. He says: "Every branch that beareth not fruit, He taketh away." Are you not named under this designation? But Christ is your ultimate judge. If there be not enough of Christianity in you to fear and mistrust the deceitfulness of your own heart and the slimy ways and wiles of the devil, and to heed the Word of the Lord, then you may know, without any other criterion, that you are already trapped and securely caged by the evil one. True Christians have a spirit of godliness which causes them to examine themselves whether they be in the faith.

Possibly you who read this know that you are a good Christian. No one has a word of warning to give you. Nevertheless, hear what He says who shall come in great glory and judge all nations. It is a poor sign of your own spiritual condition, if you think only of others and forget yourself when the Lord speaks of true piety.

It may well be that another person who reads these lines is obsessed with a spirit of fear and uncertainty. He never feels certain in regard to his interest and participation in Christ. His thoughts revolve continually about his many sins and shortcomings. He thinks every error is a monstrous sin, a sign of spiritual decay. He draws no distinction between defects which are the sign of spiritual decline and death, and those that are not such portentous signs. Ponder, friend, the words of Jesus about the Vine and the Branches. In that wonderful illustration He tells you what in your soul operates toward death, and what does not so operate. In the study of these words of Jesus, you may gain assurance in this important concern of your soul's salvation.

Observe, in the first place, the glorious and comforting relation of the soul to Christ as presented in the parable of the Vine and the Branches. It portrays the intimate unity that subsists between Jesus and His believers. For He says: "I am the Vine, ye are the branches" (John 15: 5). What is more closely united than a tree and its branches? It is in reality one body: the same sap and life pass through the stock and all the branches, clear out to the tiniest leaflet. Such is the union, says the Lord, between Himself and His believing disciples. When He says, "I am the Vine, ye are the branches," I could wish to look into His heart. What mysteries of love and life are expressed in these words of Jesus! He says definitely in verse 4: "Abide in me, and I in you." In His sacerdotal prayer to the heavenly Father, He says: "I in them, and Thou in me" (John 17: 23). This intimate relation, He assures us, is not confined to the apostles: it has also reference to all believers to the end of time. For we read, verse 20: "Neither pray I for these alone, but for them also who shall believe on me through their word, that they all may be one; as Thou, Father, art in me, and I in Thee." In these words our Lord declares that all believers are one with Him. What glory! We are one with Him.

Behold here true Christianity at its best and

purest! Behold herein the mystery of the Christian life! It is not only a certain amount of knowledge concerning Christ; nor is it the generous assent to the truth of the Word of God; nor yet does it consist in a pious life, Christian activity, good works, and external observances. True Christianity is something else and something far greater. It consists primarily in a most intimate union with Christ, as the branch is intimately united with the tree. This union—call it mystical if you will—is the true source and strength of genuine Christianity. Even as Christ declares: "He that abideth in me, and I in him, the same bringeth forth much fruit: for without me ye can do nothing" (John 15: 5). "Abide in me, and I in you. As the branch cannot bear fruit of itself, except it abide in the vine; no more can ye, except ye abide in me" (verse 4).

This soul-union with Christ is the secret spring of true Christianity, of which the world knows not a thing. For this reason the world cannot understand a genuine Christian. It looks upon the life of an honest Christian as a life in galling bondage. The reason for this misconception of true Christianity is that the world is ignorant of the real foundation upon which it rests. The world is not aware of the circumstance that a Christian lives in a most intimate union with the Lord.

Here the question arises: Who are thus one with Christ? A second question follows: How may the soul be assured that it lives in this intimate union with the Lord Jesus?

There are many who assert that Jesus lives in

their hearts and that they hold sweet communion with Him. Meantime they delude themselves in their boast of converse with Christ; for in reality they hear the seductions of the wily serpent and are intoxicated by insidious whisperings of the devil. They are ready to swear that the Lord dwells in their hearts. He gives comforting answers to their anxious questionings. But they are misled by Satan and their own carnal minds. Testing them by the figure of the Vine and the Branches, they come short of their boasting claim. They manifestly deceive themselves about their spiritual condition.

Others, again, live more strictly in accord with the Word of God, but have no genuine soul and heart union with Christ. Their interest in Christ is purely intellectual or at best merely sentimental. How may I know whether I am deceived or whether I in truth live in intimate unity with Christ? The answer to these questions is given in the words of the Lord Himself. We are at liberty to trust our own wisdom if we so choose; but the day is coming when our thoughts and philosophies of life will be tried in the fire. Nothing but God's thoughts and God's Word will survive. What says the Lord? He declares: "Every branch in me that beareth not fruit He taketh away: and every branch that beareth fruit, He purgeth it, that it may bring forth more fruit" (John 15: 2).

Here we first note the ominous words: "Every branch in me that beareth not fruit shall be taken away," "cut off," and "cast into the fire." These awful words of our Lord indicate the secret death of the soul, the blind delusion which leads the soul to imagine that it lives in communion with the Savior while in reality it does not so live in Christ. The same sad condition of the soul is described in the parable of the Wedding Feast. Many were invited, but most of those invited would not come on one pretext or another. One must look to his merchandise, another to his oxen, another had just established a home, and could not come. But yet all the tables in the banqueting hall were filled with guests who had no such hindrances or who had brushed them aside. Nevertheless, among these who came was one who was "cast into outer darkness" because "he had not on a wedding garment" (Matthew 22: 11).

We should always remember that this Wedding Feast does not signify the great assemblage of all who are baptized, since no one is hindered from membership in the external communion of the Church by his business, his farm, or whatnot. Christ in this parable speaks of souls who upon the invitation of the Gospel have come to the Wedding Feast. And still He says that even among them was one—that is, a number—who was cast into outer darkness.

Our Lord frequently speaks of this secret and unhappy state of the soul which deceives itself into thinking that it is secure even if it does not live in true soul-communion with Christ. Ten virgins went forth in the night to meet the bridegroom, but one-half of the number were shut out of the Wedding Feast because they had not oil in their

lamps. He who is not utterly sunk in carnal security, allied with death and in a covenant with
hell, must shudder at such words uttered by the
Lord. He will conclude that there must be a secret,
terrible danger threatening the souls of men, since
the loving, gentle Savior speaks in such drastic
language.

BRANCHES ON THE VINE
(*Continued*)

THE THIRTIETH DAY

WHAT particular marks does the Lord give by
which we may know the genuine branches from
the worthless ones? The first and most essential
mark is that the good branches bear fruit, which
means that the true disciples of Jesus bear fruit.
The next important question is: What does the
Lord mean by the word "fruit," and by the phrase,
to "bear fruit"?

There are many who readily settle the question
by saying that "fruit" here means good works.
We need, however, to look at the question more
closely, and to note carefully what our Lord and
His apostles mean by the term. It is true that good
works are the fruit of the Spirit, and it is also—not
true. The Scriptures make much of the source and
character of our good works. He who is willing
to deceive himself and fall under the sentence of
God's judgment will take no notice of this circumstance; but a sincere Christian who desires the

salvation of his soul will heed the description given by the Lord regarding the origin of truly good works. The Scriptures draw a sharp line of distinction between "works" and "fruit." When the Apostle Paul has first made use of the expression "the works of the flesh," he continues by way of contrast to speak of "the fruit of the Spirit." By the latter term he means to designate that which develops as the result and product of the work of the Holy Spirit (Galatians 5: 19, 22). It is therefore of the most vital importance to distinguish between "works" and "fruit," between "the works of the Law," which may proceed from a kindly personality or a good education, and "the fruit of the Spirit," which are the result of the soul's intimate union with Christ.

A fine specimen of the "fruit" of the Spirit is given as the first in the long list of various kinds of fruit enumerated by Paul in the Scripture passages to which reference has just been made—love. Love is the Queen of All Virtues in the heart and life of the Christian. Love is the controlling and directing element in his thought, speech and conduct. Love is the animating and life-giving principle in every other virtue of his life. Without love, all other virtues are soulless and lifeless, shells without a kernel, corpses without life. No matter how glittering and scintillating a person's virtues may look in the admiring eyes of the world, with love lacking in the heart, they are in the eyes of God but paste and pretense. Jesus says plainly: "By this shall all men know that ye are my disciples, if ye have love one to another" (John 13: 35). The Apostle John speaks much of "love to the brethren" in his first epistle as the surest mark and criterion of a true Christian.

First, then, we must treat of Fraternal Love. Is it not a fact that many people think and remonstrate about as follows: "How can love to the brethren be a mark and sign of true Christianity? Love to the brethren? Ah, that is an easy matter. Why, to love those who like myself love God and seek His righteousness — that is the easiest and most natural thing in the world." But, friend, the world does not think so. Hypocrites do not think so. The disciples of Moses do not think so. To all these people it is no easy matter to love the believers in Christ. To love a certain individual Christian for some kind act by which their hearts have been won, that is easy — they can do that. To love one's party — they can do that. But from the heart to love all who love God — that is something which they can not do. They may be able to imitate everything else in Christianity — but they can not imitate this love. In any such attempt, they are sooner or later revealed in their true character by a deep-seated and secret hostility to true Christianity. With keen eyes and a sharp nose, they hunt around for some dereliction or shortcoming in the life of true Christians, spread it around, gossip about it, whisper it to others, gloat over it like dogs over a carcass, and enjoy the real or manufactured sin immensely.

Love does not so act. "Love rejoiceth not in

iniquity, but rejoiceth in the truth. Love is kind, envieth not, vaunteth not itself, thinketh no evil" (1 Corinthians 13: 4-6). If a Christian falls into sin, the others suffer with him, try to cover up the sin, refuse to talk about it, and endeavor in love to restore the fallen one. That is the way of love. That is in line with what the Apostle Paul writes: "Whether one member suffer, all the members suffer with it; or one member be honored, all the members rejoice with it" (1 Corinthians 12: 26).

Since now this love is not a product of the carnal mind, the question arises: Where did you get this love that seems so easy to you, a second nature to you, the impulse of your naturally proud, envious and hateful heart? Did you create this love by your own strength and will-power? Was it not rather when as a lost and wretched sinner you sought and found redemption in Christ? Very well: this new love to God and to all those who love God is the fruit of your soul-union with the Savior. It is the fruit of the Spirit. That explains why this love is so natural and easy to you. That explains why you do not have to struggle with your naturally evil heart to force love to others. This love is not the work of the Law, but the fruit of the Spirit. Here you see what it is to "serve in newness of spirit, and not in the oldness of the letter" (Romans 7: 6).

Such is also the case with the universal love of believers. While it is a fundamental trait in human nature to live selfishly, think supremely of oneself, love oneself and have no thought or care for the

welfare of others except as it may affect and influence one's own welfare, you have by your union
with Christ received the new nature that you cannot
be otherwise than zealous also for others. Even
though a certain natural sympathy with the sorrows
and sufferings of others may induce them to render
assistance, they are yet blind and utterly indifferent to the spiritual distress which surrounds
them. Hypocrites and Pharisees may talk volubly
about the sins and shortcomings of others, but to
labor in love for their conversion and salvation is
beyond their power and care.

What is the effect of grace in the heart through
the soul's union with the Savior? The effect is this:
The dullest persons, the child, the servant, as well
as the university professor, by coming to Jesus and
by becoming one with the blessed Redeemer of the
world, begin to develop interest and solicitude for
the salvation of others, which after all is the highest
good. They talk with them about sin and grace,
recommend some good book to them, pray with
them and pray secretly in their own chamber for
them. In these acts of a Christian you see some of
the fruits of the Spirit. King David said: "I believed, therefore have I spoken" (Psalm 116: 10).
Paul writes: "We having the same spirit of faith,
according as it is written, I believe, therefore have
I spoken; we also believe, and therefore speak"
(2 Corinthians 3: 13).

A believing heart can not hide the divine gift
within itself. The lips utter that which fills the
heart. The world, on the contrary, is spiritually

deaf and dumb. It can speak a thousand words about everything else but of the Savior of mankind. Hypocrites and self-righteous persons may talk of church affairs and of the sins and derelictions of other people. They say nothing about the Lamb of God, the grace and truth in Christ. Even though through admonition and exhortation they might be moved to speak of the love of God in Christ, their speech would be labored and mechanical, devoid of spirit and unction.

But now that you are united with the Savior, grace is become the most precious topic for your thought and your speech. That which formerly was dull and difficult, is now the delight of your soul. Now you no longer need to be admonished to think in love of others and to bear witness to Jesus. Though you were prohibited from witnessing for Christ under threat of imprisonment and death, you could not be restrained from speaking of your dear Savior. He has become the light of your life, the One supremely beloved. His love is second nature with you. You are a new creature in Christ. How and when did this transformation take place? That happened when as a condemned sinner you found grace and salvation through faith in Christ. Hence, it is the fruit of your union with Christ. Your confession of Christ is a fruit of the Spirit.

The same holds good in regard to the delight which you take in everything that is pleasing to God, as humility, patience, purity, and all other fruits of the Spirit. You have a new heart and a new mind. That fact is demonstrated more and more

in your daily life, however fiercely the flesh may
war against the Spirit. It is these new inner qualities, created by the union with Christ, and the
voluntary expressions of the new spirit, which in the
Scriptures are designated as "the fruit of the
Spirit." These fruits of the Spirit are spoken of
by Jesus as "the fruit" of the branches of the vine.
Specifically He mentions love as a fruit of the
Spirit. "This is my commandment, that ye love one
another, as I have loved you" (John 15: 12). And
shortly afterward: "These things I command you,
that ye love one another" (John 15: 17). Then
He mentions patience as one of the fruits of the
Spirit. (See verses 18-21.) And then witness-bear-
ing. "Ye also shall bear witness" (verse 27). This
fruit of bearing witness for Him, He emphasizes in
verse 16: "Ye have not chosen me, but I have chosen
you, and ordained you, that ye should go and bring
forth fruit, and that your fruit should remain."
But He reiterates that these fruits must flow from
the union with Himself and depend entirely upon
that mystical union. For He says: "If ye abide in
me, and my words in you, — ye shall bear much
fruit." "Abide in me, and I in you. Abide in my love."

It follows, then, as a matter of inexorable logic,
that no matter how much you have experienced,
learned, labored and suffered, if you lack the
"fruit" spoken of in the Scriptures, you are not in
personal, intimate union with Christ. Still, if you
judge yourself, and seek the true union with Christ,
all you lack is that you do not know your Savior.
You only need to know Him, to lose yourself in His

unfathomable love, to be baptized "with the Spirit and with fire." But if you have chosen to go your own way, destitute of these chief fruits of the Spirit, you are assuredly one of the branches on the vine which shall be cut off and "cast into the fire to be burned." The Lord has pronounced this sentence upon the unfruitful branch.

BRANCHES ON THE VINE
(*Continued*)

THE THIRTY-FIRST DAY

ARE the good branches of the vine perfectly clean and robust? They possess love and all the fruits of the Spirit. But are they free of all taint of evil? Christ says something quite different: "Every branch that beareth fruit, He purgeth it, that it may bring forth more fruit" (John 15: 2). Here I learn that the same souls whom the Lord commends as good, fruitful branches, are not entirely clean in themselves. There are many Christians who maintain that a fruitful tree of necessity is a clean tree. But these are two different things. As a good and precious branch which bears fruit abundantly may yet have a dry twig or a sucker which only absorbs the sap and ought to be removed, so a Christian may be rich in fruits of the Spirit, and yet not only be tainted with the universal evil of natural depravity, but also with some fault or habit which daily needs to be crucified, and which he never quite overcomes. Nevertheless, he is a different branch from the withered or decayed branches which bear no fruit. Many a man may have but few faults socially; he may have a pleasing personality, and still be a dead and fruitless branch.

Remember, then, my Christian friend, that you are not altogether clean of sin and evil propensities. They cause you daily mortification; but they shall not condemn you, provided you remain faithfully united with Christ in a humble, living faith. You realize that you may even so bear good and acceptable fruit, though you may never be perfectly satisfied with them. United with Christ, you are a "new creature" in Him (2 Corinthians 5: 17). Let me say it once again: So long as you abide in Christ, the True Vine, all your defects and shortcomings shall not condemn you. No one suffers from the sins of a Christian as much as he himself does. No one is as keenly aware of them. Nevertheless, they are clean in Christ, well-pleasing to God, and precious branches upon the Vine.

How does the heavenly Gardener deal with the branches that bear fruit? He says: "Every branch that beareth fruit, He purgeth it, that it may bring forth more fruit" (John 15: 2). Observe: "He purgeth it." That is a short sentence, but long and trying in actual practice. He cleanses the good branch. This is the second mark of the good branches. The branch that bears no fruit whatever is not purified. It grows free and untrammeled, as it pleases. It is only to be burned, anyhow. But the branch which bears fruit must be pruned and cleansed of excrescences.

How is this cleansing performed? The parable of Christ is constructive. He speaks of a "purging," a "cleansing," performed by a gardener. This cleansing is not done with water, but with knife and shears, by the use of which dry twigs, fungi, and parasitic shoots and leaves are removed. This performance illustrates graphically the experience of the believer. Are we not familiar with the gardener's knife? Do we not know the "two-edged sword" of the Word of God operating in our hearts, cutting away the sins and shortcomings of our daily lives? When negligent of our duties to God, cold and indifferent to the warnings of the Spirit, how were we not trimmed and pruned by the correction of the Spirit of God!

The gentle Gardener going about in His Vineyard makes us dissatisfied with the poor fruit that we produce. He chastises us in the inner parts. Hear King David's prayer: "Examine me, O Lord, and prove me. Try my reins and my heart" (Psalm 26: 2). Wherever the Holy Ghost dwells, this must be the case. For the Spirit will always find impurities in our hearts. Of course He must cleanse His own habitation. But that which can not be done by the inner discipline of the Word in our hearts, our faithful Lord does by external trials and tribulations, sorrows and perplexities, of which James speaks as "divers temptations" (James 1: 2). In short: A child of God must be purified. "For whom the Lord loveth He chasteneth, and scourgeth every son whom He receiveth. If ye endure chastening, God dealeth with you as with sons; for what son is

he whom the father chasteneth not? But if ye be
without chastisement, whereof all are partakers, then
are ye bastards and not sons. . . . Now, no chastening for the present seemeth to be joyous, but
grievous. Nevertheless, afterward it yieldeth the
peaceable fruit of righteousness unto them which
are exercised thereby" (Hebrews 12: 6-8, 11).

This, then, is the purpose of the Gardener's
"purging" of the branches. He takes no pleasure in
plaguing men, but when necessary, as Christ says,
He purges the fruitful branch, that it may bear more
fruit. This aim of the Gardener is attained also
through outward chastisements. Have we not seen
Christians, intelligent and upright, but spiritually
indolent and unfruitful, suddenly stricken by some
great sorrow or misadventure, or troubled spiritually to the anxious concern of their friends, finally
emerging from the ordeal purged, purified, and beginning to bear good and abundant fruit? Have we
not all seen that when selfishness, worldliness, and
the carnal mind threaten to take possession of our
hearts, some grief comes along and brings us to our
right mind again? When the Lord has again comforted us with His gracious forgiveness, we feel
cleansed as from a bath. We are ready to resume
the daily renewal of our lives with vigor and determination.

All who have become accustomed to this chastening of the heavenly Father, know very well when the
pruning-knife is to be expected. They know for a
certainty that the branches must be purged. The
Lord is filled with a holy zeal for those whom He

prepares for heaven. He would have them more
clean and fruitful. The others are left to grow after
the lusts of the flesh. In the final chapter of the
Bible, the Lord says: "He that is unjust, let him
be unjust still, and he which is filthy, let him be
filthy still, and he that is righteous, let him be righteous still, and he that is holy, let him be holy still"
(Revelation 22: 11).

Let us remember that this chastening of the Lord
of which we have spoken, is a most excellent mark
of the good branches, particularly the chastening of
the Holy Spirit in the heart of the Christian. External trials are experiences which the ungodly also
may have. But the inner chastisement of the Spirit,
rendering the believer dissatisfied with himself, and
compelling him constantly to find refuge in the
shadow of the Cross, is a fine criterion of true Christianity. For when they fail to find the fruit of the
Spirit in their lives, owing to their many shortcomings, the fact of this chastening of the Lord in one
form or another is evidence of the second fact that
they belong to the branches which the Lord prunes,
trims and cultivates as His own.

On the other hand, when an individual who seems
to be a Christian and in reality is not worldly-minded
is so well pleased with himself that he actually is
more grieved over the sins of other people than
over his own, the indications are that he does not
belong to the branches which the Lord cleanses. For
it is impossible that the Holy Spirit of God should
dwell in a heart without finding anything to correct.
The words of the apostle are definite and final: "For

if ye be without chastisement, whereof all are partakers, then are ye bastards, and not sons" (Hebrews 12: 8).

May the Holy Ghost now establish in our hearts what the Lord has said to us, and may we never forget it. May all believers gain greater assurance of their union with the Savior, saying with the apostle: "Hereby we know that we dwell in Him, and He in us, because He hath given us of His Spirit" (1 John 4: 13). May all who lack this intimate union with the Savior, never rest before they come to Him and begin to bear the fruit of the Spirit! Then, in spite of all defects and impurities, we shall be "clean" in the eyes of the Lord by virtue of justification by faith in the cleansing blood of Christ. Amen.

THE SECOND SERIES

THE REVELATION OF THE MYSTERY

Now, to Him who is of power to establish you according to my Gospel, and the preaching of Jesus Christ, according to the revelation of the mystery, which was kept secret since the world began, but now is made manifest, and by the Scriptures of the prophets, according to the commandment of the everlasting God, made known to all nations for the obedience of faith: to God only wise, be glory through Jesus Christ for ever. Amen (ROMANS 16: 25-27).

THE FIRST DAY

THE spiritual vision which discerns the undercurrents of human life, notes many deplorable and depressing facts. Nothing, however, is as heart-rending and regrettable as that which the Apostle Paul saw, and on account of which he had "great heaviness and continual sorrow" in his heart (Romans 9: 2, 3). "For," he writes, "I could wish that myself were accursed from Christ for my brethren, my kinsmen according to the flesh." What did he see? He beheld earnest souls who yet were unhappy. He beheld souls who longed for righteousness and peace with God, but sought in vain. He beheld some who, despite all their seeking, still remained unsaved, unhelped and uncomforted in life and death: they were toiling sons of the bondwoman who were to be "cast out" (Galatians 4). He saw others, comforted, safe and satisfied, and yet sadly deceived, "ignorantly in unbelief" (1 Timothy 1: 13), aroused to the knowledge of their hopeless condition too late. These were the self-deluded Pharisees, the hypocrites and false Christians. What had brought about this sad deception? They were not aware of the "mystery of revelation," did not know of its existence. It had never been revealed to their hearts.

What is the "mystery"? The whole mystery is clearly revealed by the Apostle Paul: "Israel, which followed after the Law of righteousness, hath not attained to the Law of righteousness. Wherefore? Because they sought it not by faith, but as it were by the works of the Law" (Romans 9: 31-32).

Friend, do you not know of some one who long has regretted his sins, resolved again and again to better his life, and yet has made no progress toward the realization of his purpose? He has started on the upward road, but backslidden. He is again the same weak renegade as he was before he attempted his own restoration. He has exclaimed: O wretched man that I am! Who shall deliver me from the body of this death?" (Romans 7: 24). Helpless, defeated, disheartened and reckless, he has finally given up all hope of conversion. Possibly he may have read or heard something full of sweet comfort in connection with God's forgiving mercy in Christ.

It touched his heart and he was strangely moved. But then he reasoned that such comfort was not intended for sinners such as he. It was for those only who were truly converted.

Once more he makes the attempt to save himself. He has now heard of God's loving grace. He begins to watch over himself more strenuously. He prays incessantly. He wars on the evil in his flesh. He falls. Gets up again. Falls once more. Falls again and again. He commits sins which he shunned formerly. The last state of that man is worse than the first. But sin palls and begins to disgust him. He sees others living clean and upright lives and he longs to be like them. Again there is the flickering light of hope in his darkened soul. Now at last he will repent sincerely and convert himself. Now he is going to make war on the evil within him. Now he will become a new man, born again, justified, sanctified and forgiven. His will-power will carry him through. Such is his idea of the way of salvation. But since he can never become as good as he knows that he ought to be, but does not see how he is to appropriate the grace of God. He concludes that since he has abused the grace of God once before, he cannot trust to that same grace now that he is morally and spiritually worse than ever. And so he turns his back on God and hardens his heart against the Spirit's warnings. "It's no use. The Gospel of mercy is not for me," is the miserable conclusion of his beclouded soul.

"How was this despair possible?" you say. "The poor soul had a Savior. He, too, was redeemed by

the blood of the Son of God. He was no despiser
of God and His grace. He honestly and earnestly
sought the salvation of his soul. How did it come
about that such a sincere soul was lost?"

Friend, the answer to your question is given by
the Apostle Paul in explaining the rejection of the
Jews. "For I bear them record," he writes, "that
they have a zeal of God, but not according to knowledge. For they, being ignorant of God's righteousness and going about to establish their own righteousness, have not submitted themselves unto the
righteousness of God" (Romans 10:2-3). That is
the answer to your question. A person may have zeal
without knowledge. A person may deny himself,
mortify the flesh, renounce evil, pray and seek and
struggle, and yet if he seeks salvation in a wrong
direction—in the deeds of the Law, for example—
he will never find that which he has been seeking
—peace with God.

Note here the supreme importance not only of
seeking and praying, but of hearing and obeying the
Word of God and of praying in the name and for
the sake of Christ, the atoning Savior of sinners.
Search the Scriptures. The way of salvation is so
clear that a child may find it. Faith in your own reformation, your will-power, your character, your
prayers and good works, will never save your sinful
soul. The grace of God revealed in the substitution-
ary sufferings and death of Jesus Christ, the Son
of God, is the only foundation upon which to build
your faith and trust.

Here is another picture. There is an individual

who similarly has been awakened from the torpor of sin. He realizes that the ordinary free and easy life, often spoken of as "the primrose path," does not lead to heaven. He makes up his mind to quit the life of sin, turn about, and lead the better life. He starts to read the Bible, engages in prayer. He gets busy recalling his sins, mourning over them and substituting good works in their stead. If he finds defects and shortcomings here and there in his life and conduct, he readily ascribes these to the account of weak human nature, which he finds common to all men. He sees that sin attaches to all men to the end of their days. He learns, however, that God is merciful, ready to forgive sin, partly because God pities poor human nature, especially when one is contrite and penitent, and partly because He has endowed him with the determination and the will-power to forsake the ways of sin and the wicked world about him. He now lives a clean life, and by the grace of God he will improve in every respect. With these satisfactory results already at hand, why should he for a moment doubt the goodness of God?

Such is the character of his faith and consolation. But what happens? He is laid upon a sick-bed. He dies, quietly and peacefully. He comes before the great Judgment Throne. He sees a glorious and awe-inspiring Presence upon the throne, surrounded by thousands and tens of thousands of holy angels and saints. But what does he behold upon this Man which causes him to tremble and quake? He observes wounds in His hands, His feet and side. He is terrified. In his lifetime he had taken no notice of them. He remembers their meaning and significance, however. Suddenly all the reasons for his comfort, his prayers, his good works, his fine character, his strong will-power, tumble about his ears like a house of cards. Now he realizes whom he has pierced with his self-made righteousness.

This is the species of Phariseeism to which Jesus refers in the parable of the Pharisee in the temple. The Pharisee did not begin by lauding himself. He praised God, not, however, for His grace through the atonement wrought by Christ, but because he was better than others. Hear him: "God, I thank Thee, that I am not as other men are, extortioners, unjust, adulterers, or even as this publican. I fast twice a week, I give tithes of all that I possess" (Luke 18: 11-12). In this connection, Bishop Erick Pontoppidan has written: "A man may show great industry in his office, admirable probity in word and act. He may be well versed in the Bible and confess his faith in the Bible as the inspired Word of God. He may courageously defend the true doctrines of the Church, yea, seal his faith with his blood. If the sad condition of the Church required it, and if it were the will of God, he would perform miracles in the name of Jesus. And yet he might lack the true mark of the children of God—justifying and saving faith in Christ, and be eternally cast out with all his sham virtues."

We have now seen a few deplorable cases of self-delusion. We have seen how the words of Jesus are actualized: "Many, I say, will seek to enter in, and shall not be able" (Luke 13: 24). We have learned that the reason for the loss of so many honest, seeking souls is their ignorance of the mystery of the Gospel. We now ask in all fairness: Why have they not learned to know this mystery? The answer is: (1) Because it is a mystery and not easily learned. (2) Because it is regarded as easily learned. (3) Because it is "kept secret" (Romans 16: 25), and maligned as was the Promised Land by the spies.

This "mystery of revelation" is indeed hidden and hard to learn. He who readily believes it does not comprehend its real meaning and content. He who sees its real meaning is unable to believe it. So great and glorious are the things contained in it. To gain an historical knowledge of the outstanding facts contained in the Gospel is an easy matter. To gain the inner spiritual meaning of the Gospel, however, is beyond the power of natural reason and intellect—none but the Holy Spirit can reveal that to the soul, mind and heart of man. For even though we read of "the revelation of the mystery" (Romans 16: 25), "the mystery of godliness, God manifest in the flesh, justified in the Spirit, seen of angels, preached unto the gentiles, believed on in the world, the pillar and ground of the truth" (1 Timothy 3: 15-16), "Who hath believed our report? and to whom is the arm of the Lord revealed?" (Isaiah 53: 1), the trouble is, that nothing seems more readily learned than this profound revelation to mankind. For as soon as one has acquired the historical knowledge of the facts of the Gospel, he thinks that he has grasped the mystery and knows it to the bottom.

Pretty soon, like the Athenians of old, he is looking for "some new thing" (Acts 17: 19), even though he has no more than the historical knowledge of the "mystery" which impenitent and conceited intellectuals also possess. These individuals fail to comprehend the mystery because the Holy Ghost reveals it to none but penitent, humble and praying souls, be they learned or unlearned. These learned folk who suffer from the idolatry of intellectual pride, reason about like this: Certainly. Who does not know that Christ died for the sin of the world, and that we are justified before God through faith without the works of the Law? Very well. Your head has the historical and doctrinal knowledge—but what of your heart? If from the heart you believed that you are perfectly justified and forgiven for the sake of the suffering and death of Christ upon the cross, as the Word of God declares, surely your heart would burn within you for love to such a Savior. You would be baptized with the Spirit and with fire. You would be born again.

As long as your soul has not been regenerated; as long as your faith is dead historical knowledge without power of action, you have had no "revelation of the mystery": you do not know Christ. In your carnal security, an historical, dead faith is easy enough. Wake up, friend! Rouse yourself and realize that you are a lost and condemned sinner. Then believe in the atonement wrought by the blood of the Son of God, and you shall discover to your

dismay that genuine, living, personal faith in Jesus
as your only Savior from sin, death, and damnation,
is not an easy matter.

Alas! this precious mystery is not only hidden: it
is also suppressed and calumniated. The state of
Zion, the Church of the living God, is quite deplorable. Well-meaning souls sit at the feet of
Moses and shun this supreme fact of the Gospel as
if it were a poison to the soul. They are deceived
and led astray by reason, which teaches that men
must be driven, threatened and frightened by the
Law, forgetting that men must be "born again of
water and the Spirit," and that "the Spirit is received by the hearing of faith" alone (Galatians 3:
2). Or they find comfort in their own righteousness.
They place a construction upon the Law so tenuous
and liberal, that any sinner may pick up not only
crumbs of comfort but great chunks of it by the
mere external conformity to the letter of the Law.
It happens, though, that really awakened souls who
find no comfort in their work-righteousness, are utterly destitute of all comfort. They are wretched
and unhappy, finding no benefit or consolation in the
merits of the Savior. They are in no better condition than the heathen, who know nothing of Christ.

THE REVELATION OF THE MYSTERY
(*Continued*)

THE SECOND DAY

IF any one should ask: Will you not explain this mystery of which you have spoken so clearly and lucidly that everybody must understand it? To which request I must answer: It is quite impossible to explain it in such a way as to make it clear to everybody. This mystery is of such a character that it cannot be understood simply by reading or hearing the Word of God. The reader or the hearer must humble himself before God and pray Him to grant the revelation of the mystery. True, it may be clearly enough expressed in words, and committed to memory and recited; but the saving and comforting revelation of the mystery is the work of the Holy Spirit alone. As a rule, the heart must be made receptive by the discouraging effort to better oneself under the Law.

If, now, we were to explain the mystery, we might do so in a few words or in many words. Here is the revelation of the mystery in one short sentence: "To-wit, God was in Christ, reconciling the world unto Himself, not imputing their trespasses unto them; and hath committed unto us the word of reconciliation" (2 Corinthians 5: 19). Here you have the solution of the mystery: From the moment that the Son of God took upon Himself the sin of the world, God has been reconciled with the world and has continually called the world to His loving arms. Here again is the revelation of the mystery:

The only thing of any value in the salvation of a sinner is the atoning blood of the Son of God. "He that hath the Son hath life, and he that hath not the Son of God hath not life" (1 John 5 : 12). "He that hath the Son hath life," even though he may be the most unworthy sinner on earth. "He that hath not the Son of God hath not life," though he may be as pious as all the saints rolled into one. Here again is the revelation of the mystery: All the sins that have grieved you, and the sins which grieve you to-day, were atoned for on the day of the death of Christ upon the cross. There is nothing with God to hinder you from coming immediately to the Mercy-seat. You may come as ignorant as you are, as humbled as you are, as hard-hearted as you are, as godly as you are, as ungodly as you are, as young as you are, as old as you are, as sinful as you are, as unhappy as you are, and you shall obtain grace, the grace of God in Christ given for our justification and sanctification.

All this may be presented still more lucidly by the story of the atonement of Christ for the sin of the world:

When Adam through the wiles of the devil had transgressed the commandment of God, thereby hurling himself and the entire human race into sin and death, the wrath of God and the curse of the Law, into agony of conscience, plagues and other punishments, and finally into eternal death, the Son of God had compassion on fallen mankind. He became the Mediator between God and man. In order that God's justice might be satisfied, and one man pay for the transgressions of all men, He became incarnate of the Virgin Mary, and took upon Himself the penalty for the guilt of all humanity.

The Triune God having chosen this marvellous counsel, by which the justice and the righteousness of God are divinely united, the Son came to earth, became man, and surrendered Himself to suffering and death for the sin of the world. Thus by His death He saved the whole human race from its guilt and punishment, from death and damnation. By His blood He has purchased that righteousness which alone avails before God.

This is "the revelation of the mystery" of which the evangelist speaks in the brief but comforting passage: "For God so loved the world, that He gave His only begotten Son, that whosoever believeth in Him should not perish, but have everlasting life" (John 3: 16).

Such is the message which God gave the world by a host of evangelists, angels, prophets and apostles, throughout all the Old Testament and New Testament ages. Such is the mystery which all the saints have believed, and in the faith of which they lived and died. God had promised on the day of the Fall: "The Seed of the woman shall bruise the serpent's head" (Genesis 3: 15). The Prophet Isaiah says: "Surely He hath borne our griefs, and carried our sorrows: yet we did esteem Him stricken, smitten of God, and afflicted. But He was wounded for our transgressions, He was bruised for our iniquities: the chastisement of our peace was upon Him, and with His stripes we are healed"

(Isaiah 53: 4, 5). The angel Gabriel says: "Seventy weeks are determined upon Thy people and upon Thy holy city, to finish the transgression, and to make an end of sins, and to make reconciliation for iniquity, and to bring in everlasting righteousness, and to seal up vision and prophecy, and to anoint the Most High" (Daniel 9: 24). The Prophet Zechariah says: "In that day there shall be a fountain opened to the house of David and to the inhabitants of Jerusalem for sin and for uncleanness" (Zechariah 13: 1). The Prophet Micah says: "He will turn again, He will have compassion upon us; He will subdue our iniquities; and Thou wilt cast all their sins into the depths of the sea" (Micah 7: 19). John the Baptist says: "Behold the Lamb of God, which taketh away the sin of the world" (John 1: 29). The Apostle Peter says: "Who His own self bare our sins in His own body on the tree, that we, being dead to sins, should live unto righteousness: by whose stripes ye were healed" (1 Peter 2: 24). The Apostle Paul says: "Christ hath redeemed us from the curse of the Law, being made a curse for us: as it is written, Cursed is every one that hangeth on a tree" (Galatians 3: 13). John the Beloved says: "The blood of Jesus Christ His Son cleanseth us from all sin" (1 John 1: 7).

All these sacred testimonies, selected from a multitude of similar ones, are as clear as the sun, as firm as the mountains. They all present the great doctrine of salvation, that redemption has been purchased with the blood of the Son of God. They all teach that God has been reconciled by the blood of Christ.

They are at one in teaching that our works do not merit the grace of God, nor do our sins debar us from the grace of God. All that now remains is that sinners return to our reconciled God and by faith accept the merits of Christ unto righteousness. This righteousness covers our sins, quiets conscience, rejoices and regenerates the heart, makes it burning, alive and holy, ready and willing to do all good works.

No one, however, arrives at this stage of spiritual development before the Law has done its proper work in arousing in his conscience a keen sense of sin and caused him anguish of soul on account of his pride, self-righteousness and indifference. When sin becomes a living, horrible reality to his soul; when lusts are recognized in the light of God's holy Law; when sin becomes "abundant," he comes to the conclusion that he is a lost soul. It is by this process that the glory for the salvation of sinners is ascribed to the cleansing blood of the Lamb of God alone. Then one is no longer a past master in the knowledge of the mystery of the atonement. Then the aroused sinner finds it no easy matter to believe the Gospel, in spite of the fact that he knows about Christ and His Apostle Paul. Then the top-lofty assurance is vanished. He realizes that the mystery contains other mysteries, too deep to fathom, hard knots too difficult to untie. With the gracious assistance of the spirit of God we would now attempt to find the solution to some of these problems.

These difficulties in the mystery of the Gospel constitute the thongs and chains of the Evil One, by means of which he binds the soul and holds it fast, after he has been permitted to enter the heart. The saintly Hollazius remarks that it is of no help to you to be loosed from six chains if you are held by a seventh. These difficulties usually revolve about the error, that, while appreciating and glorifying the doctrine of grace, it is in practice repudiated in connection with its appropriation. This is done by all kinds of misunderstandings regarding repentance, regeneration, faith, personal fitness or unfitness, worthiness or unworthiness. A very common difficulty presents itself when the free, unbounded and universal grace of God in Christ is offered to a penitent and humbled sinner who, like the publican in the temple, dares not lift up his eyes to heaven for very shame. He reasons in this manner:

"The Gospel message is true and beautiful for those to whom it rightly belongs, the converted and regenerated people, the good people, the pure and holy. But I am not in their class. I have no right to take the Gospel to my own heart." This is a mixture of truth and error. It is true that the contemners of the grace of God have no right to His mercy so long as they despise the atonement on the cross of Christ. But it is a most grievous error to think that they may not come to Christ and receive His pardoning grace when contrition for sin overwhelms them. It is an error to think that a person must be regenerated before he may dare to come to Christ. If regeneration before coming to Christ were a condition of salvation, not a soul on earth would or could be saved.

The truth is, that as soon as you feel the need of a Savior; as soon as you realize that you can not continue in your life of wickedness and worldliness: as soon as you start out to go back to the Father's house—then are you sufficiently converted to accept the comfort, not of your perfect conversion, but of the great truth that you are redeemed by the blood of the Son of God, redeemed and ransomed just as you are. When from the hunger and thirst of your wretched soul you stretch the weak arms of faith toward Jesus, or when the mystery of the atonement is suddenly revealed as a flash of light in the darkness of your soul, and you find to your exceeding joy that you already believe in Him, then the great regeneration has taken place in your heart and you are "a new creature in Christ Jesus."

From the day of your second birth, the rebirth of your soul, a new world opens before your astonished eyes. Your mind is crowded with new, clean thoughts, thoughts that are constructive and sanctifying, bringing peace and gladness in their train. Your heart is directed by new desires and motives; your conduct and conversation by new principles. Regeneration does not occur before you come to faith: it follows faith, and is the product of faith. Doctor Martin Luther says: "Faith is the work of God in us. Faith changes the heart. It regenerates the heart. It creates us anew and makes us new men." It is not as a converted and regenerated soul that you are to come to Christ, but as "ungodly," as lost and condemned (Romans 4: 5). Christ will help you, not when you are as good as you ought to be, but when you neither are good and holy nor can be good and holy. When you are weak, Christ is mighty to save.

THE REVELATION OF THE MYSTERY
(*Continued*)

THE THIRD DAY

SHOULD anyone ask the question: "Does not salvation really take place before I come to faith and before my sins are blotted out?"——the answer is: Salvation in reality took place nineteen hundred years ago on Golgotha, the Place of Execution, outside the walls of Jerusalem. Concerning this historical event, we read: "When Jesus therefore had received the vinegar, He said, 'It is finished': and He bowed His head, and gave up the ghost" (John 9: 30). Mark you: "It is finished." Behold in these words the salvation of the world! When these words were uttered by the dying Savior, God's eternal justice was satisfied. Humanity was redeemed and ransomed by the blood of the Son of God on the cross. Then occurred the "blotting out of the handwriting of ordinances that was against us, which was contrary to us, and He took it out of the way, nailing it to the cross, and having spoiled principalities and powers, He made a show of them openly, triumphing over them" (Colossians 2: 14-15). Behold on the cross the price of the redemption of mankind! No man can lay another foundation.

The death of the Son of God is an atonement for sin so perfect that the Triune God according to the Law is absolutely satisfied. No sinner who comes to God in the name of Jesus will be turned away. Atonement has been made for the sin of the world. The punishment for all the sins of every sinner has been suffered by Christ. He bore them all in His body on the tree. Now God calls out everywhere: Return, all ye backsliders, and ye shall receive double at the hand of the Lord for all your transgressions. Your sin is taken away. Your iniquity is atoned. Eternal righteousness has been purchased for you by the blood of the Son of God Himself. "Come unto me, all ye that labor and are heavy laden, and I will give you rest" (Matthew 11: 28).

All that remains now is to believe. "He that believeth and is baptized shall be saved, but he that believeth not shall be damned" (Mark 16: 16). He who would know himself to be saved must turn in faith back to that which transpired nineteen hundred years ago on Golgotha.

> *"My soul is saved from sin and shame,*
> *For I believe in His dear name."*

He who would be saved must turn his faith to the suffering Christ on the shameful cross. He must look to what took place there—not to that which may take place in himself.

"But," you remonstrate, "I read in my Bible: 'Repent ye therefore, and be converted, that your sins may be blotted out, when the time of refreshing shall come from the presence of the Lord' (Acts

3 : 19). Granted, that repentance is not the same as regeneration, sanctification and the cleansing of the heart, for which we find no strength under the Law, yet God requires repentance, that is, contrition and sorrow for sin. I am afraid that I am not as repentant as I should be. I am callous and hard. How, then, am I to believe?" *Answer*: Repentance is indeed necessary. It begins with a sensitiveness of conscience, a feeling of sinfulness. Under the various attempts at betterment, this feeling of sinfulness develops into the living knowledge of sin, soul-poverty with no substantial and abiding comfort in anything. In order that you may know whether your repentance is as it should be, you must consider its purpose; for that which attains its purpose is sufficient.

What is the end and purpose of repentance? God's purpose in your repentance is by no means that you are to make yourself fit and worthy of His pardoning grace, but rather that you be driven to Christ. Paul, the apostle, says: "Wherefore the Law was our schoolmaster to bring us unto Christ, that we might be justified by faith" (Galatians 3 : 24). If, then, you are capable of remaining away from Christ, away in your carnal security, with no desire to beseech God for mercy and pardon in the name of Jesus, your knowledge of sin and guilt before the all-seeing eye of God is certainly shallow and superficial. If you still seek salvation in your own betterment, the improvement of your character, your remorse and your prayers, your knowledge of sin and guilt before the living God is sadly defective. But as soon as you find no peace; as soon as you cannot conform to the ways of the world, uncertain about the mercy of God, with no comfort in your heart, in your contrition, in your self-improvement, throwing yourself upon the mercy of God in Christ alone, just as you are, then is your repentance as it should be; for it attains its purpose, which was to drive you to Christ. In Him you find peace and rest and safety. You are secure in the city of refuge. "He who hath the Son, hath life."

You understand, friend, that in order that your knowledge of sin may be right, it must not be of your own making. You might find comfort in your own remorse. All such artificial comfort must be taken from you. True repentance involves dissatisfaction with your repentance. It comprises a sense of spiritual callousness, imperviousness to the approaches of the Spirit of God, carnal security, and the inner corruption. You are constrained by the facts in the case to judge yourself as worldly-minded, secure, ungodly, condemned by the righteous Law of God. Not until you have reached this stage of self-damnation are you ready to give Christ the honor of saving your soul.

If anyone should ask: "How much remorse and sorrow for sin must I have before I am fit to come to Christ?" the answer is: You need only so much sorrow for sin as to feel your need of Christ, that you can not live without Him, that you can find no peace before you come to Him. No greater sorrow for sin is required—and no less will suffice. It is an error, though, to believe that remorse must first have its time; then there comes the time for faith; then the time for peace, joy and holiness. Begin, friend, by believing in Christ. Then follow Him in a daily renewal of your life and conduct. One result will be that you will know the sin in your flesh more keenly than you ever did formerly.

However, one of the shrewdest tricks of the devil is the following: A man believes in a general way that the Bible is the Inspired Word of God. The Book is God's Word from cover to cover. In it he seeks comfort and encouragement for his heart, light and strength for his daily life and walk. But there is one particular sin weighing upon his conscience. Then comes the devil and suggests to him the following line of reasoning: "The Gospel is the very truth of God. The grace of God in Christ is universal and comprises all sinners. All sin has been atoned for and taken away by Christ, so that ordinary sinners may be pardoned and receive mercy at the hands of God. But you are an exception to the rule: You know yourself what you have done. If it had not been for that particular sin or many sins against the Fifth, Sixth or Seventh Commandment, you too might be forgiven. But your sin is too black. You are an exceptional sinner. You do not come within the scope of God's merciful compassion." The phrase: "You are an exception," is the most venomous thrust of the ancient serpent. Truly, as Jesus says: "He was a murderer from the beginning, and abode not in the truth, because there is no truth in him. When he speaketh a lie, he speaketh of his own; for he is a liar, and the father of it" (John 8: 44).

The truth is that there is no exception among sinners. The mercy of God is over them all. There is no sin that has not abundantly been atoned for by the blood of the Son of God. All that is necessary is that the sinner, whoever he or she may be, or whatever he or she may have done, repents of the sin or the sins, turns to Christ and of Him receives grace for grace. The pardoning grace of God in Christ is the very heart and core of the Gospel. Both the Old Testament and the New Testament testify to the universal grace of God, and that by word and example without number. "Come, now, and let us reason together, saith the Lord: Though your sins be as scarlet, they shall be as white as snow; though they be red like crimson, they shall be as wool" (Isaiah 1: 18). King David, guilty of adultery and murder, Manasse, the robber on the cross, the woman who was "a sinner in the city," Peter the denier, all these are striking examples to prove that with God there are no exceptions among sinners. He invites them all to share in His grace, however sinful and guilty they may be.

Indeed, it was precisely for the blackest sins and the vilest sinners, for whom there is no salvation anywhere, that the Son of God became incarnate, bled and died, in order that "whosoever believeth in Him should not perish, but have everlasting life." To summarize: You have never sinned so horribly, never sunk so low, but that the blood of the Son of God can cleanse you, providing only that you repent and accept the forgiveness of God in the Savior. But that your heart and conscience may find rest and peace, it is a blessed privilege, in the case of gross sin especially, to make confession to your pastor or to some other Christian. The pressing burden will as a rule fall from the conscience.

THE REVELATION OF THE MYSTERY
(*Continued*)

THE FOURTH DAY

A SINCERE Christian may find himself in perplexity upon realizing that, even though he trusts implicitly in the grace of God as revealed in Christ Jesus, he has no vivid feeling of this grace in his heart, but is instead troubled by the consciousness of his sins and shortcomings. Here we would let Doctor Luther answer by an excerpt from his sermon on Easter:

"Now comes the question: Since Christ has died and taken away our sins, how does it come that we still feel that sin and death are within us? For sin gnaws at the conscience, and an evil conscience causes us to fear the judgment. *Answer*: I have already said that it is one thing to feel, and quite another thing to believe. Faith clings to the Word in despite of feelings and reason. Feeling operates against faith, and faith against feeling. For this reason you must set reason aside and listen only to the Word, permit the Spirit to inscribe the Word upon your heart and believe it. Hold to the Word, even though you have no feeling that your sins are forgiven, and even despite the fact that you feel the power of sin within you. You must not go by your feelings. You must hold fast the truth that sin, death and the devil are conquered, even though you feel that you are held back by sin, death and the devil. For though there still is in you a feeling of the strength of sin, that should drive you all the more to faith and make you strong in faith. Disregard your feeling of sin and guilt before God and take Him at His word. Then let your heart and conscience rest in Christ. Thus faith leads us, in spite of our feeling and the strictures of reason, through sin, death and hell. As a consequence, you shall see God's redemption. You shall realize thoroughly what you formerly believed, namely, that sin, death and all evil have been taken away from you.

"Let me draw a comparison from the fish in a net. When they are enclosed in the net, they are drawn so gently on ship-board, that they do not realize that they are caught. They imagine that they are in the water. Very quickly, however, they begin to squirm and tumble about, realizing that they are in captivity. So also with the souls that are caught in the net of the Gospel. Jesus compares the Gospel to a net: 'The Kingdom of heaven is like unto a net that was cast into the sea, and gathered of every kind' (Matthew 13: 48). When the Gospel takes possession of the heart, it binds the heart to Christ, and leads it so quietly and unnoticeably out of hell and the love of sin, that the soul scarcely realizes that it has been delivered from the power of sin and death.

"Presently a conflict arises between feeling and faith. The more faith increases, the more the remonstrances of feeling decrease, and *vice versa*. Sin still clings to us, in spite of our faith and trust in the promises of the Word of God. Pride, avarice, anger, and other sins, still torment us, but only to drive us to faith, in order that faith may increase and grow stronger day by day." Thus far Luther.

Jesus taught His disciple Thomas the same lesson when He said: "Thomas, because thou hast seen me, thou hast believed: Blessed are they that have not seen, and yet have believed" (John 20:29).

There are spiritual perplexities of a more puerile character. The following is an example: "I certainly believe that my sins are all forgiven. But I do not conduct myself in my daily life and conversation as I ought to do, according to the Word and will of God. The result is that I am a little uncertain as to whether I stand in the grace and friendship of God." *Answer*: It is, in the first place, a great error to think that only in your great conversion did you receive the forgiveness of your sins, particularly of the sins which you committed in unbelief and spiritual darkness, and that you after that event would be enabled by the grace of God to live so sinless and pure, that by your holy life you would retain the friendship of God. You must know that the greatest saints have always stood in need of the daily forgiveness of their sins. For this reason Jesus taught them to include in their daily Lord's Prayer the petition: "Forgive us our trespasses as we forgive those who trespass against us." The holiest saints have daily committed sin, real sin, not imaginary sin. "If we say that we have no sin, we deceive ourselves, and the truth is not in us" (1 John 1: 8).

But it is equally certain that in Christ we have a perfect righteousness before God. This righteousness covers not only all our former sins, but also our present daily sins, that is to say, all the defects, faults and shortcomings of our daily life. The Apostle Paul writes: "For what the Law could not do, in that it was weak through the flesh, God sending His own Son in the likeness of sinful flesh, and for sin, condemned sin in the flesh, that the righteousness of the Law might be fulfilled in us, who walk not after the flesh but after the Spirit" (Romans 8:3, 4). Observe: We have already now in Christ the righteousness before God which the Law demands. The defects of your daily life are precisely the sins for which you have daily forgiveness.

"According to what you have just said," some one interposes, "we do not need to live the Christian life. We do not need to leave off sin and sinful habits, since we have begun to believe in Christ. Since through faith we possess the righteousness of Christ which we could not produce by our good works under the Law, we may live as we please, may we not?" *Answer*: You may not live in sin if you would live in Christ. That would be the same as repudiating the merits of Christ. Paul says: "I do not frustrate the grace of God: for if righteousness comes by the Law, then Christ is dead in vain" (Galatians 2:21).

We are bound to live the Christian life for an entirely different reason, namely, gratitude to God for His pardoning grace. Christ says: "He that loveth me, he will keep my Words, and the Word which ye hear is not mine, but the Father's which sent me" (John 14:23, 24). In other words: There are two things in the life of a Christian which must be kept apart. The one is his life and conduct, his thoughts, desires, words and deeds. As regards his life, the Christian can never be too severe and critical. Self-criticism in the light of God's Word and Law will be his daily and continuous practice. The other factor is his state of grace with God. The adoption into the holy fellowship of God and all believers is attested by the Spirit of God. In this state of adoption as a child of God, he deprecates his own works and merits, but magnifies Christ. He looks away from his own merits and excellencies, and sees nothing but the Crucified Christ.

As regards our life and daily conduct, we need to be circumspect and exacting. As a rule, however, we are only too gentle and merciful in judging ourselves. As regards our state of grace we should be happy and secure in the merits of Christ. But here, again, we are inclined to be legalistic and fearful. This condition is intimated by the apostle: "My little children, these things write I unto you, that ye sin not. And if any man sin, we have an Advocate with the Father, Jesus Christ the Righteous" (1 John 2:1).

THE REVELATION OF THE MYSTERY
(*Continued*)

THE FIFTH DAY

IT is an error to believe that the doctrine of God's free grace in Christ produces carnal security and contempt for good works. The Gospel never bears such fruit. It is the devil, in collusion with fallen man, who contrives to make of the Gospel a pillow for carnal security. Then, too, the Gospel is not for secure and impenitent sinners. The Gospel is preached to the "poor," that is, the poor in spirit. Spiritually poor and contrite sinners always find greater joy and strength in the new life the more their faith develops and increases. Jesus shows this in connection with the narrative of the woman who washed His feet with her tears and wiped them with the hairs of her head: "Wherefore I say unto thee: Her sins, which are many, are forgiven; for she loved much; but to whom little is forgiven, the same loveth little" (Luke 7:41-47). Since, therefore, the Gospel is the power of God unto salvation to poor, penitent sinners, it must be preached for their sake, despite the fact that it is a savor of death to dull, drowsy, secure and carnally-minded men.

Still another perplexed soul says: "To sin against one's own conscience is to sin on purpose, is it not? And how can that harmonize with being in the state of grace? But that is exactly what I have done. I can not believe that I am a child of grace on account of such sins." *Answer:* To sin against conscience and better knowledge is indeed a heinous sin. It were far better that you never had committed such sins, but rather had kept your heart in godliness by prayer and watchfulness. Nevertheless it must not be forgotten that even these most reprehensible sins have been expiated by the blood of the Son of God. Since you heartily repent of your sin and wish nothing more than that you never had committed the sin, and since you honestly purpose never to repeat the sin, and since you seek mercy and forgiveness in the blood of the Lamb of God, it can not be denied that your sin is taken away, forgiven and forgotten of God. Otherwise Christ were not a perfect Savior and Redeemer, and the Gospel would not be anything else than the justice of the Law.

In the nineteenth chapter of Deuteronomy we read that he who had accidentally slain anyone or committed any other sin ignorantly or unwittingly, might flee to one of the three cities of refuge and find safety from the avenger of blood. The Law itself liberated those who had sinned unwittingly. Ordinary human sense of justice passes the same judgment. But we will not overlook the difference between mercy and justice. Nor will we forget the mercy which has been purchased at so great a price. It comprises within its scope the remission of sins, which the Law never could grant us. Hence the apostle says: "If by grace, then it is no more of works: otherwise grace is no more grace" (Romans 11:6).

Besides, it can never truthfully be said that a

Christian sins deliberately and on purpose to transgress the Law of God. If he sins knowingly, he has simply been overwhelmed by the temptation, by the "law in my members," as Paul terms it: "Now, if I do that I would not, it is no more I that do it, but sin that dwelleth in me" (Romans 7: 20). In the hour of temptation, however, when the struggling spirit already has been overcome, it seems to the Christian that he sins deliberately, since his will to do right has been conquered and subdued by the evil spirit of his flesh. O what tortures an honest soul endures in such an ordeal! How he wishes himself the master of the temptation and the occasion for sin!

It is to be noted, however, that even though deliberate sins may be forgiven when they are sincerely regretted, it by no means follows that continued sins receive continued remission. Deliberate and continued sin implies a deliberately impenitent mind, a condition of heart which Christ with all His merit has never condoned. A boundary wall of fire has been erected by the Word of God and His Holy Spirit between deliberate impenitence and the pardoning grace of God.

Finally, we would consider still another mystery: You are living in secret sin. You sin deliberately but clandestinely. You do not want to be damned, nor do you want to give up your pet sin. Your conscience is awakened to the extent that you find no peace of mind in a false and self-made comfort. You have no apology or excuse for your deliberate

and continued impenitence. You go to the Gospel
for comfort. You hear of the boundless mercy of
God and try to make it cover your soul and your
life in sin. But no peace comes to your heart. Your
sin gnaws at the soul and cuts it as does a grain of
sand the eye. While others rejoice in the pardoning grace of God, your heart is ill at ease and your
soul is troubled.

What is the reason for this disquietude of heart
and mind? Like Jonah, who "lay fast asleep" in
the bottom of the ship, your pet sin lies at the bottom
of your heart. It must be cast out if the sea is to be
quieted and the ship of your soul to be saved and not
perish. But you remonstrate: "I have not the
strength to rid myself of this pet sin." By that kind
of speech you demonstrate that you are not fit to
enter the Kingdom of God. Jesus says: "If any
man will come after me, let him deny himself, and
take up his cross daily, and follow me. For whosoever will save his life shall lose it: but whosoever
will lose his life for my sake, the same shall save it"
(Luke 9:23-24).

Meanwhile, if the work of grace prospers in your
soul, the day will come when you surrender to the
Holy Spirit unconditionally. You will pluck out the
eye which offends you and see only the holy will of
God. It is expensive to cast into the sea a cargo of
costly wares. This is never done in fine weather.
But when a hurricane hits the ship, threatening to
destroy it and all on board, the wares are thrown
into the sea, in order to save that which is more

valuable. When you realize that you are in imminent danger of being engulfed in the depths of the tumbling sea, and when you are weary of a torturing conscience, your selfwill shattered in the storm of the soul, it becomes an easy matter to surrender the favorite sin, or at least the stubborn adherence to it and the dishonest endeavor to palliate its heinousness. The temptation may still be there; defeat and triumph may alternate in the struggle going on in your soul; but you are headed in the right direction, and to your unspeakable joy you shall one day discover that Christ has set your soul free.

It is a notable fact that as soon as the heart of a man becomes perfectly honest with itself, the Gospel brings comfort and delight, even though there is an occasional lapse from righteousness. But so long as the spirit of a man is false and dishonest, there can be no suggestion of peace in his heart. True, there is another road to peace beside the thorny road of repentance and conversion — the road which the Bible speaks of as hardening of the heart. That soul-condition comes about when it resists the Holy Ghost deliberately and drives Him away. Then, of course, you may keep your pet sin—it remains securely in the ship's hold of your soul. However, the apostle reminds you that your "damnation slumbereth not" (2 Peter 2:3).

Once again I would remind you that we are speaking of the deliberate and determined cherishment of sin. For you will not immediately be entirely rid of sin. You will yet complain with the great apostle:

"But I see another law in my members, warring against the law of my mind, and bringing me into captivity to the law of sin which is in my members. O wretched man that I am. Who shall deliver me from the body of this death?" (Romans 7:23-24). This is the lamentation of all believers as long as they live on earth.

Especially is sin powerful as long as the legalistic mind controls the heart. You sin frequently and grossly, even though you honestly strive to avoid the sin. Then when your rashness or recklessness brings you renewed humiliation, the devil again has the opportunity of sifting and defeating you. We are not here speaking of the dishonest mind which purposes to hold fast to sin. He who proceeds in that manner will get no comfort from the Gospel.

But who is able to enumerate all the difficulties with which the devil and the deceitful heart overshadow the Gospel, in order to confuse the mind and undermine our faith? If we are to be saved from all these perplexities, there is nothing for us to do but to close our eyes and ears against everything which fails to agree with God's Word. We must look away from everything else and fix our eyes solely upon the Word of God. We must see Jesus only. We must behold the Crucified Son of God, and the grace and righteousness which He has purchased and won for us. This concentration on Christ, however, is a difficult matter. Without the grace of God it is impossible for awakened souls, and here we speak only of them. Hence we must humble ourselves before God and beseech Him to impart to us the Spirit of wisdom and revelation, that we may be enlightened in the true knowledge of Him.

Now, since Christ has given a special assurance that the Holy Spirit shall be given to all who ask (Luke 11:13), let us often include that petition in our prayers. Let us pray for the enlightenment of the Spirit, and we shall see marvellous things in the Gospel. Our heart shall rejoice and our spirit shall be exalted. "Now to Him that is of power to establish you according to my Gospel, and the preaching of Jesus Christ, according to the revelation of the mystery, which was kept secret since the world began, but now is made manifest, and by the Scriptures of the prophets, according to the commandment of the everlasting God, made known to all nations for the obedience of faith: to God only wise, be glory through Jesus Christ forever. Amen" (Romans 16: 25-27).

THE ASSURANCE OF THE REMISSION OF SINS

THE SIXTH DAY

HE who would be a Christian and does not seek the assurance of his adoption with God, who is content to remain in uncertainty as to his state of grace, is surely not an awakened soul: he is either a slumbering hypocrite or a drowsy Christian. This

lies in the nature of the case. The bride who is
satisfied to live in uncertainty as to the love of her
bridegroom, can have no true love for him. It is
therefore a manifest sign of impenitence and one
of the excuses for impenitence, that such a person
denies the possibility and the actuality of the
assurance of the forgiveness of sins. He de-
cries this assurance as purely imaginary and
the evidence of spiritual pride. Says Doctor
Luther: "When the Cainite saints hear this
confession, they cross their heart and exclaim,
'God deliver me from the delusion of claiming to be
a child of God! No, rather let me humble myself,
and remain nothing but a poor sinner. For God
exalteth the humble.' But the Bible says: 'We
know that we have passed from death unto life, because we love the brethren' (1 John 3: 15). 'Hereby we know that we are of the truth, and shall assure our hearts before Him' (verse 19). 'Hereby
we know that He abideth in us, by the Spirit which
He hath given us' (verse 24). 'We know that we
are of God' (1 John 5: 19). 'We know that the Son
of God is come, and hath given us an understanding,
that we may know Him that is true, and we are in
Him that is true, even in His Son Jesus Christ. This
is the true God, and eternal life' (1 John 5: 20)."

The apostle again and again makes the positive
statement: "We know." "We know" that we are
the children of God. "We know" that we have the
forgiveness of our sins. "We know" that we have
eternal life. "Therefore," Luther says, "we should
thoroughly root out this pernicious error, with

which the world is deluded, that a man may not know for a certainty whether he is in the state of grace or not" (Luther's *Exposition of the Epistle to the Galatians,* chapter 4, verse 6). This error does not come from the intellect, but from the heart; not from any obscurity in the Word of God, for the Scriptures everywhere speak very clearly upon this topic. The error comes from the impenitence and unbelief of the heart.

"They who neither possess nor seek to gain this assurance of the grace of God abiding in them naturally deny its possibility. But even though we do not deny the possibility of this certainty of adoption with God, it is nevertheless a bad sign if we are content to live on in uncertainty regarding our state of grace. It is quite another matter when a person seeks this assurance and absolute certainty of the forgiveness of his sins and of God's continued grace and does not immediately realize it. This, however, is no reason for discouragement. But never to seek assurance of salvation in Christ and definite certainty of grace, is always a sign of carnal security."

Again: However honest a soul may be, and however sincerely he hungers and thirsts after righteousness, it still is a serious defect in his Christianity that he remains in uncertainty regarding the actuality of his restoration to the state of grace. It is true that he desires grace and the remission of his sins. It is true, as Luther says, that "the remission of sins is of two kinds, namely, on the one hand, secret in the counsels of God, and on the other

hand, recognized and manifest to the soul." Christ
had already pardoned the woman "who was a sinner," lying at His feet, and had said so to Simon
Peter, before He turned to her and said: "Thy sins
are forgiven" (Luke 7: 48). A soul that hungers
for the mercy of God may thus possess the forgiveness of sins before he is fully aware of it or believes it to be true. "Blessed are they which hunger
and thirst after righteousness" (Matthew 5:6).
That is all very true. But the soul is never in the
right relation with God before it possesses the certainty of pardon and sonship with God. Until that
assurance fills and thrills the soul, the Kingdom of
God has not fully entered the heart.

"The Kingdom of God is righteousness, and
peace and joy in the Holy Ghost" (Romans 14:17).
Until this has been actualized in the soul, a person
has no power truly to love and praise God, and to
walk with Him in the beauty of holiness. To be
sure, one has the righteousness of Christ whether
one's faith be strong or weak, but one has not the
same power of sanctification in his daily life. For
the daily renewal, the new spiritual power, and the
fruits of faith always proceed from the certainty
of faith. "The joy of the Lord is thy strength."
It is therefore of the greatest importance that every
sincere soul arrives at the full assurance of his state
of grace.

But he who would have this blessed assurance of
faith should learn the right way to obtain it. When
we would make sure of the pardoning grace of God,
we begin to examine and re-examine our conversion,

our faith, our spirituality, whether we have had the standard experiences, whether we have the correct marks of true Christianity. If we find these things, we shall believe assuredly that we are the children of grace. This is not the right road to assurance and peace. When a person by this method seeks assurance of grace and pardon, he takes upon himself a difficult task. He soon grows discouraged. It is not an easy matter to find the fruit of faith as long as one has not arrived at a living faith. Even though a person may attain a certain kind of peace by this process of rigid self-examination, it is nothing more than a tottering peace which fails in the time of spiritual distress and struggle. There is no solid foundation for enduring peace and comfort.

Furthermore: This labored peace is an impure peace. It is not altogether founded upon Christ. It resembles the image which King Nebuchadnezzar saw, as described and explained by Daniel: "This image's head was of fine gold, his breast and his arms of silver, his belly and his thighs of brass, his legs of iron, his feet part of iron and part of clay. Thou sawest till that a stone was cut out without hands, which smote the image upon his feet that were of iron and clay, and brake them to pieces. Then was the iron, the clay, the brass, the silver, and the gold, broken to pieces together, and became like the chaff of the summer threshing-floors; and the wind carried them away, that no place was found for them: and the stone that smote the image became a mountain, and filled the whole earth" (Daniel 2:32-35).

The genuine assurance of faith is built upon the Word of Christ alone. Nothing perdures in the storm and stress of the soul but the words and acts of Almighty God—the words and the acts which concern the "ungodly" on the one hand, and the "lost sinners" on the other hand. The only right way to assurance of faith is complete trust in the Word and promises of God; or, in other words, that you in full confidence repeat the words of God after Him. One of the church fathers expresses it as follows: "How safe and secure I am when in faith I simply repeat what God has said before me." Saint Paul teaches us that "faith cometh by hearing" (Romans 10:17).

Such faith and assurance come through the comfort and joy I gain from the grace of God as revealed in Christ. I gain this comfort, not because I deem myself worthy of it, but because I realize how poor and sinful I am, afraid even of believing and trusting God, or of taking Him at His word. The prodigal son was afar off when the father surprised him with pardon and restoration (Luke 15). When you have found comfort in Christ through the Word, you will discover the fruits of faith in your heart and life. Saint John says: "He that believeth on the Son of God hath the witness in himself" (1 John 5:10). But the essential assurance of faith always arises from the Word prior to the manifestations and fruits of faith.

Whatever more we have to say regarding this

topic, we shall cull from the writings of the well-known C. H. Bogatzky of Germany. We shall not quote him verbatim. He writes about as follows: I do not say, nor shall I ever say, that a person who has not perfect assurance of the mercy of God, is therefore utterly impenitent and unbelieving. By such language we should render troubled souls yet more troubled and uncertain. Nevertheless, this much is certain: If a person is genuinely repentant and rightly knows his soul-peril, he will earnestly and persistently seek true peace and assurance for his soul. He will long for nothing in the world with such fervor as for grace and pardon. He will surrender everything rather than continue in uncertainty and insecurity.

He who has not found true peace for his soul, who does not even strive to attain it, but rather seeks peace and comfort in the world, its pleasures and pretences, is not truly penitent. In that condition he will never find peace. But he who finds no rest before he finds comfort in the wounds of Christ and for a certainty knows that his sins are forgiven, has found that which his soul has sought. In him is fulfilled the promise of Christ: "For every one that asketh receiveth; and he that seeketh findeth; and to him that knocketh it shall be opened" (Matthew 7:9).

He who regards the assurance of pardon and grace as the greatest blessing on earth; who hears that it is a supreme privilege to possess this assurance; that it is the earnest will of God that he ought to seek his certainty of forgiveness and mercy, and that it is within his reach, will arouse himself and take the Kingdom of Heaven "by force" (Matthew 11:12). Now, "the Kingdom of God is not meat and drink, but righteousness, and peace and joy in the Holy Ghost" (Romans 14:17). He who through penitence and faith is justified before God may also be endowed with peace, joy, and assurance that he is a child of God. He is prepared at any time to make oath that his sins are all forgiven by God in heaven, and that God regards him in Christ Jesus as if he never had committed one single sin in all his life. Before God he is garbed in the snow-white garment of Christ's righteousness. The prophet confirms this statement: "I have sworn by myself; the word is gone out of my mouth in righteousness, and shall not return, that unto me every knee shall bow, every tongue shall swear. Surely shall one say: In the Lord have I righteousness and strength; even to Him shall men come, and all that are incensed against Him shall be ashamed. In the Lord shall all the seed of Israel be justified, and shall glory" (Isaiah 45:23-25). In the Lord is my righteousness and strength. That confidence is based upon the oath of Almighty God. A believer may be sure of himself, because he builds his faith upon the Word of God. For God keeps His oath and His promises. He has sworn that He does not desire the death of a sinner, but rather that he turn from his wickedness and live. He is ever ready to forgive and let mercy supplant justice to the penitent, because the Son of God has fulfilled all righteousness for all men.

THE ASSURANCE OF THE REMISSION OF SINS
(*Continued*)

THE SEVENTH DAY

THE repentant sinner knows that he needs the grace of God. He realizes that he does not desire false comfort. He has no intention of misusing the pardoning grace of God as a covering for carnal security. He intends to abandon all his sins.

But first he must be certain of the grace of God and the forgiveness of his sins. God has installed Christ, His Highpriest, in his sacerdotal office. He has sealed the installation with an oath, as we read in His word: "For those priests were made without an oath, but this with an oath by Him that said unto Him, The Lord sware and will not repent: Thou art a priest forever after the Order of Melchisedec—by so much was Jesus made a surety of a better testament. . . . For the Law maketh men high priests which have infirmity, but the word of the oath, which was since the Law, maketh the Son, who is consecrated for evermore" (Hebrews 7:21, 22, 28). Consequently God has established and confirmed Christ's mediatorial office and declared: As I live, my Son is a perfect and an eternal High Priest. As I live, all sinners are reconciled with me by Him, their guilt is atoned for by His blood. As I live, all penitent and believing sinners have the remission of sin in His name. "To Him give all the prophets witness that through His name whosoever believeth in Him shall receive re-

mission of sins" (Acts 10:43). The penitent ought
then surely gain assurance of his state of grace and
pardon, since God has assured him of His grace by
an oath. God does not violate His oath.

Seeking God in Christ alone, I need not doubt
nor feel uncertain. I need not suspect that He may
not keep His promises and His oath. Scriptures
speak with assurance. "We know that we have
passed from death unto life" (1 John 3:14). "We
know that we are of God" (1 John 5:19). "We
know that the Son of God is come, and hath given
us an understanding, that we may know Him that is
true, and we are in Him that is true, even in His
Son Jesus Christ" (1 John 3:20). That is: We
know that God is true. He keeps His covenant and
His oath. We know that we are "in Him that is
true," even in His Son Jesus Christ. Then listen to
this logical conclusion: "There is therefore now no
condemnation to them which are in Christ Jesus,
who walk not after the flesh, but after the Spirit"
(Romans 8: 1). There is now no sin upon Christ
to condemn Him to death: He is in heaven without
sin. The believer who is in Him is also without
sin. He is regarded as if he were without sin.
Since he is without sin or since his sins are forgiven
and blotted out, then the Law can no more accuse
him on account of his sins.

But if the Law can no more accuse and condemn
him, then has he no longer an evil conscience. He
has a satisfied and "perfect" conscience. The
worshippers, once purged, should have had no more
conscience of sins (Hebrews 10:2). The be-

liever sees his sins upon Christ, the Lamb of God, who has paid their guilt with His blood. "For with one offering He hath perfected forever them that are sanctified" (Hebrews 10:14). He need have no fear, nor need he come again under the yoke of bondage. Christ has satisfied the exacting justice of God's holy Law. He has paid the ransom for all sinners collectively and for each one individually. He has taken upon Himself the sins of all mankind. He has suffered the penalty for the sins of all. He has "tasted death for all men" (Hebrews 2:9). God is reconciled in Christ with all men. He punishes no one for sin who by faith accepts the perfect sacrifice made by Christ. Nothing but deliberate unbelief condemns a man. Yea, every human being is regarded as though he himself had been nailed to the cross, had died, had suffered the penalty for his sins, had been buried, and his sins with him, had risen from the dead with Christ, had been set free from sin and guilt, had been "made to sit in heavenly places in Christ Jesus" (Ephesians 2:6), and had "passed from death unto life." Therefore he can as little die and perish as Christ can die and perish—providing he remain in Christ, who is his life.

In Christ he is certain of pardon and salvation. In and with Christ he is without sin and guilt, hence free from the condemnation of the Law. He is liberated from the accusations of an evil conscience, free from the peril of eternal death. Yea, he already possesses eternal life. He no longer needs to

listen to the criminations of the Law and an evil
conscience. Rather does he defend himself with "the
shield of faith and the breastplate of righteousness"
(Ephesians 6:14-16). No law is able to force itself into his conscience, which is now cleansed with
the blood of the Son of God. For the believing
conscience is, as Luther says, "the bridal chamber
of Christ, where He dwells alone with His bride."

It is true that the Law rebukes and restrains the
flesh from doing its will and gratifying the evil desires. But the Law has no right to enter the conscience with its threatenings and condemnations.
It may transpire, though, that we yield to the flesh
and do its bidding. Simultaneously we permit the
Law to enter the conscience, where it has no right
of entrance. It leads us to fear and bondage. We
are free where we ought not to be free, that is, in
yielding to the evil propensities of the flesh. We
are in bondage where we ought to be free, that is, in
Christ. The liberty which permits us to violate
God's Law, is false. It places us again under the
Law and into the spirit of bondage. For even
though peace of heart does not depend upon the degree of our piety but rather upon Christ, peace of
heart and soul can not articulate with a life of the
flesh. Peace with God does not harmonize with
peace in sin. God's Word clearly tells us that
Christ has not shed His blood to comfort us in
willful sin.

If there be a spark of faith in the soul of a person
who sins deliberately and willfully, conscience will

condemn the sin as willful, since there was no
earnest struggle against the sin. Luther says in
his sermon on the First Sunday after Trinity:
" 'There is no fear in love; but perfect love casteth
out fear, because fear hath torment. He that fear-
eth is not made perfect in love' (I John 4:18).
This Bible passage shows you what fear and dread
it will cost you in case you do not walk in love, but
permit yourself to be uncharitable and unfair to
your neighbor. You may not necessarily perish in
your sins. You may save your soul alive, provided
you know how to hold the 'shield of faith' against
the fiery darts of your conscience, and say: 'Though
my Christianity break down, yet Christ will hold me
fast.' Your soul may be saved—but it is going to
cost you a good sweat-bath."

Awakened souls, however, who have not attained
to peace with God and assurance of pardon, may be
classified under three heads.

The first class consists of such persons as do not
realize the natural depravity of the heart. They
have a number of secret methods of self-justification.
They are rich in excuses and palliations of their way
of life. They are not spiritually unclothed of the
love of sin. They label a great many practices as
"innocent" and "permissible" which are questionable,
to say the least. They protect themselves with the
fig leaves of expostulation and excuse. They complain bitterly of this or that hindrance to their
Christian life. They blame this person and that person for causing them to sin. They blame their

environment and associates for their delinquencies. They never dream of accusing themselves, closing their lips, and confessing themselves personally guilty before God.

These people have no real interest in their souls. They are not persistent in prayer and in the use of the Means of Grace. They are satisfied with an occasional glimpse of the mercies of God. They readily find their supreme delight in nature and the things of this world. They are a happy-go-lucky lot, with no serious thought of God and the judgment.

Since they are not truly regenerated, nor thoroughly sincere, not ingenuous, but cherish many impure purposes, yield to their passions, and have no "single" eye to salvation, they of course never arrive at a state of peace and certitude. It behooves such persons to quit excusing themselves and blaming others. They need to learn and to confess that they themselves are to blame for their sins and no one else. They need to realize that the circumstances of life in which they find themselves by the leadings of God, are, after all, the best for them, and that nothing can possibly harm them spiritually if only they seek that which is good. Everything will subserve their truest interests, further their spiritual development, sanctify their hearts and lives, and enhance their peace with God in Christ Jesus.

Superficial Christians need to realize that "the one thing needful" is the salvation of the soul.

This should become their chief care and constant solicitude. Nothing in the world should be permitted to interfere with the salvation of the soul. They must quit playing the weathercock, pretending piety among the pious, and conforming to the world when among worldly people. They must shun a false and self-made peace as they would their direst enemy. They must not pretend to more than they really are. They must not seek only to please mén, for that shall profit them nothing. Like Enoch, they should learn to walk with God. Let them seek praise of their own conscience, and not of men.

If these thoughtless and frivolous persons permit the Lord to arouse them from their spiritual lethargy, they will prosper and develop spiritually. They shall become assured of their state of grace, if only they earnestly begin to live unto the Lord. They shall find rest and peace in the merits of the Crucified Savior. But until they arrive at that stage of spiritual development, the Lord will continue to cause them fear and anxiety of soul. He would lead them to an earnest solicitude for their salvation. He would make them serious-minded and God-fearing. He would cause them to cast aside all their excuses, pretexts and palliations, their reservations and conditions, their double-mindedness and equivocations, and learn to love the Lord Jesus with their whole heart.

THE ASSURANCE OF THE REMISSION OF SINS
(*Continued*)

THE EIGHTH DAY

THE second class consists of those who, as a rule, are sincere in their seeking after God, but chained down by the fetters of some idolatrous love or favorite sin. They have no genuine peace of mind and heart, because they are uncertain of the pardoning grace of God. The love of their idol or pet sin is so strong that they are not even sure that they wish to be rid of the sin that holds them fast. The result is that their hearts are closed tight against the grace of God: their idol is too attractive, their pet sin too fascinating. So long as the heart never has tasted the entrancing love of God, it remains in bondage to its idolatrous love. This is a deplorable condition. No human help is possible. The victims themselves and their spiritually-minded friends are on the brink of despair as to the redemption of these unfortunates.

But the power of the Lord is great, and His faithfulness is able to liberate these slaves of sin. If they but hear the Word of God, their troubled conscience and distress of soul will eventually render them so weary that their idol or pet sin finally becomes nauseating to their better nature, and they turn from it in horror and disgust. Suddenly or gradually the "abundant grace" of God looks marvellously attractive to them. No sooner have they in trembling faith realized that the Lord is good and merciful than the idol falls from the pedestal of their heart: their incipient faith has saved them. Or they may only have realized the possibility of redemption from the slavery of sin, and upon that strange discovery have learned to seek the Lord and His salvation by the way of "faith" (Hebrews 11).

The third class of those who do not readily find peace of heart and mind is of an entirely different character from the two preceding classes. They realize deeply their spiritual corruption. They are very much in earnest about their salvation. They are diligent in prayer. They yearn for the consciousness of the pardoning grace of God. They long for peace of mind and heart. Naturally, however, they are anxious and timid. More than others they incline to legalism and exaggeration. The enemy sows the seed of skepticism and doubt in their hearts. They are filled with many strange notions and theories about themselves and about God. They are spiritually in a blind alley. They are keenly alive to their sins, their distrust of God's gracious promises and their unbelief. They feel that there is no hope for them.

Such distressed souls should be encouraged and cheered with the love of Christ for sinners. Their sins should not be magnified and exaggerated. Sincerely desiring to be liberated from sin and guilt; determined to give up all sin, even the most cherished sin; hungering and thirsting for the mercy of God; praying for forgiveness and assurance of pardon;

eager to accept the grace of God in Christ alone as
the only way to peace of soul and heart, but afraid
of appropriating to themselves the gracious promises of God on account of their unworthiness—such
souls should know that their faith is far greater than
they imagine.   Their faith is not a strong, courageous faith, but it is a trembling and timid faith.
The hunger and thirst after God, the yearning and
longing for righteousness, however deeply hidden
and timorous, is yet the beginning of true faith.
"Lord, Thou hast heard the desire of the humble;
Thou wilt prepare their heart; Thou wilt cause
Thine ear to hear" (Psalm 10:17).   "They looked
unto Him, and were enlightened; and their faces
were not ashamed" (Psalm 34:5).

Jesus says: "Blessed are the poor in spirit: for
theirs is the Kingdom of Heaven.   Blessed are they
that mourn: for they shall be comforted.   Blessed
are they which do hunger and thirst after righteousness: for they shall be filled" (Matthew 5:3, 4, 6.).
"A bruised reed shall He not break, and the smoking flax shall He not quench" (Isaiah 42:3).   God
will look "unto them that mourn in Zion, to give
unto them beauty for ashes, the oil of joy for mourning, the garment of praise for the spirit of heaviness, that they might be called trees of righteousness" (Isaiah 61:3).   Why should this be said to
these timid souls? Because their "iniquity is pardoned" (Isaiah 40:2).   Let all such distressed
minds remember these words.   They give assurance
and consolation.   "We have also a more sure word

of prophecy: whereunto ye do well that ye take heed, as unto a light that shineth in a dark place, until the day dawn, and the day star arise in your hearts" (2 Peter 1:19).

These timorous souls make the mistake of gazing too long and too intently upon their sins and their evil propensities, even as the frivolous and thoughtless do not look upon them long enough for their own good. It is well that they realize their corruption, unbelief, darkness and hardness of heart. It is well that they are not content with a false, shallow kind of comfort. But they should not stop at this point. They must move on from the Law to the Gospel. It is the Gospel that enlightens, invigorates and softens the heart. Let them also look away from their sins and look to Christ, who has atoned for the sin of the world. Let the consciousness of sin and depravity serve to drive them to Christ, the Crucified One. Let them realize that He has suffered the penalty of the Law for their sins, unbelief, hardness of heart, blindness and corruption, and thus purchased forgiveness with God for all their sins.

Why, then, does the penitent soul doubt that God is ready and willing to forgive all his sins? It costs God nothing now to forgive: the guilt of sin has been atoned for by Christ. His blood is the costly price paid for our ransom. Because the ransom has been fully paid, God now readily forgives the sins of every soul that comes to Him in faith or even in a prayerful longing for grace. God's eternal jus-

tice will not permit Him to require a double payment for the sin of the world. "If we confess our
sins, He is faithful and just to forgive us our sins,
and to cleanse us from all unrighteousness" (1 John
1:9). The repentant sinner should not waste time
in gazing upon his dead, dark body of sin, but rather
let him look to Christ, the Prince of Peace. Let him
mourn his unbelief before Christ and say with the
anxious father who petitioned Jesus for his epileptic
child: "Lord, I believe; help Thou mine unbelief"
(Mark 9:24). Let him comprehend that God will
impart to him as large a measure of grace as his
poor, narrow heart can hold. Let him understand
that his unworthiness need not deter him from coming to Christ. The fact is, that in no other way can
he receive the forgiveness of his sins than by coming
as an unworthy sinner. Not as a worthy, good and
pious sinner must he come to God, but rather as an
ungodly person, who prays only for mercy through
the merits of Christ. Let him simply believe on
Him "who justifieth the ungodly" (Romans 4:5).

"We pray," says Luther, "because we are unworthy to pray or to receive grace. For this reason
we become worthy to pray and to receive grace. For
this reason we shall also be heard and our prayers
shall be granted. Since we believe that we are unworthy, and trust only to God's faithfulness, He will
answer our petitions." Let such a soul continue
faithfully to make use of the Means of Grace, to
hold fast to God's promises of pardon, and comfort
his fearful heart with the mercy of God in Christ

Jesus. Let him know for a certainty that God requires no merit or worthiness of him, but that of sheer grace and mercy He will pardon all his sins and assure him of salvation.

THE ASSURANCE OF THE REMISSION OF SINS

(*Continued*)

THE NINTH DAY

A SINNER who sincerely desires to be saved by grace is saved already, whether he knows it or not. Let him follow Christ as his faithful Shepherd, and he shall receive grace for grace. He shall have the grace of forgiveness, the grace of victory over sin and the sinful passions of his nature, the grace of sanctification. The Lord will give him all these mercies without money and without price. Therefore let him only come with confidence and say:

> "*Lord Jesus, my Shepherd, I come unto Thee;*
> *Have mercy, and let me Thy follower be.*
> *I hold to Thy promises, faithful and true,*
> *Thy mercies each day Thou wilt ever renew.*
> *Thou seest how poor and how wretched I am,*
> *I come, then, confiding in Thy blessed name.*"

Let him know that all his sins are forgiven, the great and the small, the secret and the open—all of them. When God forgives, He forgives completely and entirely, for time and eternity. The righteous-

ness of Christ imputed to the penitent and believing
soul is likewise a perfect righteousness. It proceeds
from our perfect High Priest, who has "an unchangeable priesthood," and of whom it is said:
"Wherefore He is able also to save them to the
uttermost that come unto God by Him, seeing He
ever liveth to make intercession for them" (Hebrews 7:25). The prophet says that Christ made
"reconciliation for iniquity" and "brought in everlasting righteousness" (Daniel 11:24). The Psalmist sings: "I will sing of the mercies of the Lord forever: with my mouth will I make known Thy faithfulness to all generations. For I have said, Mercy
shall be built up for ever" (Psalm 89:1-2). All sins
are forgiven the believer. "Wherefore I say unto
you, All manner of sin and blasphemy shall be forgiven unto men: but the blasphemy against the Holy
Ghost shall not be forgiven unto men" (Matthew
12:31). "Who forgiveth all thine iniquities"
(Psalm 103:3). God forgives "iniquity and transgression and sin" (Exodus 14: 7). All sin has been
laid upon the Son of God, who bore our sins in His
body "on the tree." Christ is the Mediator between
God and man. He has paid the price of our redemption. Not one single sin is unpaid and un-
atoned. Consequently, the forgiveness of sin is provided for all sinners.

God forgives all our sins at once, not one to-day,
a second to-morrow, and so on. No, they are all
forgiven simultaneously and forever. "I, even I, am
He that blotteth out thy transgressions for mine own

sake, and will not remember thy sins" (Isaiah 43:25). "He will have compassion upon us. He will subdue our iniquities; and Thou wilt cast all their sins into the depths of the sea" (Micah 7:19). "I have blotted out, as a thick cloud, thy transgressions, and, as a cloud, thy sins: return unto me, for I have redeemed thee" (Isaiah 42:22). "As far as the East is from the West, so far hath He removed our transgressions from us" (Psalm 103:12). Through justification by grace, or by the remission of sins, God imputes the perfect righteousness of Christ to the believing sinner. Now, the merits of Christ cover every sin, past, present, and future, and are accounted to the believer for righteousness as long as he remains in the faith.

Thus a believer is continually justified. He has the daily and eternal remission of his sins. All his sins, deficiencies and shortcomings are and remain forgiven. "In whom we have redemption through His blood, the forgiveness of sins, according to the riches of His grace" (Ephesians 1:7). The mercy of God is as great and rich as God Himself is great and rich. For this reason the believer lives in the grace of God. Even with all his errors, he is still assured of his salvation. For he does not build his hope of salvation upon his good works, his fine character, his service of love to humanity, but rather upon the rich, free and abundant grace of God in Christ Jesus. Without this foundation for his faith, he would have no assurance of salvation, no genuine peace of heart, no ground for joy and hope. Yea,

the believer could not for one moment feel assured
of the blotting out of his sins, if he did not know that
God requires absolutely nothing of him by way of
merit or worthiness and only asks him to find
refuge in the merits of Christ. For, as Luther says,
"Where there is remission of sins, there is also life
and salvation."

Since the believer knows this, and lives solely in
the pardoning grace of God, surrounded as it were
by His forgiving love, he remains assured of salvation, with the peace of God in his heart. If he fal-
ters, the reason lies in his weak faith which does not
invariably look to Christ. If at times he stumbles
and falls, the reason is that he does not dwell continually in the grace of God as the home and abiding-place of his soul, but strays away to other
things which occupy his heart and mind, or because
he finds something in himself which serves him in
the way of excuse or comfort. August Hermann
Francke in his book, *The Safe and Sacred Way of
Faith,* refers to this state of mind in the following
beautiful words: "As long as the heart finds nothing
meritorious in itself, but everything in Christ, it
moves in the realm of celestial bliss, and God is
present with comfort and strength. But when the
heart no longer seeks salvation in the gracious forgiveness of sins through confidence in the merit of
Christ, it is on the wrong track and finds no peace."

It is of the greatest importance, even after one
has received grace and pardon, constantly to regard
oneself by nature as a depraved, lost and condemned

sinner. It remains necessary to recognize the fact that one is naturally a sinner, who needs to pray with the Psalmist: "Enter not into judgment with Thy servant: for in Thy sight shall no man living be justified" (Psalm 143:2). In the entire pilgrimage of life there is then nothing left to us but Christ and remission of sins in His name. On Him alone may we build our confidence. As poor and naked sinners we must be clothed with Christ's righteousness alone. It must remain our joy and consolation, that our sins are blotted out and that we are the objects of the mercy of God. Luther says: "We regard the Kingdom of God as a beautiful canopy above us, shielding and protecting us from the wrath of God. It resembles the vault of heaven, wherein the sun of grace and pardon shines out upon the whole world. All the sins of all the world are as a drop in the ocean. Though your sin oppresses you, it can not harm you—it will melt away under the sunlight of God's love."

Beginners in the Christian life usually find some degree of comfort in their new outlook upon life. They rejoice in the changed mind and purpose. They are happy in the improvement of their conduct, the gifts of grace, and their victories over sin and temptation. They are intent upon sanctification. But since they find greater delight in these feeble evidences of betterment than in Christ, they soon grow weary and powerless, restless and uncertain of themselves. They realize that there are many and great defects in their Christian development. They are humiliated in the discovery that they have scarcely made a beginning in the Christian life. They are sorely distressed and at a loss to evaluate their spiritual condition.

In order that beginners in the Christian life may not remain in this state of despondency on account of their discovery of the lack of progress, let them come back to the Fountain of Life and drink of its life-giving waters. Let them find peace in contemplating the Wounded Christ. Let them ponder the gracious promises of God. Thus shall they be revived and satisfied with the grace of God alone. The danger is, that unless I constantly believe in the complete and daily forgiveness of my sins, and look upon myself as justified through faith in Christ, the Law may again force itself into my conscience and once more make me uneasy and uncertain, restless and unhappy. Thus the whole Christian life suffers and there can be no true progress in the daily renewal.

Even in the following after "holiness, without which no man shall see the Lord," the forgiveness of sin must be basic and come first, as Jesus indicates: "As the branch can not bear fruit of itself, except it abide in the vine, no more can ye, except ye abide in me. I am the Vine, ye are the branches. He that abideth in me, and I in him, the same bringeth forth much fruit: for without me ye can do nothing" (John 15: 4, 5). May He who is the author and finisher of our faith help us to the true faith and keep us therein until the end. Amen.

THE USE OF GOD'S WORD

THE TENTH DAY

IN view of the importance of this subject, as also of the treatment which God's Word too often receives, one can not deal with it without a large measure of anxiety. The Christian's heart grieves in contemplation of the abuse to which the Word of God is subjected. But what is to be done? Lord Jesus, Thou art the Shepherd of the flock; Thou art the Bishop of souls. Help us, we pray Thee, to use Thy Word aright.

We would consider first of all the dangers arising from many confusing voices that come to us through the selection of teachers and books. We children of men are like sheep in a wilderness, hearing voices calling us from all directions. "Here is the way! Here is the way." "Of making of many books there is no end" (Ecclesiastes 12: 12). In our day especially is there an ocean of books dealing with religion, shrieking with every wind of doctrine. "Beloved, believe not every spirit, but try the spirits whether they are of God; because many false prophets are gone out into the world" (1 John 4:1). Thus writes the apostle, and with good reason. The fact is, that our spiritual welfare, our eternal destiny, depends in great measure upon the books we read, and the teachers we have learned to love. False doctrine is to the soul what poison is to the body—it destroys the soul for time and eternity.

"But to him who believes the Bible to be the

Word of God there is no danger," some one will remonstrate. In a sense this is true. He who uses the Bible as the Word of God, reading it devoutly, humbly,obediently,and with prayer for the enlightenment of the Holy Spirit, as the Word of God requires, shall of a certainty find the Water of Life and be refreshed. By the mercy of God he shall be saved from error. But alas: the well is deep. We need interpreters to lift the mysteries of the Word into the light of day. And here lies the danger to us who believe the Bible to be the Inspired Word of God. For there are many kinds of interpreters. The devil himself makes use of Bible passages, as, for instance, when he tempted Christ. The devil's apostles and all heretics do likewise. Luther refers to this fact when he says that the Bible is "the heretics' book." It is forced to lend its sacred words to the heretic.

What is to be done about it? Where are we to turn for help against these marauders? First and above all, in a matter of such transcendent importance you must not rely upon human judgment. All men may err. How do you know whose judgment you are to believe? Your own judgment may be the most dangerous of all. If you like a book or a teacher, you are liable to decide that that book or that teacher is the best. Fortunately, however, we have a rule to go by in the choice of books and teachers which has greater authentication than the opinions of all men together. Here is the rule: If you seek the doctrine of Christ, look for the signs of the doctrine of Christ.

Christ's doctrine has always had certain signs or marks accompanying it. The presence of these signs is more conclusive evidence of the genuineness of the doctrine than is the opinion of men. These signs are twofold:

I. Wherever Christ comes with His doctrine, souls are always won for heaven. They are transformed from careless, ungodly worldlings to pious, believing and happy souls. They are kept by the power of the Word.

II. The second sign is, that where the doctrine of Christ comes, Satan and his crew begin to rave and rage, and the world grows hostile, regarding the doctrine as insanity.

Beware of the doctrine that has not these marks, at least in some degree, no matter how good the doctrine seems to be. If the question is about books, consult history regarding them. The study of history will guide you to good and salutary books, as, for example, those written at the time of the Reformation by men about whom the battle raged. The teacher whom the world loves does no harm to the world. The books which the world adores do not injure the Kingdom of Darkness. Make a note of this fact. Corroboration of this rule is to be read in the history of the progress of the Gospel and in the history of the Church in all ages.

It is well for us if we go by this rule. We are wise if we do not judge of men and books by our individual taste, for our taste may be erroneous. Even our taste needs to be judged by the signs of the doctrine of Christ. Though His doctrine may not be to our taste, it is yet wholesome. Using it faithfully, we shall be fashioned in its image and likeness. Soon we shall develop a taste for such books. They will grow more and more attractive, as is often the case with Luther's works, for example. They do not please the beginner, but if they are read thoughtfully, they will in time become very precious. "Tell me who your associates are, and I will tell you who you are." The reading of evangelical books makes evangelical Christians, and *vice versa.*

Secondly, we would consider the correct use of the Word of God. Possibly you have heard and read the Word of God many a time, but rather to your soul's hurt than good. Many unknown perils surround us. It is perilous to hear or to read God's Word unless we hear and read as we ought. As a sharp knife, rightly used, may do much good, but wrongly used, may do great harm, so is the Word of God. It may be "the savor of death unto death or the savor of life unto life" (2 Corinthians 2:16). The Word of God is never without some effect when it penetrates the mind. It either brings a blessing to the hearer or the reader, or it effects the very opposite. It operates like the sun. The light of the sun is to the creatures of the day a means to growth, development, joy and activity; but the birds of the night are blinded by it. The heat of the sun melts the wax and makes the clay hard.

So dissimilar is the effect of the Word of God.

The Jews, it is true, were spiritually hardened before Christ came to them. But while He was with them, and the sun was at his zenith, their blindness, hardness of heart, and wickedness became frightful. Call to mind the traitor Judas. His spiritual condition was terrifying. Jesus foretold to him his danger, warned him, and said: "Woe to that man by whom the Son of Man is betrayed" (Matthew 26: 24). But Judas braved the danger. And yet Judas during his discipleship of three years had had the richest opportunity of realizing that not one word from the lips of Jesus was ever lost but always fulfilled to the letter. When He had said to the fig-tree: "Let no fruit grow on thee henceforward forever," the fig-tree soon had "withered away" (Matthew 21:19). When He had said to the sea: "Peace, be still: the wind ceased, and there was a great calm" (Mark 4:39). When He had said to the stinking Lazarus in the grave: "Lazarus, come forth!" "He that was dead came forth, bound hand and foot with graveclothes, and his face was bound about with a napkin, and Jesus said unto them: 'Loose him and let him go' " (John 11:43, 44). Judas had seen all these evidences of the power and efficacy of the Word of the Lord. He had furthermore heard the most excellent sermons ever preached on earth. Possibly he had said: whatever the Lord says is done. But he made one exception when that Word concerned himself.

After this manner the Word of God is disregarded by all blinded and hardened hypocrites. The question now arises: How had this hardening of the heart come to maturity in the case of Judas? Well, Judas had been one of the Twelve. He had seen, heard and experienced a great deal; but he had made poor use of what he had seen and heard. Similarly to-day. There are many who by daily reading know the Bible almost by heart, and yet they are steeped in sin and carnal security. Others, like Judas, have walked with Jesus and His disciples, but they have lost the life of God in their hearts. The power of the Gospel is lacking in their daily lives, in spite of the fact that they constantly read their Bibles. These individuals are not only as dead as if they never had heard the Word of God, but they are "seven-fold" worse, as the Scriptures say. Such are the fruits of the wrong use of the Word of God.

How is the Word of God used rightly? The answer is brief, but so comprehensive that if you observe it, you shall not hear or read God's Word in vain. You make the right use of God's Word when you accept it in faith and child-like obedience. God requires this of you. The Word of God is not only to be read and heard, but also believed and obeyed. Do this, friend, and you shall not be put to shame. The greatest abuse of God's Word is to hear it and not to live according to it. This was the way of Judas to his own damnation. You are to put into practice what you hear and read in the Word. You realize that you are in need of spiritual enlightenment. Pray God for light. You see that you ought to relinquish some certain sin. Do so right away. For by hearing and not doing, you harden your heart.

When are you to obey God's Word if not now? Of what use is the Bible if you are not to live according to its precepts? You had better immediately give up reading the Bible and hearing the Word of God and go to the devil, if you do not intend to live according to God's Word. Why should you not order your life in harmony with God's Word if you have any hope of salvation? The way of damnation for the world that now is and for the world to come is to disregard the statutes of the Lord. If you say: "I am unable to live according to the will and Word of God," I answer: Does God require too much of you? Is He unfair in His requirements? Is it unfair of Him to ask you to love Him above all things and your neighbor as yourself? That is all He asks. Have you earnestly tried to do the will of God? Possibly you have not tried very hard. Possibly you have been careless and given yourself over to sin and frivolity. Are you entirely fair to yourself in despising the Word of God? If you tried to obey that Word and to cleanse yourself from sin and deviltry, you would soon discover your sad estate. Your pride and intellectual self-sufficiency would take a tumble. You would awaken from the narcotics of self-delusion and sin. You would realize that sin is of the devil and that you are in the service of Satan, the enemy of mankind

A "godly sorrow" would enter your heart, and you would soon be on the way to salvation.

When fruitlessly exerting all your powers in the desperate attempt to do the will of God, you shall ultimately be impelled to pray for the Spirit of God to help you. Then shall you in the school of experience receive the true light upon the Word of God —the Light from heaven. Without this experience, the highbrows and scribes are blind as bats in things spiritual. Without the Holy Spirit, the Word of God is not understood. Luther says: "When God gave His Word, He said: I shall let it be plainly written and preached, but I shall so arrange matters, that it shall depend upon my Spirit as to who shall understand it. Hence we see that they who think that they are able to understand the saving doctrine of their own mental astuteness, remain in spiritual darkness."

THE USE OF GOD'S WORD
(*Continued*)

THE ELEVENTH DAY

AS your awakening from the sleep of sin resulted from the contemplation of God's Word, so shall you come to the true faith when, realizing that you can not save yourself, you hearken to the good tidings of pardoning grace in Christ. Faith will arise in your heart when you permit this message from heaven to count more than all the objections and contradictions of your reason. The same principle holds good all through life. Let God's Word control your intellect, your heart and your life. Pray for the Spirit of God whenever you go to hear the Word of God or sit down to read its wondrous pages, and you shall not hear and read in vain.

Finally we would consider the benefit and the necessity of the right use of the Word of God. At this point, however, we confess to an utter inability to speak as we ought to speak, both on account of the weighty matter in hand, as also in view of the powerful enemies which present themselves, namely, the sluggish flesh, the seductive world, and the malicious Satan. Here I could wish that my words would burn themselves into every heart. For who recognizes the fact that neglect of the Word of God is the reason for all the spiritual misery in the world, the lethargy of the Church, the ineffectiveness of its individual members, and the general moral turpitude? Who realizes the fact that the faithful use of God's Word is the cause of every spiritual good in the world?

It is true that man is fallen. It is true that the results of the Fall are deplorable; unbelief, sin, darkness, carnal security and hardness of heart. But all this evil might be remedied. The compassion of God would not leave mankind in this sad estate without providing the means of restoration. He gave us the Means of Grace, a precious seed which, when sown in the hearts of men, is able to produce a harvest of righteousness in their lives; a

restorative of the original image of God in their immortal souls; a light to clear up their darkened intellect; a medium by the use of which the Spirit of
the living God creates in man the will to holiness,
and endows him with heavenly gifts and powers.

You are callous, self-willed, and chained to sin—
you may be made over into a decent human being,
pure, upright, and honorable, by the means which
God has sent down from heaven. You may be made
unselfish, trusting, and liberated from the power of
sin, by this instrumentality. But without the use of
this means, you have not the power in you to overcome your sin. You will never be restored to what
you might be unless you make use of the Means of
Grace. All your good resolutions, prayers, watch-
ing and will-power, will prove but as chaff before
the wind, unless you permit God's Word to recreate
you into a new manhood. With all your fine
character, your own righteousness, and your eminent
services to your day and generation, unless the Word
of God is your staff and stay, you will be swept away
by the irresistible flood of your evil passions.

All experience testifies to this fact. There are
churches and communities which are blessed with
faithful pastors, who plow and plant the seed with
prayers and tears; but the harvest is next to nothing.
Among the people there is little evidence of the
power of the Gospel; no sign of faith; no genuine
Christianity; nothing but a boastful intellectualism
or a mushy emotionalism.

What is the reason for this condition? Investigate, and you shall discover the fact that the people do not read the Bible in their homes; there is no family altar. Where this neglect of the Scriptures obtains in the homes of the parishioners, that which they hear from the pulpit flies away and bears no fruit. There are localities and seasons where powerful revivals have occurred. The people were strangely moved. The fields were green and blossoming. There is great rejoicing in the prospect of much fruit from this planting of the Lord. A few years pass. You visit the district again. You do not recognize it. You look out upon the barren land with sorrow. You see nothing but thorns and thistles, mixed with audacity and ungodliness. What do you suppose the reason is? Well, a laborer in the vineyard died or moved away from the community, and there was no one to care for the people. They had neglected to use the Word in their homes and hearts.

Then again you will find other communities where no one in particular has held the leadership in the work of the Lord. But the people had begun to edify themselves by the use of God's Word. You are happy and surprised to see that the work of the Lord has not only been conserved, but increased, extended and matured. These phenomena are so common that anyone who has any comprehension of the Kingdom of God may readily observe the facts in each case.

How are we to explain these phenomena? Recall your personal experience as a Christian. You have been a pupil in the school of the Holy Ghost. Of what do you boast as the means by which your inner life was nourished and prospered? Have you put your trust in your will-power, your watchfulness, your intellectuality, your steadfastness in the overcoming of temptation? Not at all. With the apostle, you will boast of God's faithfulness. But God is equally faithful to all. It was not on account of any lack in God's faithfulness that the Christian life died out here and there. No. The difference is in the circumstance that they neglected the Means of Grace, while you made use of it. However secure and forgetful you may have been, you still occasionally read and heard God's Word, meditated upon it and allowed it to work in your heart.

You have discovered that the blessing was in proportion to the use that you made of the Word. Have you not learned by experience that, after a long period of neglect of God's Word, your heart has become dried up and cold, indifferent to the welfare of your soul, weak in the presence of temptation, carnal and worldly-minded? At other times when you diligently made use of your Bible, have you not realized that the inner life in you grew strong and vigorous?

Further: Has it not frequently occurred, when you were on the brink of falling into sin or carnal security, that a Scripture passage, a sermon, or even a hymn, awakened you from slumber and saved you? Has it not happened, when your heart seemed dead and cold, and the world seemed dreary, and you read a verse or a chapter in the Bible or a portion of some good book, or you met a friend who quoted a Scripture promise of good cheer, that new light dispelled the gloom upon your soul and a new encouragement invigorated your heart? Have you not under such circumstances had the same experience as King David: "Unless Thy Law had been my delights, I should then have perished in my affliction" (Psalm 109:92). You know from experience that God's Word has been the means by which your spiritual life has been sustained. The same is the case with the Church, that is, with all other believers. The Word of God is not called "a Means of Grace" in vain.

How cruelly they deal with their souls who thrust aside the Bread of Life, the heavenly food, God's Word. God has of grace given us a visible means, in which He dwells and comes to us: a means through which He calls, gathers and enlightens us, a means upon the right use of which our eternal welfare depends. And what do we behold? Not only does the blind and raw worldling trample these pearls of great price under his brutal feet, but what is still worse, they "who have tasted the good Word of God and the powers of the world to come" "fall away." They permit the world and the flesh to hinder them in the perusal of God's Word. Entire days and weeks pass by without any contemplation of God's Word whatever. The soul is left to starve. Or, even if some little time is given to the reading or hearing of the Word, the mind and the heart are so occupied with the things of the world that the soul, like the tumbling ocean, can not be warmed by the rays of the sun of the heavenly Father's love. The fruit of such treatment of the Word is only a greater aversion to its use. The Word of God must be received in a quiet, devout spirit if it is to warm and vivify the heart.

THE USE OF GOD'S WORD
(*Continued*)

THE TWELFTH DAY

MANY are hindered from the use of God's Word by worldly affairs. In the parable Jesus speaks of these worldly hindrances as "the thorns" that spring up and "choke the good seed." He explains these thorns as "the care of this world and the deceitfulness of riches" (Matthew 13:7, 22). The cares and allurements of worldly interests naturally produce indifference to spiritual interests. From this follows carnal security. Earthly matters become to the blinded soul of far greater importance than heavenly treasures. "I have no time for the reading of God's Word nor for church-going. I am so busy that I even need my Sundays for doing odds and ends of work about the house or at the office. As for family prayers, we are all too busy during the rest of the week to even think of anything but work. We bolt our breakfast, and off we start to work. At night we are too tired for the reading of the Bible, or else we have engagements of one kind or another." Such is the apology of the worldling and of the spurious Christian.

"But," you remonstrate, "our work is a sacred duty and may not be neglected. The Good Book says: 'But if any provide not for his own, and especially for those of his own house, he hath denied the faith, and is worse than an infidel' (1 Timothy 5:8)." But Jesus says that we are to do the one and not neglect the other. You may attend to your calling in life with the greatest zeal and industry, but if you neglect your soul, your industry is not going to save you on the Day of Judgment. If you pretend that your business would suffer if you took some time for the contemplation of God's Word, you are simply deceived by the old Serpent, who keeps alive the heathen in your heart. It is the unbelief of your soul which disregards the heavenly things. Your worldly mind more readily wastes ten hours in frivolity and nonsense than it utilizes one hour in the interest of your immortal soul.

What worse than pagan contempt for the living God and His Holy Word! You are given the unspeakable privilege and honor of communing with the Lord of heaven and earth, the Redeemer of your sinful and guilty soul, and you have not the time. You are too busy with earthly matters. He would speak to you through His Word of Revelation, and you may speak to Him through prayer, but you are too busy to commune with Him who has your life in His hands entirely. You have plenty of time for the

vanities of this passing world, but no time to listen
to the voice of God Almighty. Do you not realize
that your eyes are blinded by the devil? You have
not the time to devote one hour of the twenty-four
to the nourishment of your starving soul. Suppose
the Lord laid you upon a sick-bed for a year or two.
The world would swing along as usual without you.
It would not stop to bother about you, nor care very
much whether you lived or died. Meantime you have
despised God and His Word. Surely you have no
right to expect any help from Him? You have had
no use for Him in the days of your strength.

The result of the neglect of God's Word is in-
evitably the decline of the inner man, the decay of
faith, the debilitation of the gifts of grace. You
complain of your spiritual weakness and lack of
power in the face of temptations, which threaten to
overcome you. What else can you expect? Neither
God nor man expects you to overcome the power
of sin in you without the means for overcoming, and
the only possible Means of Grace for overcoming is
the Word of God used in prayer. By the diligent
use of the Means of Grace, however, you shall lack
nothing necessary to salvation. If you say that you
have read the Bible, but to no avail, one of two
things is at fault: Either you do not understand that
conversion as a rule is a process of humiliation and
abasement in which you do not find yourself better
and better, but rather the opposite; or you are in
reality still a slave of sin, without the new life in
Christ, without the new desire and the heavenly

powers. You have not made the right use of the Word of God. You have inverted God's order. You have tried to conquer the evil in you before accepting the grace of God in the merits of Christ. You have tried to bear fruit before being grafted in Christ.

Begin by obeying God's Word. First go to Jesus and beseech Him for pardon and grace. Then shall you be granted the will and the power to overcome sin and temptation. Let go of your self-righteousness. Throw yourself into His loving embrace just as you are, with all your sins and apologies, and you shall find to your immeasurable surprise and joy that "where sin hath abounded, grace hath much more abounded." The joy of this discovery will so change your heart that you will find no more pleasure in the sin which formerly held you in its iron grip. The good which you could not do, you now do naturally and cheerfully. It is your soul's delight. Such is the teaching of God's Word. Obey the Word implicitly, and you shall find that nothing is impossible.

You say that you have frequently heard and read God's Word without experiencing any effect upon your heart: you remained callous and indifferent. I would answer you thus: If you are content to hear the Word of God unfeelingly, it is a sign that your heart is unrepentant and hardened. If, however, you are distressed in heart because of your listlessness; if you try to hear the Word devoutly and understandingly, your anxiety about your spiritual callousness is a sure mark of the honest mind of a disciple. Note, further, that you shall not read or hear God's Word in vain. It will humble you and cause you much dissatisfaction with yourself, but it will also sow good seed in the dry soil of your heart, which with the early or latter rains will sprout and bear fruit.

In other words: While you may only receive the Word intellectually and find no application for it in your heart at the time being, other circumstances will cause it to spring into life and activity. That is the way the Spirit operates through the Word. That is what Jesus means when He says: "The Holy Ghost shall teach you all things, and bring all things to your remembrance, whatsoever I have said unto you" (John 14:26). Such was the experience of the disciples. They did not understand all that Jesus told them; but later when something intervened to make His words fit the circumstances, "they remembered what Jesus had said." It may not suit the happy-go-lucky individual to listen to a consolatory sermon, but when trouble and grief overwhelm him, such a sermon may prove very useful to him. This is the case with all the Word of God. The Word is never heard without some fruit, providing it is heard and remembered thoughtfully.

"But," you say, "I don't need to read the Bible any more, nor do I need to hear any more sermons. I know all I need to know. If only I could live according to what I know!" O my perverted friend!

God's Word is not only to furnish you knowledge, but also the power to live as you read and hear. You say that you know all that you need to know? Very well. All that remains, then, is that you live according to the Word. But nothing in the world can give you this power but the Word itself. There may be a good light in your head, but only darkness in your selfish heart. Your heart may be sorely lacking in love to God and man, in peace and joy, in patience and humility. Is your faith perfect? Have you succeeded in believing all that you ought to believe? Is your love so burning that you need no replenishment from God's holy Word? Have you quite enough of confident trust in times of trial and temptation? Enough of peace and joy in the Holy Ghost?

You have learned from experience that it is the Word of God alone which produces these results. Are not these blessings worth increasing? If you knew of a field where costly pearls and gold coins were to be found, would you not make use of every hour in order to find the treasures? But what pearls and coins are as precious as the spiritual gifts of faith, peace, joy, love, patience and hope? All these you may seek and find every day in God's Word. God's Word is the true Gold Coast, where the heavenly treasures are to be found. But man is carnal, of the earth, earthy. He places a small valuation upon the spiritual and heavenly riches. The time will come, however, when you will gladly exchange all your gold and silver for one sin-

gle comforting word of God, for instance, when at
your death-bed the physician no longer can give you
any hope of life.

In short, the spiritual life is not only a matter of
intellectual knowledge. It is not even a life in accordance with certain fundamental principles and
resolutions. It is a genuine life from above, which,
like all other forms of life, needs to be sustained
with its own appropriate food, namely, the Bread
of Life, which is "from heaven" (John 6:32).
This life is a spiritual life, a soul-life, which can not
be sustained by human conditions or earthly food of
any kind, material or intellectual or esthetic or ethical, but only by the heavenly food of the Word of
God. Many an honest soul looks anxiously forward
to the coming years with their concomitant temptations, and he thinks: "How am I to stand fast in the
grace of God and preserve my spiritual life?" Your
spiritual life, my friend, does not depend upon the
conditions and circumstances of your life, but solely
upon your faithful use of the Means of Grace.

Christ Himself, the faithful Shepherd, will provide for the nourishment of your soul. How often
do we not see that weak and naturally melancholy individuals, under much discouragement and in perilous surroundings, as lambs among wolves, nevertheless are protected and preserved by the faithfulness of the Good Shepherd! But not only this: they
even make wonderful spiritual progress in all that
which is good, simply because they make daily and
devout use of God's Word. Other more favored

persons, endowed with happy natures and moving in pleasant surroundings conducive to spiritual growth and improvement, gradually decline into spiritual apathy and death, again, simply because they neglected to hearken to the Word and voice of God. Therefore, of two brothers in the Lord, the one who loves God's Word, reads it, hears it, and meditates upon it, will grow in grace and all spiritual gifts; while the other, who neglected the Word, will decline spiritually. For the Holy Spirit dwells in the Word and works through the Word.

If you would gain eternal life, you must sustain your spiritual life. If you have no time to meditate upon the Word of God as you should, you ought to set aside some period or periods for that purpose either from the day or from the night. "One thing is needful." If you can not do this, it may as well be said to you that you can have no grounded hope of salvation. From the moment that you decide that you have no time for the perusal of the Bible, you will of course cease to think about heaven and your immortal soul. For without the proper use of God's Word, your spiritual life must of necessity decay, and you have no reason to look forward to eternal life. If you were incarcerated where the Word of God were denied you, God would no doubt provide some method by which your soul-life might be sustained, but not as long as you have access to His Word. It is for you to determine which you regard as the more precious, the earthly or the heavenly treasures.

THE USE OF GOD'S WORD
(*Continued*)

THE THIRTEENTH DAY

OH, that all true Christians, who are the true pastors whether in the holy office or not, might untiringly encourage their fellowmen in the use of the Word of God. You who feed a poor and hungering person are doing a good deed, but you are doing him a far greater service if you put him in the way of earning his own daily bread. This is precisely the service which he renders who induces the people to read, hear, and study God's Word. Where is the shepherd who with his own hands can properly feed the entire flock? Does he not with much anxiety think upon his parish, the many and variant members entrusted to his care? Who is able personally to care for all these? But if he can prevail upon the people to feed themselves with the Word of God, then has he led them to the "green pastures" indeed. Would not this fact be a satisfaction to the heart and conscience of a faithful shepherd?

Possibly the most important point in this matter has been omitted. We have considered the Marks of the True Doctrine; the Right Use of God's Word; and finally, the Use and Necessity of the Word. Let us now for the sake of the unlearned attach a few remarks appertaining perhaps more to the external aspect of the topic, and yet of great importance.

1) As in everything else, order should be observed in the use of God's Word. Instead of read-

ing disconnectedly here and there in the Bible, take a certain portion of the Scriptures or a book, and read it continuously to the end. In this way you get a prospectus of the whole and grasp the central thought of each book, chapter, or portion. This again gives you more delight in the Word and saves you from the puerility of not knowing where to begin your reading. If you are not well acquainted with the Bible, begin with the New Testament. It concerns us most directly, and is easier to understand than is the Old Testament. If possible, set aside definite periods for your meditation upon God's Word. Otherwise you will be drawn from one distraction to another, and your complaint will be: "I did not find time to read my Bible to-day."

2) Do not always read to yourself alone. Share the study of God's Word with others. It will come with redoubled power to your own heart, and you are thereby doing your neighbor a service. That the Word has the greater power to move the hearts when fellow-believers share it with one another, all experience has proved in every age. From the earliest Christian era it has been customary for "brethren to dwell together in unity" (Psalm 133: 1), praying, reading, speaking and singing the Word of the Lord. How great a blessing this custom may be to others, you may never know in this life. If thus you have become the instrumentality for the salvation of one soul, your reward will be great in heaven. An insignificant beginning has frequently resulted in a great awakening. "The Kingdom of heaven is like to a grain of mustard seed, which a man took, and

sowed in his field: which indeed is the least of all seeds; but when it is grown, it is the greatest among herbs, and becometh a tree, so that the birds of the air come and lodge in the branches thereof" (Matthew 13: 32-34). Such is the Kingdom of God.

3) If you are a father or a mother, you have a peculiar responsibility for the souls of your children. Hear the command of God to every father and mother: "And thou shalt teach these words diligently unto thy children, and shalt talk of them when thou sittest in thine house, and when thou walkest by the way, and when thou liest down, and when thou risest up" (Deuteronomy 7: 7). Sometimes parents go too far in their anxiety to fulfil this commandment. Let them not be too fearful, but only do what the Lord tells them to do, and then cast all their cares and anxieties upon the Lord. This Scripture passage only requires that you have a concern for the souls committed to your care, and that you impress the Word of God upon their hearts in season and out of season; for they need godly admonitions every day.

These duties are, alas! all too frequently neglected, though not hard to perform. For this reason Jehovah continues: "And thou shalt bind them for a sign upon thine hand, and they shall be as frontlets between thine eyes. And thou shalt write them upon the posts of thy house, and on thy gates" (verses 8, 9). If, then, you are diligent in inculcating the Word of God, and your children refuse to obey the Word, you are at least free of their blood. If, however, you neglect to warn and admonish them with God's Word, you assume a tremendous responsibility.

But now arises this question: How am I to perform this duty? Recall what was said above about the advantage of an orderly use of the Bible. Why not dedicate a certain daily period to family worship? But that arrangement does not exclude the duty of making use of other opportunities for the assembling of the family about the family altar. "When thou walkest by the way," "When thou sittest in thine house," when at work with your people, anywhere and at any time when suitable opportunity offers, you are to inculcate the Word of the Lord by precept and example. But the regular daily assembling for family worship at a definite period should be observed inviolate. Have you done your duty to your family in this respect? Possibly you have not. Do you propose to continue in the neglect of this supreme responsibility? Are you not called to be the pastor of your own household? Do you propose to let your children pass through the world without your personal spiritual guidance? Is there not to be an altar in your home dedicated to the living God, where He may be worshipped and adored?

It is true that after long neglect it is no easy matter to establish or even reestablish the family altar. The devil will offer resistance. The carnal mind will sneer and create embarrassment. But is a Christian to become so worldly-minded that a period of family communion with the Lord of the household should be a disagreeable performance?

Right here is conclusive evidence as to the need and importance of daily family worship. You realize that this beneficent custom requires earnestness of purpose and the discontinuance of evil habits. Evil becomes yet more evil in the presence of holiness. Unrest and conflict arise in the soul when you come into the presence of God after the commission of sin. Conscience is in tumult when after communion with God you go and sin.

"It is to be noted, that it is precisely the secret love of certain pet sins that hinders family worship. But there is perhaps no greater evidence of spiritual degeneracy than the fear of being held back from the commission of sin." Luther says in the preface to the Greater Catechism: "Doubtless you shall find no stronger barrier against the devil than the use of the Word of God. That is the sign and holy water which he dreads."

Perhaps you fear that the daily family worship may become a mere habit, resulting in work-righteousness, hypocrisy and hardness of heart. That indeed may happen. But that may also result from the use of any of the Means of Grace. We ask: Will they who misuse the Means of Grace be improved without the use of these same means? Are we to discard all the means to salvation, the Gospel, the Sacraments, church-going, because they are frequently misused? Far from it; for by the use of the Means of Grace some may and will be saved, but without them not a soul is saved. There is no better mark of the integrity of a family or of a nation than that "the Word of Christ dwelleth in you rich-ly" (Colossians 3 : 16).

But we have been harping long enough upon this string. We would close with the following notations: Would you not wish to have a court preacher in your home, who might preach daily to yourself and your family for instruction, repentance, comfort and consolation? Very well. If you so desire, such a one is offered to you. Without paying great salaries, you may have the greatest court preachers at your service in your own home—kings and prophets, who will not flatter you, but tell you the truth to your face; Christ Himself with the holy apostles—all these will be only too glad to serve you, if you so desire. Ought you not to be ashamed of yourself and bitterly regret that you have so long despised so great an offer? Woe to the unbelief and spiritual darkness which prevent us from realizing the abundant grace thus offered to us! Think of the great preachers whom you may hear in the Bible and other good books! How thoughtless and shallow-minded men are!

Suppose we were informed that on the top of a certain mountain an angel from heaven were preaching the Word of God, and that there was reason to believe in the truthfulness of the news. Would we not hasten to the mountain, no matter what the difficulties might be? Now, suppose that on the road we were met by the returning multitudes, who informed us: "You come too late. The angel with the shining wings has ascended to heaven." Would we not anxiously inquire: "But do you not remember the words which he spoke?" And they would answer: "Oh, yes. Here we have his entire speech written down." Would we not give everything we possessed in order to see and hear the words which the angel had uttered?

Friend, that is precisely what has happened. God Himself, His angels and prophets, the Son of God also, have all spoken on the mountains of the East. They have spoken in the homes and in the temple. And their words have been written down and preserved in the Holy Bible. This is not fiction. It is the very truth of God. Ought we not love, cherish and diligently use God's Word? Ought we not mount it in gold, or, like the Emperor Theodosius, "copy it in letters of gold upon parchment"? Or better still, ought we not permit the Spirit of God to indite it upon our hearts and remain faithful and true to God's Word in life and death?

SPIRITUAL DROWSINESS AND CARNAL SECURITY

THE FOURTEENTH DAY

IN the twenty-fifth chapter of the Gospel according to St. Matthew, at verse 5, Jesus says concerning the Ten Virgins, both the wise and the foolish: "While the bridegroom tarried, they all slumbered and slept." We see a repetition of this phenomenon daily in the incomprehensible drowsiness and spiritual lukewarmness which obtains in Christendom. The world is secure and obdurate. The hypocrite deceives himself year in, year out, with a spurious Christianity and a false hope. The believers grow forgetful, drowsy, negligent, make tottering steps, stop half way, or lapse into spiritual death. And the reason for this deplorable condition is: The Bridegroom tarries. Nothing of an exceptional character happens. One year is very much like another. There are no special signs indicating the second coming of the Lord. The ungodly flourish and rejoice in their prosperity. They seem happy, secure and confident. He who loves the Lord and seeks the heavenly treasures is laughed at and ridiculed as a fool, frequently suffers adversity. A thousand allurements attract him, and his heart is bowed down. Everything argues for the world. Nobody utters the word of warning, of exhortation or of comfort. The Word of God is sorely neglected. Prayer, testimony, witnessing for Christ, suffering for His name's sake—all these are absent. The evil day is here. The powers of darkness rule. Even the elect become drowsy, cold, listless. The oil in their lamps is constantly diminishing: gradually it will disappear and the lamps will go dry. Christians are growing worldly-minded, careless, and spiritually indifferent.

The listlessness into which Christians are sinking is shown by the circumstance that spiritual things are becoming insignificant and unimportant, while the world and worldly things are becoming of prime importance to them. It is demonstrated by the fact that the Christian has become perfectly satisfied with himself. He relies upon himself. He feels no burden of sin. He has no conflict between the spirit and the flesh, no fear of the enemy, no doubt as to himself. He resembles Peter, when he assured the Lord: "Though all men should be offended because of Thee, yet will I never be offended" (Matthew 13: 33). A few hours later he denied his Master. He resembles King David, when from the roof of his palace he cast lustful eyes upon the woman, without dreaming of danger. Too many Christians have no concern about their steady advancement in that which is good. The grace of God in Christ no longer warms the soul as in the early days of the Christian life. The Word of God becomes insipid and tasteless.

But that which differentiates an honest soul from the dishonest one is, that the living Christian soon becomes anxious about himself, sees the warning look of the Master, goes out from the world, and weeps bitterly. If his carnal security has progressed so far that God must use external tribulations, or some reprimanding Nathan, to effect an awakening, the honest Christian will accept the ordeal to his own good. He will take the warning or the chastisement to heart, confess his sins and his spiritual indolence, and amend his life by a closer walk with God.

1.

It is, on the contrary, a mark of the transition from spiritual drowsiness and security to death and obduracy, that a person refuses to be warned, and remains self-satisfied and carnally secure. Either, like Judas Ishkarioth, he continues in sin, conceals it, defends it, denies it, or, like the foolish virgins, he leads an outwardly respectable life, but is utterly lacking in spiritual life. Thus he goes on, a false Christian, until the door is shut. A person is in a frightful soul-condition when he no longer is capable of serious thought, no longer possesses the ability to stop and consider the most important things of life, no longer has any concern for his soul and the Judgment Day.

But such is human nature,—a dreadful demonstration of death which was to be the penalty for sin and disobedience: "In the day that thou eatest thereof, thou shalt surely die" (Genesis 2:17); the result of the condition described by the apostle: "There is no fear of God before their eyes" (Romans 3:18). They hear God's Word. They read it. They believe that while others may deceive themselves, they are safe and secure. They have no fear of being lost. They are hypnotized by the allurements of the world, and laugh at the admonitions of the Spirit.

Here are a few illustrations: A God-fearing wife one morning said to her husband: "I never hear you speak of Jesus as you used to do in the early days of your conversion. Nor do you ever regret your shortcomings. Nor do you read the Bible. How is it with your soul? Do you never pray to God?" The husband's face flushed. He turned abruptly to his wife and said: "Please do not trouble yourself about my soul, my dear." He walked away, humming a frivolous song. Such is the way of carnal security. He repulsed his Christian wife's concern for his salvation, though he was slipping farther and farther away from God. He was fast joining the careless crowd of whom the apostle said: "There is no fear of God before their eyes."

Here is another example: A young man who had been away from his home community a long time, was awakened and became a sincere Christian. He returned to his home and talked with his brothers and sisters regarding their spiritual condition. He talked with his sister concerning the necessity of the new birth. He quoted the words of the Lord to Nicodemus: "Except a man be born again, he cannot see the Kingdom of God" (John 3: 3). He asked her: "Do you know in your heart that you have been born again?" She avoided a direct answer and sidetracked the question. An elder brother was very religious and generally regarded as a Christian man. When among Christian people, he was pious and unctious. When among the worldly at social functions, he had a way of conforming smoothly with their ways and customs.

One day the younger brother said to the older: "Brother, I am afraid that you are leading many innocent souls astray. Among Christians you are regarded as a true believer, and among worldly people you are as worldly as any of them. I would advise you to give up the name of Christian, declare war on the believers, and conduct yourself consistently as a man of the world. Then you would deceive nobody, and nobody would be led astray by your duplicity. The Bible says: 'Come ye out from among them, and be ye separate, saith the Lord, and touch not the unclean thing, and I will receive you, and will be a Father to you, and ye shall be my sons and daughters, saith the Lord Almighty' (2 Corinthians 6: 17-18). We also read: 'Be ye not unequally yoked together with unbelievers: for what fellowship hath righteousness with unrighteousness? And what communion hath light with darkness? And what concord hath Christ with Belial? Or what part hath he that believeth with an infidel?' (2 Corinthians 6: 14-15). Again: 'Know ye not that the friendship of the world is enmity with God? Whosoever, therefore, will be a friend of the world is the enemy of God' (James 4: 4)."

The elder brother was somewhat offended, and said that he understood these Scripture passages in a different sense. He maintained that they referred only to the inner soul-life of a man. The younger brother now asked him if he had not by his double life encouraged the ungodly in their worldliness, while at the same time he had caused offense among all true Christians. Again there was the same evasion of the real issue, precisely as in the case of the sister. The religious elder brother repeated that he revered God's Word most highly, but placed a different construction upon the passages which the younger man had cited. "There is no fear of God before their eyes," thought the young man, as he sadly walked away. His conclusion was, that the misinterpretation of God's Word is to be ascribed not so much to any lack of intellectual comprehension as to an unwillingness to obey the Word.

2.

There are numberless examples of such hardness
of heart. Perhaps the most striking one is that of
Judas Ishkarioth. He was one of Jesus' disciples,
one of the Twelve, one of whom the Lord might say
as He said to David: "Yea, mine own familiar
friend, in whom I trusted, which did eat of my
bread, hath lifted up his heel against me" (Psalm
41 : 9). Judas's hardness of heart began by his gradually habituating himself to sin, "because he was a
thief and had the bag" (Luke 12 : 6). Judging by all
the circumstances, his thieving was carried on very
cautiously, gradually increasing as time passed on
and opportunity offered. As in the case of the ordinary sinner, and especially in the case of a Christian,
the retrogression usually begins with a minor sin before he is able to commit the grosser sins. So also
with Judas. He had for three years had the best
of opportunity to witness the fact that whatever
Jesus foretold would most certainly come to pass.
And yet we see him so hardened in his wicked purpose that he must hear these most awful words addressed to him particularly: "Woe unto that man
by whom the Son of Man is betrayed. It had been
good for that man if he had not been born"
(Matthew 26 :24).

We marvel that Judas could hear these awful
words without falling to the earth dead. But he
was quite capable of hearing them without fear,
without altering his bloody resolution. He was
hardy enough to greet his Master with a kiss at

the moment when the deputies laid hands upon His
sacred body. When the heart is hardened, neither
reason nor intelligence avails. With seeing eyes,
Judas could yet not see. With all his knowledge of
Jesus, with every opportunity for repentance and
restoration, yea, with seeing eyes wide open, he
walked with firm steps to his eternal doom—he
went "to his own place" (Acts 1:25). What he
lacked was a watchful and God-fearing heart. There
is a word spoken by the Holy Ghost, which every
one who has heard the Gospel should keep in mind:
"Woe also to them when I depart from them"
(Hosea 9:12).

3.

Luther says: "He who fears not himself has the
greatest reason to fear." Not to fear oneself; not
to suspect oneself; to live in secret sin, not regarding it as perilous; to be content with one's own
piety—these are some of the signs of hidden spiritual death, the prelude to eternal misery. It is
precisely an excellent mark of live Christians that
they have the spirit of fear. They fear even when
there is no danger. They suspect themselves. They
are afraid of deceiving themselves. They are dissatisfied with themselves. Realizing that they are
drowsy and forgetful Christians, they are fearful
on that account.

This spirit of fear is genuine watchfulness. It
causes the sheep to keep close to the Shepherd;
the chickens to hide under the wings of the hen; the
Christians to clothe themselves daily in the **gar-**

ment of Christ's righteousness. Thus only are they protected from the world, always garbed and ready to stand before the Son of Man. What says the apostle? "Many are weak and sickly among you, and many sleep. For if we would judge ourselves, we should not be judged. But we arc judged, we are chastened of the Lord, that we should not be condemned with the world" (1 Corinthians 11:30-32). What says the Lord Jesus? "Behold, I come as a thief. Blessed is he that watcheth, and keepeth his garments, lest he walk naked, and they see his shame" (Revelation 16:15). "And what I say unto you I say unto all—Watch" (Mark 13:37).

AM I DEBTOR TO MY BROTHER'S SOUL?

> *Thou shalt love thy neighbor as thyself* (Mark 12:31).

THE FIFTEENTH DAY

CAN you possibly love your neighbor if you see him going to perdition without warning him by a single word? It is our sacred duty to seek our neighbor's salvation, next to our own; to "love" our neighbor as we love ourselves; to be sincere in our love. We cannot silently witness the destruction of our brethren. We shall try to arouse them to a sense of their danger, and make use of all means to attain this end. We are familiar with the profound truths, that every unconverted soul is on the way to eternal death; that that same soul may by conversion become an heir to the glories of heaven; that the lowliest Christian may be an instrumentality for the salvation of that endangered soul.

We know the Lord's will in this matter. "He that gathereth not with me scattereth abroad" (Matthew 12:30). The apostle says: "He which converteth the sinner from the error of his way shall save a soul from death, and shall hide a multitude of sins" (James 5:20). We are familiar with the royal mandate: "Thou shalt love thy neighbor as thyself." We know the commandment, but how do we obey it? It is a sad commentary upon human nature, that even sincere Christians overlook this prime Christian duty. We are daily surrounded by souls who in their ignorance are under the damnation of the Law. "They know not what they do." We understand their plight, however. We have in terror fled from "the wrath to come." And yet we have no word of warning or admonition to utter to these people. How does this reticence argue for our love to our neighbor? Is there any rime or reason in this attitude of silence? Are we alive or are we spiritually dead or moribund?

There is, to be sure, great difference between Christians in regard to their attitude toward others. Some are greatly concerned about their unfortunate brethren. They labor diligently for their salvation.

Others, again, subside into a dense obliviousness of their neighbor and his spiritual need. They are utterly indifferent as to the fate of their neighbor: he means nothing to them. They are looking out for their own comfort of mind, body, and soul. They are "spiritual egotists," living supremely unto themselves. We ask such Christians: Are you really growing spiritually? Are you truly living in Him who was always about His heavenly Father's "business," the saving of immortal souls? Christians of course do something for their fellow men, but as a rule, very much less than they might do.

What does Jesus say in regard to this great commandment of love? He says: "He that believeth on me, as the Scripture hath said, out of his belly shall flow rivers of living water" (John 7:38). And in another connection He says: "Whosoever drinketh of the water that I shall give him shall never thirst; but the water that I shall give him shall be in him a well of water springing up into everlasting life" (John 4:14). A spring wells forth continuously with pure, fresh water. It operates by a law of nature. It produces rills and rivulets and cannot be restrained. Hence King David says about the compelling power of the Holy Ghost: "I have preached righteousness in the great congregation: lo, I have not refrained my lips, O Lord, Thou knowest. I have not hid Thy righteousness within my heart; I have declared Thy faithfulness and Thy salvation: I have not concealed Thy loving kindness and Thy truth from the great congregation" (Psalm 40:9-10). The spring is the source of the river. Where the spring is, the water gushes forth cool and clear as crystal to all who live near it. Where there is no spring, all labor is in vain for the production of the water of life.

There are two infallible signs of this futile effort to produce the spiritual life mechanically. The one is characterized by external means and methods, reinforced by an artificial enthusiasm of a frothy and unsubstantial quality. This sort of witnessing never produces abiding results. It fails because it relies upon human intellect and emotionalism instead of depending upon the Holy Spirit. It is superficial and fabricated, and therefore futile and void of thorough conversions. The other sign of a spurious conversion, whether individual or in greater number, is that which is characterized by insipidity, sentimentalism and lack of power. It is devoid of life—a painted carcass.

Let all who would work for souls remember the repeated words of Christ that their work must depend upon the spring, the fountain, the source of spiritual life. The spring from which the living waters flow is the personal life of faith in Christ, who alone giveth the world life. "That which is born of flesh is flesh; and that which is born of the Spirit is spirit" (John 3: 6). Hear what the Apostle Paul says about this spring in activity: "For the love of Christ constraineth us; because we thus judge, that if one died for all, then were all dead, and that He died for all, that they which live should not henceforth live unto themselves, but unto Him which died for them, and rose again" (2 Corinthians 5: 14-15).

How the heart of the apostle must have tasted the love of Christ! It must have been a high and glorious experience thus to be united in love with

Christ. This oneness with Christ explains the tireless zeal of the apostle. He could not have labored as he did unless Christ had revealed His love to him. It was this love of Christ which made the apostle so burning in the spirit. It is not enough that we intellectually appreciate the love of the Son of God. If this love is to become a compelling force in the heart, it must be embraced in faith and used as a light which none but the Holy Ghost can produce in the heart. It must fill the soul with peace and joy in the Holy Ghost. It is the flowering of the heart's individual knowledge of Jesus and His love. Thus His love becomes a spring in the heart, from which by the law of necessity the waters of life flow out to bless other souls. The apostle has explained his own personal relation to Christ in the words: "I am crucified with Christ: nevertheless I live. Yet not I, but Christ liveth in me; and the life which I now live in the flesh, I live by the faith of the Son of God, who loved me, and gave Himself for me" (Galatians 2:20).

But what was it really which the apostle saw in the light of the Spirit, since the love of Christ had so completely captivated his heart? He tells us: "Because we thus judge, that if one died for all, then were all dead" (2 Corinthians 5: 14). This is the blessed vision. It is the mystery of the atonement. Christ is so fully our substitute that He died upon the cross for our sins. His death is as valid with God as if we had died. Christ was so completely in our place that God saw us all in Christ.

He saw not Christ, but us suffering death upon the cross.

There are some who explain this passage thus: Since Christ died for all, then all should die from sin. Or thus: This verse refers to believers only, who are dead to the world and to sin. Both interpretations are incorrect. The apostle does not say: Since one died for all, then all ought to be dead. He says: "Then are all dead." Nor does he say: All believers. He says: "all." The word "all" of course has the same meaning in the conditional clause as it has in the main sentence. Now, since we know, as the Apostle John says, that "He is the propitiation for our sins, and not for ours only, but also for the sins of the whole world," the word "all" as used in the passage referred to must retain its entire and unabridged content and meaning, namely, that Christ died for the world, for all mankind, for all men, the good and the evil without distinction, and that all human beings are regarded by God as having died in the death of Christ. It means that the guilt of all men has been blotted out. It means that no one will be condemned on account of his guilt. It means that every soul will be tested and tried in accordance with his relationship to Christ.

Christ Himself has clearly stated that he only who does not believe is already condemned: "He that believeth on Him is not condemned; but he that believeth not is condemned already, because he hath not believed in the name of the only begotten Son of God" (John 3:18). Again He says:

"Of sin, because they believed not on me" (John 16: 9). But why adduce further Bible passages to prove the universality of Christ's redemption? Do we not understand the apostle's meaning when he says: "If one died for all, then were all dead"? Further on he says: "For He hath made Him to be sin for us who knew no sin, that we might be made the righteousness of God in Him" (2 Corinthians 5:21). Thus the apostle expresses the same truth. One, the Holy One, the Sinless One, is made sin for us, in order that we might be made the righteousness of God in Him. His death must then be our death. Since He died not for Himself but for us, it follows that we all died in Him.

O the inexpressible love of Christ! When Christ went to His passion He said: "For their sakes I sanctify myself, that they also might be sanctified through the truth" (John 17:19). Hearken! "For their sakes I sanctify myself," not for my own sake. Praised be His holy name! Christ for us, and we in Christ. Thanks be to God. This was what the apostle knew. It was this fact which filled him with a spirit on fire for Christ, with love and joy. It was this fact which became the driving force in the hearts of all the apostles. For this love they suffered anything and everything, if only they might win souls for Christ. "The love of Christ constraineth us, because we thus judge, that if one died for all, then were all dead" (2 Corinthians 5: 14).

Similarly the love of Christ will constrain us also if the Holy Spirit is poured out upon our hearts, and our faith is something more than a voluntary assent or an intellectual approbation. In three ways, especially, will the love of Christ constrain us to love the brethren. *First,* as already demonstrated, when this love of Christ becomes a fountain of love spontaneously welling forth the waters of life. *Secondly,* when every human being appears to us in a new light, namely, as one who has been redeemed from sin, having already suffered death upon Calvary, but also as one who must be lost if he remains away from the wedding-feast of the Lamb of God. When, with this illumination in our hearts, we see a poor, ignorant soul living without God and without hope in the world, we think in deepest compassion: Oh, if you only knew that your sins are blotted out; if you only knew that you already have died with Christ on the cross, that you no longer need to die if only you would come and take possession of your inheritance! You may receive it at any time, and for nothing. When in faith I consider this love of Christ, these words keep ringing in my heart: "And the Spirit and the bride say, Come. And let him that heareth say, Come. And let him that is athirst come. And whosoever will, let him take the water of life freely" (Revelation 22:17). *Thirdly,* this love of Christ involves a sacred obligation upon every Christian not to live unto himself, but for Him who has purchased us with His blood.

The apostle continues: "And that He died for all, that they which live should not henceforth live unto themselves, but unto Him which died for them, and rose again" (2 Corinthians 5:15). A Christian will no longer regard himself as belonging to himself, or as justified in serving himself only. He is "purchased with a price." His life, his soul, mind, and body, his gifts and talents, all belong to His Master. From childhood he has confessed that "Jesus Christ is my Lord, who has purchased and won me from sin, death and the devil. . . . . that I might be His own, live under Him in His Kingdom, and serve Him in everlasting righteousness and blessedness."

When, now, you ask Him: Lord, what wouldest Thou have me do? He answers: The acts which I do, you are also to do. The poor ye have with you always, the spiritually blind, the halt, the maimed, the deaf. "Whatsoever ye have done to one of the least of these my brethren, ye have done it unto me." Christ would have us in His stead upon earth. He would have us minister as He ministered. For this purpose He died, that we are to serve as He served. We are to live, not unto ourselves but unto Him and for Him. Such is the relation between Christ and the Christians. They live for each other. Christ lives for us, and we live for Him. The Christians are regarded by God as in Christ, and Christ is regarded by the world as being in the Christians. Christ has zeal for them and they for Him. Christ confesses them before the Father, and they confess Christ before the world (Matthew 10:32).

Christ will see to it that no sin whatever shall condemn you. The evil which still is in your life will not bring you to the judgment. You shall not be judged by the Law but by grace. Christ will see to that. But what He wants of you is that you live for Him, that you are zealous for His honor and for the ransomed souls about you, that you hearken to His voice, watch and pray. With these minor matters you are to occupy yourself, while He as the great High Priest attends to the atonement for your sins and intercedes for you at the throne of God. Blessed exchange of service!

Christ has no more precious possessions on earth than the souls which He has redeemed with His blood. You must know then, what He expects of you. No matter what your calling may be, or what your station in life may be, He expects that you from the love of souls utilize every opportunity in the service of their salvation. He wants you to speak the truth in love and humbleness of mind. He asks you to counsel them, guide them in the matter of their salvation, hand them a good book, and do whatever your judgment and tact indicate. Only see to it that the love of Christ constrains you. Have a care that you walk in the Spirit. Seek wisdom from God in prayer, and the Lord Himself will furnish you the opportunity, the words you are to use, the deeds you are to perform, and crown your endeavors with His blessing.

THE BELIEVER'S SPIRITUAL CLEANNESS

> *Ye are clean through the word which I have spoken unto you* (JOHN 15: 3).

THE SIXTEENTH DAY

WHEN Jesus, as recorded in verse 2, had said, "And every branch that beareth fruit, He purgeth it, that it may bring forth more fruit," He added: "Now ye are clean through the Word which I have spoken unto you" (John 15:3). This is remarkable language, dark and obscure, especially to those who do not believe the sacred content of the Scripture quotation. What a strange juxtaposition of words: "clean through the Word"! What is the meaning? "Ye are clean through the Word which I have spoken unto you." These words are extremely important. In the first place, they are the words of our adorable Lord and Savior, and His words are always of the greatest moment to us. In the second place, they treat of a most important topic, our spiritual cleanness before God, without which no one shall see God.

Jesus speaks of a quality of spiritual cleanness which is acceptable to the Eternal Judge. He Himself speaks these words. That which He designates as cleanness has perfect validity in heaven and earth. Otherwise we could never be sure that what we regard as cleanness would be recognized as cleanness also by Him. Everything depends upon His acknowledgment. "It is God that justifieth." It is

God who shall judge us. If I am in possession of a cleanness of soul which God recognizes, it matters nothing if I and all other men see only uncleanness in me. The heavenly Voice said to the Apostle Peter at Joppa: "What God hath cleansed, that call not thou common" (Acts 10:15). Let me therefore investigate what Christ means by these words. Possibly I may find some fount of comfort in them. Suppose that there were a relationship in which, without my knowledge I am regarded by God as perfectly pure and sinless! Suppose that there were a secret relationship in which God is perfectly pleased with me, looking upon me as innocent, holy and acceptable to Him, while I go on regarding myself as impure, sinful, abominable! O that I might know for a certainty that before God I am clean, innocent and pleasing to Him! Therefore let us study these mysterious words of Christ.

The first thing we would note is, that the Lord speaks of a spiritual cleanness, cleanness before God. No one would possibly imagine that the Lord in the middle of a profoundly spiritual discourse would speak of an outward ecclesiastical cleanness or physical cleanness. For Jesus speaks of a cleanness which was theirs through the Word that He had spoken. Of necessity, then, He speaks of a spiritual cleanness. But how is this cleanness to be understood? How were these disciples clean through His Word?

The Scriptures speak of two kinds of spiritual purity only. The one is the purity created in the heart by God. He refers to this kind of purity

thus: "purifying their hearts by faith" (Acts 15:9).
This purity of heart signifies an indwelling purity.
The other kind of purity is a liberation from sin
and guilt which has been secured by a sacrifice. By
this liberation I am justified before God. Saint
John speaks of this freedom from sin and guilt
when he says: "The blood of Jesus Christ, His Son,
cleanseth us from all sin" (1 John 1: 7). This
cleansing is portrayed in the Old Testament by the
sacrifices for sin when the high priest enumerated
the sins of himself and the people, transferring
them to the animal to be sacrificed. The prophet
Isaiah says in speaking of the Messiah: "The Lord
hath laid upon Him the iniquity of us all" (Isaiah
51:6). John the Baptist says, pointing to Jesus:
"Behold the Lamb of God, which taketh away the
sin of the world" (John 1:29). This cleansing
from sin is also produced by the Word of God, as
the apostle says: "That He might sanctify and
cleanse the Church with the washing of water by
the Word" (Ephesians 5:26).

Let us now look at the character of each of these
two kinds of cleanness or purification and see which
one of them Jesus meant in the words at the head
of our meditation. Since there are many who fear
that believers are too much inclined to comfort
themselves with the imputed righteousness of
Christ, setting aside the cleansing of the heart, we
would carefully look into this subject.

There has been a great deal of controversy
among spiritually-minded people regarding this indwelling purity as created by the Spirit of God.

There are those who go to the extreme of insisting that Christians by faith, prayer and the daily renewal, may become so pure at heart that they are practically sinless. Others again go to the other extreme, and practically deny any indwelling purity. They speak of the Christians as if they were precisely like the unconverted, with only this difference that they believe in Christ and thus possess justification by faith.

That these latter controversialists are in error is easily proved by a few plain words from Scripture, as, for instance, the words which we quoted above: "purifying their hearts by faiths." The reference here is not to the blotting out of sin, but to the hearts. Again the Lord says: "Then will I sprinkle clean water upon you, and ye shall be clean: from all your filthiness, and from all your idols, will I cleanse you. A new heart also will I give you, and a new spirit will I put within you: and I will take away the stony heart out of your flesh, and I will give you a heart of flesh. And I will put my Spirit within you, and cause you to walk in my statutes, and ye shall keep my judgments, and do them" (Ezekiel 36:25-27). Here the Lord speaks expressly about "a new heart." Finally, the apostle writes: "For they that are after the flesh do mind the things of the flesh, but they that are after the Spirit the things of the Spirit" (Romans 8:5). He therefore says that there is a difference between those who live after the flesh and those who live after the Spirit in their mind and heart.

It is consequently an error to say that the Christians have no personal purity which differentiates them from unbelievers. The error is a gross and dangerous one because it furnishes the excuse for degrading the Christian life to a life of the flesh. The truth is, that the believers have a new, clean heart, a new, holy spirit.

Now the others come and say: "Since you have a clean heart, there can be no sin or evil in you. Jesus says: 'Out of the heart proceed evil thoughts, murders, adulteries, fornications, thefts, false witness, blasphemy' (Matthew 15: 19). If the heart is clean, there can be no evil thoughts in it. For sin does not lie in the body, but in the heart. How do you harmonize your claim to cleanness of heart with that Bible passage?" Here we must distinguish between "heart" and "heart." What is the new, clean spirit but the "willing Spirit" (Matthew 26:41); the Spirit of Christ in our hearts, which "warreth against the flesh" (Galatians 5:17)? For the word "flesh" in this connection does not signify the physical body, nor any one definite sin, but it means "that which is born of the flesh" (John 3:6) the corrupt nature which we have inherited from Adam by birth. It signifies the inner spiritual evil which is the source of all evil in our hearts and lives. It signifies the old heart, from which proceed evil thoughts, desires and lusts.

Now, the Bible nowhere says that "the flesh" in the believers is holy. On the contrary, it says that the flesh makes such desperate war upon the spirit in the heart of believers, that "they can not do the things that they would" (Galatians 5:17).

Hence the same apostle says: "They that are Christ's have crucified the flesh with the affections and lusts" (Galatians 5:24). Note that he speaks of those who "are Christ's." He does not say that they are clean from lusts and evil desires, but, on the contrary, that they have these evil desires. Their "flesh" is so evil that it must be constantly "crucified." And this the apostle says of those who "are Christ's".

THE BELIEVER'S SPIRITUAL CLEANNESS
(*Continued*)

THE SEVENTEENTH DAY

THEY who speak for the sinlessness of the Christian say: "That only is sin which I voluntarily commit against a clear commandment of God. That which we do not do in full liberty is not sin." Admitting this definition of sin, we are willing to concede that the believer in a certain sense is sinless. For the believer does not sin wilfully. "For if we sin wilfully after that we have received the knowledge of the truth, there remaineth no more sacrifice for sin" (Hebrews 10: 26). The believer can not sin wilfully against a manifest commandment of God. If he does something which in itself is sin, he does it either in ignorance of the true character of the deed, or incited by ensnaring surprise of the enemy, or by the overpowering force of a mighty temptation, as was the case with the disciple Peter. Saint Paul refers to such a time of sifting when he writes: "For that which I do I allow not; for what I would, that I do not; but what I hate, that do I" (Romans 7: 15). Thus also we must construe the episode between Paul and Barnabas: "The contention was so sharp between them that they departed asunder one from the other" (Acts 15: 39). Likewise, when Peter in the house of the high priest three times denied his Master, and when later in Antioch he acted the hypocrite, so that Paul publicly reprimanded him. "And when I saw that they walked not uprightly according to the truth of the Gospel, I said unto Peter before them all: If thou, being a Jew, livest after the manner of the Gentiles, and not as do the Jews, why compellest thou the Gentiles to live as do the Jews?" (Galatians 2: 14).

Now Saint Paul says: "If I do that I would not, it is no more I that do it, but sin that dwelleth in me" (Romans 7: 20). In this way it is true that a Christian, or his new "I," does not commit sin. Saint John writes: "Whosoever abideth in Him sinneth not; whosoever sinneth hath not seen Him, neither known Him. Whosoever is born of God doth not commit sin; for his seed remaineth in him, and he cannot sin, because he is born of God" (1 John 6: 9). Sin is not his business, but rather his torture.

With all this, however, no apostle has ever said that we are sinless in ourselves. John says expressly: "If we say that we have no sin, we deceive ourselves, and the truth is not in us" (1 John 1: 8). No. Our human nature is saturated with sin. We do not even realize that we sin. The old uncleanness attaches to all that we do and say and think, even when we do that which is good. The Bible says that our own righteousness is as "filthy rags," and we realize that the statement is literally true. For instance: that we do not believe in God as stead- fastly as we ought; that we do not love Him with all our heart and soul and strength and mind as we ought; that we permit our thoughts to fly away to many sinful and worthless things; that we do not pray as unceasingly and as sincerely as we ought; that we do not search the Scriptures as diligently and devoutly as we ought; that our mind too readily is moved to impatience, anger, selfishness, pride and impure desires; that we are not animated by that zeal for the honor of our Lord and the salvation of souls which we ought to have. All of this is sin and spiritual uncleanness.

Add to this register of sins the periods of actual temptation when the Lord permits us, like Peter, to be "sifted by Satan." In such times we are so beset by temptation that it seems to us as if the enemy of souls had us utterly in his evil power. The Holy Spirit seems to have departed from us. We mourn and grieve as though we were lost and eter- nally condemned. Such has been the experience of some of God's greatest saints. David's psalms of repentance demonstrate this truth. The great apos- tle prays for deliverance from "the body of this death."

And yet how clean is not their new heart, their new mind, in the midst of all their sins and defects! Listen to their mournings, their self-denunciations, their prayers! Behold their tears, their genuflections, their conflicts! Most wretched is their depression when they do not find in their heart the will to cleanness, the sincere hatred of sin, but rather discover to their horror that they love sin, and yield to temptation. What an awful condition of soul when even the best of saints must confess to himself that he loves sin! But is not the spirit which thus complains a pure and holy spirit?

Observe the difference in the spirit of those who live after the flesh and that of those who live after the Spirit. The former are perfectly content with their life of sin, defend it, apologize for it, and continue in sin. The latter mourn their sins, repent of them, regard them as their bitterest experiences, as a chastisement and a torment. In this condition of shame and selfreproach they need sympathy and encouragement rather than denunciation and condemnation. They have enough of damnation in their own heart. Whatever the Bible has of reprimand and threatening is directed not against those who mourn their sins and damn themselves, but against arrogant sinners who glory in their shame. "And ye are puffed up, and have not rather mourned" (1 Corinthians 5: 2). As soon as the Corinthians repented, there was nothing but comfort and consolation in the words of the apostle: "Now I rejoice, not that ye were made sorry, but that ye sorrowed to repentance; for ye were made sorry after a godly manner, that ye might receive damage by us in nothing. For godly sorrow worketh repentance to salvation not to be repented of, but the sorrow of

the world worketh death" (2 Corinthians 7: 9-10).
That is what the Scriptures mean by the "clean
heart."

It is true that the disciples of Jesus had this clean
mind through the Word of their Lord on the evening when He uttered these words: "Ye are clean
through the Word which I have spoken to you"
(John 15: 3). We see this in Peter when he went
out and "wept bitterly," having denied His Master.
We learn this fact from his whole history. He was
not the one to deny the Lord, to swear and curse.
Therefore these words, "Ye are clean," also apply
to him.

There is one circumstance which proves that Jesus
speaks of another "cleanness." It is the fact that
Jesus earlier in the evening had said precisely the
same thing about them. But then He said it in a
connection which definitely shows that He referred
to that high, perfect cleanness which alone avails
before the Judgment Throne of God. He refers to
the cleanness or righteousness which we have through
faith in His blood. It was when He washed the
feet of the disciples. He said: "He that is washed
needeth not save to wash his feet, but is clean every
whit. And ye are clean, but not all" (John 13: 10).
John adds the annotation: "For He knew who
should betray Him; therefore said He, Ye are not
all clean."

We learn from this explanatory sentence by the
evangelist, that Jesus speaks of a soul-cleanness
which the traitorous Judas could not possess. We
note that Jesus in the beautiful words which He ut-

tered in connection with the washing of the feet of the disciples speaks of the spiritual cleanness which avails before God. Aside from the exclusion of Judas, we know this to be the fact, as He did not seem to care chiefly about the cleanness of their feet but rather of their souls. What else can be the significance of the foot-washing than, as Luther says, their daily life and its purification? Now I see in the whole connection of the words of Jesus and the foot-washing something very precious. He expresses it thus: It is your walk only that is unclean, your daily life: it must be cleansed constantly. You have, however, another cleanness, which is perfect. You have previously been washed in such a manner as to render a second washing superfluous. "Ye are altogether clean."

THE BELIEVER'S SPIRITUAL CLEANNESS
(Continued)

THE EIGHTEENTH DAY

WE ought carefully to consider the words of the Lord: "He that is washed needeth not save to wash his feet, but is clean every whit: and ye are clean, but not all" (John 13: 10). The Lord distinguishes between the cleanness of their feet, that is, their daily life, which needs to be purified constantly, and the cleanness which was theirs by another washing, by which they were altogether clean. When therefore He says: "Ye are clean," He means this latter, perfect cleanness. This distinction we also understand from the circumstance that He who utters the words is He who goes to shed His blood for the redemption of mankind. It was He who had said shortly before on that same evening: "This is my blood of the New Testament, which is shed for many for the remission of sins" (Matthew 26: 28). The fact that we are at all mystified by the words of the Lord in connection with the washing of the feet of the disciples, proves that we have not penetrated into the counsel of God regarding our redemption. If we only remember what Jesus now purposed in His heart, we should immediately understand what He meant by saying to His disciples: "Ye are clean." If we only understand the greatest fact of all in heaven and earth, that God gave His only-begotten Son as the atoning sacrifice for the sin of the world, we should not be in doubt as to the meaning of His words to the disciples: "Ye are clean." If we only would recall to our mind that God during a period of four thousand years by means of numberless bloody sacrifices, purifications and cleansings, portrayed to His people the coming Sacrifice of Atonement for the sin of the world, we should not for a moment suppose that Jesus now spoke of any other cleanness to His disciples than the cleanness resulting from the washing away of their sins by His blood.

If we were in heaven and realized that the one great topic of the glory-song of the white-robed choir of the redeemed is: "Thou wast slain, and hast redeemed us to God by Thy blood out of every kindred, and tongue, and people, and nation; and

hast made us unto our God kings and priests"
(Revelation 5 : 9-10) ; if we could realize that the
only-begotten Son of God has shed His blood on
Calvary for the remission of the sin of the world,
we would not ask what the Savior meant when, as
He was going to the shedding of His blood, He
said: "He that is washed is clean," wholly, perfectly clean. Had we been with Jesus on the Mount of
Transfiguration and heard the heavenly visitants,
Moses and Elias, talk with Him "of His decease
which He should accomplish at Jerusalem" (Luke
9: 31), we would understand that nothing else is
great in heaven. If we lived in faith and had an
adequate conception of this atonement for sin, we
should have surmised what Moses and Elias talked
about without being informed by the evangelist.

Our understanding of the words of the Lord thus
depends upon how closely our mind articulates with
His mind. There is no need of guessing at His
meaning. His words clearly show that He distinguishes between two kinds of cleanness. He first
speaks of an imperfect cleanness and a continuous
cleansing. Then He speaks of a perfect cleanness:
"Ye are clean," a cleanness which needs no improvement. At the foot-washing He intimates that they
needed a constant cleansing in their walk of life.
Thereupon He addresses them as being perfectly
clean. In the parable of the Vine and the Branches
He says: "Every branch that beareth fruit, he purgeth it, that it may bring forth more fruit" (John
15: 2). Again He speaks of a perfect cleanness
which the disciples already possessed. In both figures

of speech, the foot-washing and the branches, He speaks of the same thing.

Finally, we note that Jesus never praises our indwelling cleanness or purification. He rather warns against glorying about our special gifts and graces. We see this on that same evening when Peter, trusting to his own courage, said: "I will lay down my life for Thy sake" (John 13: 37), and the Lord answered him: "The cock shall not crow till thou hast denied me thrice." He warned His disciple against overconfidence and trust in his own strength. Again we see this same deprecation of indwelling gifts and graces when the disciples returned and boasted of the fact that "even the devils are subject unto us through Thy name." He corrected their personal glorification thus: "In this rejoice not that the spirits are subject unto you; but rather rejoice because your names are written in heaven" (Luke 10: 20). Nothing but their unmerited salvation, the universal grace common to all sinners, was to be the subject of their rejoicing. When, again, He represents to them the man who stood in the temple and thanked God—thanked God, mind you—that he was better than other men, it was the publican, who dared not lift his eyes to heaven for very shame, who "went down to his house justified rather than the Pharisee."

We realize from these examples that he who rejoices more in God's gifts and graces in us than he does in the atonement for sin by the blood of the Son of God, is farther from the mind of Christ than is he who feels nothing but infirmity in himself and finds all comfort in Christ alone. He would be all our cleanness and comfort who has purchased us to God by His precious blood.

We return to our subject. We understand, then, what Jesus meant when He said: "Ye are clean through the Word which I have spoken to you." Who can fail to comprehend His meaning? The meaning is the same as that expressed in the words of our Lord on the sending out of His apostles: "He that believeth and is baptized shall be saved." It is the same Lord of whom His apostle said: "That He might sanctify and cleanse the Church with the washing of water by the Word" (Ephesians 5: 26). Here, then, we have the two Means of Grace— Baptism and the Word—by which we are cleansed in the blood of the Son of God.

But we have explanations enough. What we now need is the prayerful meditation upon the words of Christ and the living, personal faith in His blood, which cleanseth from all sin.

See how Christ confirms the great chief doctrine of the Scriptures—justification by faith alone. Saint Paul says: "Faith cometh by hearing," that is, the preaching of the Word. Jesus says: "And ye are clean by the Word which I have spoken unto you." You have done nothing more than that you have heard me preach the Gospel of salvation. Through my preaching faith has been created in your hearts. As a consequence you are clean. God regards you in Christ as though you never had committed any sin. "Ye are clean." These are the Words of Christ, who shall judge all men on the Last Day. Every sinner ought to rejoice in his inmost soul that Christ has said: "Ye are clean through the Word which I have spoken unto you." He says never a word about works and gifts and graces and fine character and our excellencies as cause for boasting. He speaks only of His Word as the means by which the disciples are made clean before God. By the Word of God are they made clean, because the Word has created faith in their hearts, and faith in the Crucified Son of God brings cleanness and righteousness before God. Nothing else avails.

THE BELIEVER'S SPIRITUAL CLEANNESS
(*Continued*)

THE NINETEENTH DAY

SINCE the entire Scriptures bind the salvation of man to the word "faith," we would now concentrate our attention upon this one topic and ask: How do we come to faith? What is faith? Every awakened and seeking soul depends for salvation upon the correct answer to these questions. Hear, then, what Christ says: "Ye are clean through the word which I have spoken unto you" (John 15: 3). Thus says the Spirit of the living God: "Incline your ear, and come unto me: hear and your soul shall live; and I will make an everlasting covenant with you" (Isaiah 55: 3). "Hear!" Only hear! Faith comes by hearing. Faith does not come of itself. It is to the wretched confusion and injury of all awakened souls that they think and think and

cogitate and ruminate and speculate and philos-
ophize instead of hearing what God says. Faith does
not come by thinking nor yet by waiting and waiting for the Holy Ghost, nor by belaboring one's
heart to bring it unto faith. Not at all. Jesus says:
"Through my Word." Stop and listen to what God
says. Take Him at His Word. Trust His promises. He does not lie nor deceive. Rely upon His
Word, no matter how defective your life is, no matter how unregenerate your heart is. If only you
take God at His Word and believe what He says
of His Son, Christ becomes your Savior with all the
blessedness that act of faith implies.

Read these precious words of the Apostle Paul:
"But the righteousness which is of faith speaketh
on this wise: Say not in thine heart, Who shall ascend into heaven? that is, to bring Christ down
from above; or, Who shall descend into the deep?
that is, to bring Christ up again from the dead; but
what saith it? The Word is nigh thee, even in thy
mouth, and in thy heart, that is, the Word of Faith,
which we preach, that if thou shalt confess with thy
mouth the Lord Jesus, and shalt believe in thine
heart that God hath raised Him from the dead, thou
shalt be saved. For with the heart man believeth
unto righteousness, and with the mouth confession
is made unto salvation" (Romans 10: 6-10).

Hear that doctrine! Do not gaze about in this
direction and in that direction, the apostle would
say. Do not look toward far distant, hazy and uncertain regions. "The Word is nigh thee." You
have the Word, the Word of Faith. But what about

Christ? Do you not hear? You have the Word. Take the Word and you have Christ. It seems to you that Christ is far off, away off in the blue sky of heaven, away behind the stars, or deep down in the lowest depths. Now you know where He is. You know how and when He may become your Savior. You do not reach out to the distant horizons for Him. The Word is nigh thee, and that Word creates faith. If you accept the Word, you accept Christ. At the moment when the Word of Christ gains entrance into your heart, Christ enters your heart also.

That is the meaning of the words of Christ: "Now are ye clean through the Word which I have spoken unto you." Through my Word ye are clean. In this manner are we saved by faith. God speaks a Word to you. You accept that Word, and you are in possession of that which the Word contains. Jesus would impress this upon our hearts as He went about helping sinners by His Word. He spoke a Word. They believed His Word, and immediately they were helped. Especially instructive is the example of the "nobleman whose son was sick at Capernaum" (John 4: 46-53). His son "was at the point of death." He went to Jesus and "besought Him that He would come down and heal his son." Jesus begins by reprimanding their unbelief. "Except ye see signs and wonders, ye will not believe." Nevertheless the nobleman reiterates his prayer. But Jesus does not go with him. But what does He do? He "saith unto him: 'Go thy way; thy son liveth.' And the man believed the word that

Jesus had spoken unto him, and he went his way. And as he was going down, his servants met him, and told him, saying: 'Thy son liveth.' Then enquired he of them the hour when he began to amend. And they told him, 'Yesterday at the seventh hour the fever left him.' So the father knew that it was at the same hour in which Jesus said unto him, 'Thy son liveth.' And himself believed and his whole house."

Here we see what it is to "walk by faith." The man saw no miracle performed. Jesus did not go with him, nor did He send any medicine with him. He received nothing that could be handled and felt. He received only a Word. With this Word he went till the following day. During the long, sleepless night he must be content with that Word. Later he received the testimony of his servant. In the very same manner we too are to be content with one single Word of the Lord. We are to walk in faith, without seeing the fulfilment of the Word. But we are to remember that in heaven all is well with us through our faith in the Word of God. The soul is clean and well. Even though we must walk in darkness of soul, if only we hold fast to the Word, we shall on the morning of eternity behold with our eyes that the words and promises of God were fulfilled every one. That is what Jesus would teach us. "Now ye are clean through the Word which I have spoken unto you." He would always turn our eyes to His Word.

It is of the highest importance to remember that the Lord would have us look to His Word for guidance in the way of salvation. It is well-nigh incomprehensible what an amount of anguish it costs many a soul to get away from feelings and emotions to a sturdy faith in God's Word. We think that we must feel thus and so, that we must have this and that experience of the spiritual life, before we dare believe the Word as it reads. These experiences can not come to us in full integrity before we learn to hear and trust the Written Word.

But how may I know that I have this faith? Christ died for all. The Word is preached to all. But all are not saved. The Lord also said: "Ye are not all clean."

Answer: Hear the Word! Pay attention to the Word of God. Nothing but God's Word can give you this assurance. "Faith cometh by hearing." "He that believeth on the Son of God hath the witness in himself" (1 John 5:10). That all men are not saved comes from the fact that they do not believe. If Judas had believed the words of the Master, he too would have been among those whom Jesus pronounced "clean." But he believed only his own notions and the evil impulses of Satan and despised the words of Christ. Heed the Word of God, and you shall know whom He judges to be saved and whom lost. You may read with your own eyes what the Scriptures mean by saving faith. It is not a drug that puts the soul to sleep upon the pillow of dead knowledge. On the contrary, faith is the grateful appropriation of the assurances of God's grace by a poor sinner.

You may see this in the life of all who are saved.

Sin and condemnation terrified them. But the Word
of Christ drew them to Him, and He said: "Thy
faith hath saved thee." To find comfort in the
promises of grace, and thereupon under all tribulations to experience the peace of God in the same
promises, is faith. Faith binds the soul to Christ and
His Word so intimately that it cannot live without
Him. Faith cometh by hearing. If your faith is
built upon the wind, upon the emotions of your
heart, upon your thoughts and surmises, it is nothing
else than carnal security. Therefore Jesus uses the
term, "through my Word." He does not even mention faith. He speaks only of His Word. He wants
to fix our undivided attention upon the Word. We
are to understand that we are not saved by a faith
which grows out of our own thoughts. We are
saved only by that faith which is created in the
heart by God's Word.

THE BELIEVER'S SPIRITUAL CLEANNESS
(*Continued*)

THE TWENTIETH DAY

WHEN you are worried about your sins, your
evil heart, your spiritual indifference, callousness, and conformity to the world; when you are
ashamed of your own defective life, and then hear
the Word about the love of Christ, captivating your
heart, intellect and affections, giving you peace, comfort and hope, it is faith which has saved you.
Jesus says: "For God so loved the world, that He

gave His only-begotten Son, that whosoever believeth in Him should not perish, but have eternal
life" (John 3:16). Now, you are one of the world
of humanity; hence God gave His Son also for you.
If this great truth gains possession of your heart
and mind, then you are a believer. Then Christ
says: "Whosoever believeth in Him should not perish, but have eternal life." Believing this word,
you have eternal life.

Faith stands upon God's Word. Faith imparts
to your soul all that the Word carries and contains.
Consider, for instance, the disciples to whom Jesus
said: "Now ye are clean." You have here the
Lord's own testimony regarding certain individuals
who were still on earth. You know their history.
You may thus conclude how they are whom Jesus
pronounces "clean." They were the eleven disciples,
and they believed in Him. The concentrated hatred
of their countrymen, together with Christ's warnings of suffering and persecution for His name's
sake, could not turn them away from Him. They believed in Him, not only as "Christ, the Son of the
living God" (Matthew 16:16), but also as their
Savior from sin and guilt, however dimly they saw
His glory. Through this faith, they separated themselves from the world. They lived and died for their
Master. They belonged to Him.

But at the side of this "clean heart," we see their
corrupt nature asserting itself in many weaknesses
of life. On that very evening when Jesus designated
them as "clean," He told them beforehand: "All
ye shall be offended because of me this night"

(Matthew 26: 31), and Peter denied Him thrice. Nevertheless He added these words: "But I have prayed for thee, that thy faith fail not; and when thou art converted, strengthen thy brethren" (Luke 22: 32). And yet: "Now are ye clean!"

Here you see the quality of these whom the Lord calls "clean." If you are a friend of the world, your artificial piety will do you no good. You must be His disciple. You must be "His own as a peculiar possession, live and reign with Him in His Kingdom." If the favor or disfavor of the world, the partial self-denial and halfway crucifixion of the flesh prevents you from true communion with Christ, you are in need of genuine conversion and faith. But if you have reached the stage of spiritual development when nothing matters if only you may be His, then your infirmities will not stand in the way of His pardoning grace. You have repentance enough, conversion enough. Only believe His Word, His gracious promises, and all is well with your soul. You are clean in Christ. In a word, if you are daily dissatisfied with yourself, your own slow progress in sanctification, your lapses and shortcomings, but yet believe in Him, and trust His Word, then are you clean, "altogether clean."

"But," you say, "I feel so much impurity in my soul. All kinds of sin are present with me continually. And that which is the worst of all, I cherish love for a certain sin which seems to hold me in its grip. I have no deep hatred of the sin, nor have I any real desire to be rid of it." *Answer*: All that does not sound well. The very fact that you realize the impurity in you is testimony that the Spirit of God is castigating the evil in you. You confess at least with the Apostle Paul: "In me, that is, in my flesh, dwelleth no good thing" (Romans 7: 18). The circumstance that you love a certain sin or certain sins is not strange. How can I possibly construe these temptations, lusts and evil desires otherwise than as the love of sin? If you are a Christian, you will realize that you also hate these same sins.

"How is that?" you ask. "Can I at the same time hate and love the same sin? That seems to me a contradiction in terms." Well, it is true, nevertheless. This contradiction is found in a Christian. The flesh and the spirit are in conflict with each other, and you cannot do that which you would do (Galatians 5). The fact that you possess not even the will to be rid of a sin, demonstrates that you have both hatred and love for that sin—the first after the Spirit, the second after the flesh. A Christian is not altogether spirit. He is also flesh. The life of a Christian is a divided and torn life in daily conflict with itself. For this reason he not only feels the presence of the clean heart and the holy will, but also the wretched mixture of flesh and spirit.

Selfmade and inexperienced Christians understand nothing of all this. To them it is a dark language. But look at King David's misery when he had sinned, and hear the moanings of the Apostle Paul and his sighs for redemption from "the body of this death"; hear him complain of the "law of sin" in his "members" warring against the "law of the Spirit," and you shall realize that it is precisely this soul-conflict which bears testimony to the "clean heart." The fact that you hate most the sins which you most love is the surest sign of the clean mind.

The carnal are carnally-minded. The spiritual are spiritually-minded. Believers hate the sins which they love the most—a testimony to the clean heart. My conviction is that when the disciples quarreled as to who should be the greatest among them, they were not conscious of any hatred of selfishness. When, however, they had returned to their real mind, they certainly hated their self-seeking. At one moment Peter asserted, "I know not the man"; at another, he went out and "wept bitterly."

If, then, you realize that there are times in your Christian life when the inner corruption of the heart silences the voice of Christ, then remember that the disciples had the same experience, in spite of the fact that He spoke to them as being "clean." Herein lies the whole force of our text. Consider: It is He who calls them clean, whose eyes are as flames of fire, who one day shall judge the quick and the dead. He designates them as "clean" at the moment when He foretells their defection and disloyalty. That same evening on the road to Gethsemane together with the Master, they quarreled as to who should be the greatest among them; when in His agony He sweat great drops of blood, they could not watch with Him, however much He begged them to do so; when He was arrested, they fled; when He made a "good confession," Peter denied His Lord. Now note, that of these weak disciples the Lord said that they were clean through the Word which He had spoken to them.

Oh, let me never forget this blessed fact! Here I see the very heart of the Gospel, its great central doctrine—justification by faith alone. Here I see the whole import of the heavenly message, "The blood of Christ, the Son of God, cleanseth from all sin." It runs counter to all reason, that unclean and sinful creatures such as we all are should nevertheless be clean before God. In the presence of this stupendous fact, I begin to realize that the blood of Jesus means more to God than it does to us, more to the angels of heaven than to us sinners on earth. We have not the eyes to see its overwhelming power. We despise Him and reject Him. We esteem Him not. But God esteems Him who shed His blood for the sin of the world, and has given Him all power and dominion.

Oh, if we were in heaven and could see in the light of eternal truth the glory of the Son of God, we should also see that we are but atoms as compared with the great Lord of heaven and earth, who gave Himself a ransom for our sins. We would say: All our infirmities, in reality great sins, are yet but as nothing compared with Him and the power of His blood. Therefore He could say in righteousness: "He that is washed is altogether clean." God be praised! So God declares. He that is washed is altogether clean, while at the same time he mourns his uncleanness and regards himself as utterly unclean. Praise be to God Eternal! In the midst of our infirmities we are pure, innocent and glorious in the eyes of God.

Christ Himself has said it. Though I, with my finite mind, do not comprehend the reasons and the ways of this purification in all directions, I yet see that He has made this pronouncement regarding such as walked in the weaknesses of the flesh: "Now ye are altogether clean." I see at least that they were regarded by Him as God's well-beloved children. In that same night Christ said that what applied to the eleven weak disciples applies equally to all His disciples to the end of time, to "them also which shall believe on me through the Word" (John 17: 20). Hence I will continue to study and meditate upon this mystery all the days of my life, and I will never forget, that the Lord Jesus, who is the only one whom I need to ask has said: "Now ye are clean through the Word which I have spoken unto you." Amen.

―――――――

THE PRINCIPAL FRUITS OF THE DEATH AND RESURRECTION OF CHRIST

THE TWENTY-FIRST DAY

ON the day of Jesus' resurrection I see Paradise restored. I see the portals of heaven swing open. I see the angels talking with men as with brothers and sisters. I hear that Jesus addresses sinners as His "brethren." I see that sin has been atoned for, that believers are just, pure and righteous altogether in the judgment of God Almighty. I see that Simon Peter and the other disciples in spite of their defection and unfaithfulness to their Lord, were yet by Him called His "brethren." I see that the Law does not condemn those who are in Christ Jesus. The Law can not disrupt that brotherhood. I see that death has no power to retain us, since our risen Brother "is become the firstfruits of them that slept" (1 Corinthians 15: 20). I see that as God walked with men in Paradise as with His beloved children, so Jesus walked in His glorified body with the two disciples on the way to Emmaus. Thus He comes to His heart-broken disciples through closed doors. Thus also, though invisible, He will walk with us to the end of the world.

However hidden our life may be by sin, sorrow and tribulation, a restored heaven yet lies underneath. We read of the two disciples who walked to Emmaus, that "their eyes were holden that they should not know Him" (Luke 24: 16). Such is the case frequently with us also. Our eyes are "holden." Therefore we walk full of sorrow and anxiety in the midst of glory; in the midst of wealth we are so poor that we would fain die of cares. If the Lord were permitted to open our eyes, we should see that all is prepared and ready for us as promised already in Paradise. We should see that our forfeited right to heaven has been retrieved.

Let us consider a few facts in connection with the Easter story. The first to meet us at the grave of Jesus are angels, "two men in shining garments" (Luke 24: 4). Matthew records that "the angel of the Lord descended from heaven and came and rolled back the stone from the door, and sat upon it. His countenance was as lightning, and his raiment white as snow . . . . And the angel answered and said unto the women: Fear not ye; for I know that ye seek Jesus, which was crucified. He is not here; for He is risen, as He said. Come, see the place where the Lord lay" (Matthew 28: 2-6). Thus the angels of the Lord were the first messengers of the perfected atonement, even as they were the first to announce the birth of Jesus.

Here is the fulfilment of the words of Jesus: "Hereafter ye shall see heaven open, and the angels of God ascending and descending upon the Son of Man" (John 1: 51). This surely is the gate of heaven, the ladder with "the angels of God ascending and descending on it" (Genesis 18: 12). Here come the angels of heaven, not in a dream, but before eyes awake, not in the darkness of the night but at the dawning of the day. And they are not only seen—they speak and instruct. There is no dark, mysterious connection between heaven and earth. The wall of partition between men and angels has been taken away. A manifest and perfect union between men and angels has been established. The angels may now commune with men in a human way, in order that men in a celestial manner may in eternity communicate with the angels.

What God originally had joined together has been reunited. Men and angels meet at the open grave of Jesus. The disjuncture caused by Satan has been healed and the original relationship between these two greatest of God's beings has been restored. What a happy reunion! What joy to see the angels' humble willingness to serve those who have been called to be the heirs of eternal salvation! Jesus speaks of the joy in heaven when a sinner repents and turns to God. Who can describe the joy of the angels when they were commissioned to announce Jesus' triumph over death and the completed atonement? Jesus is risen. Death is conquered. Sin is blotted out. The Law is fulfilled. The condemnation is annulled. Justice is satisfied, and God is well pleased. That which Satan has destroyed has been made good. Not hell but heaven, not the devil but the angels of God, now receive the ransomed souls of men. Therefore the heavenly hosts rejoice. Many a Lazarus soul is carried by the angels to Abraham's bosom. Whom could God rather have chosen to bring the message of salvation to men? Among all created beings the angels are the most obedient of God's servants and the most trustworthy of His messengers.

"How beautiful upon the mountains are the feet of him that bringeth good tidings, that publisheth peace; that bringeth good tidings of good; that publisheth salvation; that saith unto Zion: Thy God reigneth" (Isaiah 53: 7). Rejoice, then, ye children of Zion! Rejoice in the message of these faithful messengers from heaven. They are sent forth to minister to the heirs of eternal glory. Some time, when soul and body shall be delivered from all shackles, we shall know God better than we do now, and we shall praise Him with clearer comprehension for the guardianship of the holy angels. The apostle writes to the Church Militant on earth: "Ye are come unto Mount Zion, and unto the city of the living God, the heavenly Jerusalem, and to an innumerable company of angels, to the general assembly of the firstborn, which are written in heaven, and to God the Judge of all, and to the spirits of just men made perfect" (Hebrews 12:22-23). May we not say, then, that heaven and earth are reunited, the Fall recovered, and Paradise regained?

The second fact we note at the grave of Jesus is that He designates His disciples as "brethren." Mary the Magdalene stands at the grave of her Lord weeping. Jesus reveals Himself and says to her: "Go to my brethren, and say unto them, I ascend unto my Father and your Father, and to my God and your God" (John 20: 17). This was the first word uttered by our Lord after the completion of the work of atonement. We note that He would center attention upon the words "my brethren." For He adds, as if to emphasize the designation "brethren" and explain it: "My Father and your Father, my God and your God." Prior to His death, Jesus addressed His disciples as "friends," and declared in general terms: "Whosoever shall do the will of my Father, which is in heaven, the same is my brother, and sister, and mother" (Matthew 12: 50). But He had not definitely addressed them as "my brethren." Now, however, when the Serpent's head had been crushed, the sin of the world atoned, righteousness purchased by His blood on the cross,

He begins to speak to His disciples and of them as His "brethren."

This fact is of such importance that we must stop to consider the meaning of the appellation. The great purpose of Christ's atoning death was the restoration of the child-relationship of men with God. All else, the atonement for sin, the removal of the condemnation of the Law, the securing of eternal righteousness for sinners (Daniel 9: 24), were all preliminary to the restoration of the child-relationship of men to God. For this is the supreme fact, that man was created to be the child of God and the heir of heaven. When this child-relationship was destroyed, "the seed of the woman" was to restore and reconstruct that relation. In the relation of man to God as His beloved child lies all blessedness for time and eternity. For, "If children, then heirs, heirs of God, and joint-heirs with Christ; if so be that we suffer with Him, that we may be also glorified with him" (Romans 8: 17).

The restoration of our relation to God as His children was the great purpose of all that which Christ as the Second Adam was to do for us men. They who understand this great purpose of God should ask themselves: Has this relationship been restored? Jesus answers by saying: "My brethren; my Father and your Father, my God and your God." This is His first expression after the resurrection. Upon this term He would center our attention. He who fails to see something infinitely great and glorious in these words of the Risen

Christ, must really possess a mind that is "holden" and darkened indeed.

The wall of partition has been broken down. God and men are reunited. The child-relationship of man to God is reconstructed. The Son of God "is become the first born among many brethren" (Romans 8:29). However much we contemplate this fraternal salutation of our Lord, we shall only have made a small beginning in the profound comprehension of the terms which He uses in addressing us as His brethren, with the same heavenly Father and the same God over all. Here are depths and heights beyond our penetration. The glory is too great. Our hearts and minds are too circumscribed to compass the majesty of His words.

THE PRINCIPAL FRUITS OF THE DEATH AND RESURRECTION OF CHRIST
(*Continued*)

THE TWENTY-SECOND DAY

"MY brethren," says our Lord, "my brethren." "Ah, but," you say, "He referred to His immediate disciples only in using that loving designation. They had been with Him during a period of three years. They were good and holy men. These were the ones whom He spoke of as His 'brethren.' Of what benefit is that to us?" We would only answer: Have you not yet understood that this child-relation to Christ is precisely the same as our filial relation to God? Can you not comprehend that the restoration of the filial relation was the supreme purpose of the atonement? Was that atonement for the sins of a few of His friends, or was it accomplished for the sin of the world? Have you not thought of the meaning of the words which you have used a thousand times: "Our Father, who art in heaven"?

It seems beyond all reason that we common sinners should really become the brothers of the very Son of God. But what say the Scriptures? What says Christ Himself concerning the highest evidence of His grace, that we are to be one with Him even as He is one with the Father? In His sacerdotal prayer, He thus expresses this sublime truth: "I in them, and they in me, that they may be made perfect in one. That they all may be one, as Thou, Father, art in me, and I in Thee, that they also may be one in us" (John 17: 23, 21). Does Jesus pray for the apostles only? No, He says: "Neither pray I for these alone, but for them also which shall believe on me through their word, that they all may be one, as Thou, Father, art in me, and I in Thee, that they also may be one in us" (John 17:20-21).

This prayer, then, is for all disciples at all times, in all lands, till the end of time. That which applies to the apostles applies with equal validity to all "them also which shall believe on me through their word." The honor is too great, it is true; but Christ loves all, and has no respect of persons. Not even the mother of our Lord had any preference in this regard (Luke 8: 19-21, and Luke 11: 27, 28). It is men who are precious in His sight, not this or that individual. There is this exception, however, that the believers are His joy and delight, while unbelievers are the children of His grief, far from His loving arms.

This filial relation to God is the gift of God not only to Christ's immediate disciples, but to all of us who believe on Him through their word. What glory! What source of eternal joy! Each one of us who believes in Him as his Savior from sin and death has the same position of glory as had the first apostles, the same right to apply these words of Jesus to himself: "Ye are my brethren. My Father and your Father, my God and your God."

But the most remarkable thing about this salutation is, that it was sent to the disciples precisely at a time when they sinned more than at any other time in their lives. Let us recall how they had acted while they were with the Lord for the last time before receiving this fraternal greeting. It was on Thursday evening that He parted with them. After the Last Supper, and after the Lord had made a touching farewell address to them, what happened? Peter, from deadly fear, denied his Master, his Lord and Savior. Gross lies passed over his lips and deep damnations followed the lies. On the previous evening Peter and the other disciples had quarreled as to who should be the greatest among them. While Jesus agonized in the garden of Gethsemane and sweat great drops of blood, they could not watch one hour with Him. When He was apprehended, they fled like a flock of frightened sheep. In view of their cowardice and disloyalty, one wonders that they did not succumb from a sense of deepest shame. They realized very well the heinousness of their sin. For when Jesus had warned them that in that same night they would all be offended with Him, they assured Him that they would sooner die with Him. And when Peter had denied Him, he "went out and wept bitterly."

After all this had transpired, they had not spoken one word with Him. And lo, now they receive this fraternal salutation from Him. What an experience! What a proof of the efficacy of Christ's atonement! Here is the fruit again of the death and resurrection of Christ. The guilt of sin is invalidated. Sin no longer condemns the sinner who holds to Christ. The Law has been fulfilled. The penalty and the curse have been removed. The defections and the sins do not for one moment shake the believer's state of grace. Now we understand the meaning of the words: "It is Christ that died, yea, rather, that is risen again, who is even at the right hand of God, who also maketh intercession for us" (Romans 8: 34). "If Christ be not risen, then is our preaching in vain, and your faith is also vain" (1 Corinthians 15: 14).

The apostles fully believed that they were no more in their sins. They believed this because Christ died and rose again from the dead. "And if Christ be not raised, your faith is vain: ye are yet in your sins" (Romans 8: 17). If Christ be raised, then are ye no longer in your sins. But now is Christ risen, and He hastens to send the disciples His brotherly greeting, despite their disloyalty to Him.

In Christ we have such a Kingdom of Grace, that sin is not imputed to the sinner who abides in Christ Jesus. We need chastisement and correction. We need the rod and the tribulation. But God's forgiving grace, our filial relation to God, shall remain unshaken. His covenant continues in force and operation as long as we adhere to Christ and find in Him our all in all.

We know that the summary of the Gospel is that the blood of Christ, the Son of God, cleanseth us from all sin, and that this is a truth worthy of all acceptation. But when our knowledge is put to the test of actual experience, it falls short and we really know very little spiritually. We believe easily enough so long as our lives are unruffled and we move along a straight line. But if we, like the disciples, should be sifted by Satan and overwhelmed by sin, even to the denying of our Lord; or if we should fall to quarreling as to who should be the greatest among us, what would happen to our faith? Would it suffer utter shipwreck? We certainly would sink into the blackness of despair if we were not blinded by an imaginary faith produced by the hallucinations of the devil. And yet we see that in the midst of such unhappy experiences the blood of Christ is efficacious.

In the midst of our consternation it is well for us if we do not lose the solid footing of faith. It is well for us if we hold fast to the pardoning mercy of God, which far outweighs all sin. At such times of sifting by Satan, when the soul is tempest-tossed, it too often becomes apparent that while we may have a ship-load of Scripture knowledge in the head, we have not a mustard seed of faith in the heart. We are the sort of believers who with the lips confess that we are great sinners, trusting only to the merits of Christ, and comforting ourselves with the consciousness that we, by and large, and on the average, are tolerably good Christians. If we fall into some deplorable sin, the blood of Christ is of no avail, His righteousness counts for nothing.

It should not be so. To be depressed and thoroughly ashamed of ourselves on account of our lapse into sin, and to weep "bitterly," is quite in order. But to throw away our comfort, to lose all hope of restoration, is to undervalue the work of Christ. By such despair we fail to give glory and honor to the Lamb of God, who "taketh away the sin of the world." That is not believing in Christ, as the apostles did, and that He rose from the dead, and "liveth to make intercession for us." With a semi-faith, a lukewarm confidence, we shall never prevail in the conflict. Sooner or later in our Christian life ordeals and perplexities will come to test our confidence in Christ. It is beyond belief what terrific trials and violent temptations assault the believer. The eleven disciples illustrate the weakness of the best of believers.

With all that we have read, heard and thought about it, our own personal experience in the hour of trial is the true criterion of the genuineness of our faith. We see how the most enlightened Christians have nearly suffered shipwreck of their faith in the evil day. It is therefore of the most vital importance that we thoroughly learn to know Christ and what He has done for us, in order that we may be prepared to meet the enemy of souls and vanquish him by the sword of the Spirit. We need to watch and pray, lest we fall into temptation. We need to know more of Christ.

THE PRINCIPAL FRUITS OF THE DEATH AND RESURRECTION OF CHRIST
(Continued)

THE TWENTY-THIRD DAY

WHEN Christ rose from the dead on Easter morning, He greeted His disciples as "brethren." We ought to think and talk as Luther writes: "It is true that I have sinned. It is true that I am unworthy of any brotherhood with Christ. But if I refuse to accept this brotherhood, which neither I nor any other human being has gained for me, but which the Son of God has purchased with His death, I only add to my other sins this horrible sin of denying the work and merits of Christ. I would by such rejection accuse Christ of being a liar, from which sin may God in mercy defend me! Hence I will rather say: I know that I am an unworthy sinner. I know that I am more worthy of being a brother of the devil than of Christ. But Christ has said that I am His brother. I am His brother just as well as Peter is, since He died for me just as truly as He died for Peter. Christ wants me to believe in Him and to disregard the fact that I am unworthy and full of sin, especially since He has said that He will not remember my sins. Since now Christ will make no note of my sins but let them lie buried and forgotten, why should not I forget them and with all my heart praise, thank and love my. dear Lord for such unbounded mercy? Though I am burdened with sin, I ought not refuse His marvellous grace and His offer of brotherhood. If I do not believe this, it is to my eternal injury. My unbelief, however, does not make the truth a lie. His grace and truth remain immovable."

There is another comfortable truth in connection with Easter. We see Jesus that evening walking with His two saddened disciples on the way to Emmaus. Unknown to them, He converses with them in their sorrow and restores their wavering faith. Finally He gives their hearts a full measure of joy by revealing Himself to them at the breaking of bread. By this action He shows how He will be our companion in the way of life, particularly when in the night of doubt and unbelief we stagger away from the company of the faithful. Like a good shepherd He goes to seek and to find the wandering sheep.

We need this comforting truth. We should be lost a thousand times in this dangerous world if the Lord did not defend us. We should be destroyed if He did not seek us in our wanderings and bring us back to our former state of grace. It is impossible so to watch as not to lapse into this or that sin or error. The darkness of doubt and unbelief sometimes falls upon us and we know neither east nor

west. Then we lament: "O that I might know where
I am! My heart is dead and cold. Neither prayer
nor the Word of God has any attraction for me.
Christ is lost to me. I have strayed away from
Him. I am no longer one with Him nor with His
people. It is my own fault. I have sinned and
brought this isolation upon myself. Woe is me for
my sin!"

At such times we are in the way with the two
disciples. Though this spiritual darkness is not the
most perilous, since the soul yet longs for the
light, it is still of such a character that we should be
lost if the Lord left us to shift for ourselves. That
was the case of these two disciples. But in the
midst of their darkness, the Lord walks with them.
If anyone had told them that the Lord was at their
side, they would have regarded the information
as a hoax. They believed that He was dead. They
talked with Him about His death in all innocence.
They did not know that they were talking with Him
whom they missed so sorely.

What a portrait of ourselves in the dark hours
of life! Then are the words of Luther verified.
When you feel that you are spiritually dead, without faith, without love, and without even sincere
anxiety on account of your deplorable condition,
"then," says Luther, "God looks deeper into your
heart. He discovers that it would not be averse to
you if your heart were burning with faith and love
to Him." When it is the lack of faith and love which
causes you the greatest sorrow, faith is by no means
dead in your heart; Christ is not lost to you: He

walks with you to Emmaus. It is only later, when He opens the Scriptures and reveals Himself, that our hearts burn within us; then we understand that He was not far from us.

We have a still greater comfort in the Good Shepherd: He not only seeks, finds and consoles honest souls who are lost in the darkness—He also seeks and saves those who are really lost, in the "far country" of sin. The truth of this statement is found everywhere in His Word. There are numerous examples of His tender solicitude in the Scriptures. In whatever condition you are, He will be your helper. He only knows our condition. He alone can help in every emergency. "For the righteous God trieth the hearts and reins" (Psalm 7:9). How dare I risk the eternal welfare of my soul to my own searching and opinion? But God has promised to do this for me, and His judgment is, as David says, "righteous." When, doubting my own heart, I implore with the Psalmist: "Examine me, O Lord, and prove me; try my reins and heart," I know then that if God, who is faithful and just, conducts this examination of my heart, He will not let me continue to walk in an evil way without apprising me of it.

God only can work in me that which I need to salvation. He can awaken me and He can convict me of sin and guilt. But He is also the Author and Finisher of faith. Hence the writer of the epistle to the Hebrews writes: "The God of Peace, that brought again from the dead our Lord Jesus, that great Shepherd of the sheep, through the blood of the everlasting covenant, make you perfect in every good work to do His will, working in you that which is well-pleasing in His sight, through Jesus Christ; to whom be glory for ever and ever. Amen" (Hebrews 13: 20-21). It is God who creates faith and not we ourselves. "For it is God which worketh in you both to will and to do of His good pleasure" (Philippians 2: 13). Jesus says: "Without me ye can do nothing" (John 15: 5).

Hence, He can supply what we lack. He is the Good Shepherd and Helper. If you can not mourn your sins as you ought, He will help you to do so. If you have an evil, impure and obdurate heart, He can "create a clean heart and renew a right spirit" within you. He alone can help in every trouble. All our wretchedness proceeds from our imagining that we can create these transformations in our hearts. We forget that God alone can recreate the heart.

Why, then, are not all men saved? Why does not God regenerate the hearts of all men? "They that be whole need not a physician, but they that are sick" (Matthew 9: 12). Again observe the two disciples: they are broken-hearted as they walk in the way to Emmaus. It is in such hearts that the Lord can do His saving work. No one who faithfully uses God's Word in the times of his perplexities, particularly if he speaks with a believing brother about his loss of the Lord, shall remain unassisted and uncomforted. In the Word or in the Breaking of the Bread he shall recognize the Master and his heart shall burn within him. Such is our Elder Brother and the faithful Shepherd of our souls. Amen.

THE CHRISTIAN LIFE

Colossians, Third Chapter.

THE TWENTY-FOURTH DAY

"IF, then, ye be risen with Christ, seek those things which are above, where Christ sitteth on the right hand of God. Set your affections on things above, not on things on the earth. For ye are dead, and your life is hid with Christ in God. When God, who is our life, shall appear, then shall ye also appear with Him in glory" (Colossians 3: 1-4).

These words are too profound and uttered by too great a soul to be understood by thoughtless individuals. Nor will careless and flippant people derive any grace or benefit from them. They are, however, uttered by the apostle for the purpose of benefitting all who read them or hear them. Hence every one who would hear or read with profit, should first of all give attention to the voice of the Spirit. He who cannot spare the time or who needs nothing for his soul, may expect nothing from the reading or the hearing of these precious utterances of the apostle. For they require a sincere, earnest and truth-seeking spirit.

"If, then, ye be risen with Christ, seek those things which are above, where Christ sitteth on the right hand of God."

Here is the supreme condition for a truly Christian life.

"If, then, ye be risen with Christ . . . . For ye are dead, and your life is hid with Christ in God" (1, 3).

Sanctimonious pretense to the Christian life is the expression of a corrupt heart and has no connection with the source of life. This fact is everywhere emphasized in God's Word. And yet there are people who comfort themselves with the notion that they are different from the world, as if external plaster and tinsel were enough to deceive the all-seeing eye of God. But soon the midnight cry shall be heard: "Behold, the Bridegroom cometh. Go ye out to meet Him" (Matthew 25: 6). Then shall they be terrified who have no oil in their lamps, no faith in their starved souls, no fear or love of God in their hardened hearts. Then shall they be compelled to hear the awful sentence: "Bind him hand and foot, and take him away, and cast him into outer darkness: there shall be weeping and gnashing of teeth" (Matthew 22: 23). I knew him not. I was not his life. He had no oil in his lamp, no wedding garment to cover the nakedness of his sinful soul.

But what does it mean to be "risen with Christ"? The apostle explains this term in the preceding chapter. "Buried with Him in Baptism, wherein also ye are risen with Him through faith" (Colossians 2: 12). In the sight of God, as Christ died and rose again, so have we all died and are risen in Him. The same apostle says: "Because we thus judge that if one died for all, then were all dead" (2 Corinthians 5: 14). Since He died for all and rose for all, we all are risen from the dead—before God. Here, however, the reference is to the resurrection with Christ in our hearts, since the apostle uses the phrase: "through faith" (Colossians 2: 12).

The apostle has at sundry places spoken about how we die and rise again; how we are crucified with Christ, buried with Christ, risen with Christ: in short, how Christ becomes our life. He writes, for example: "For I through the Law am dead to the Law, that I might live unto God. I am crucified with Christ. Nevertheless I live. Yet not I, but Christ liveth in me; and the life which I now live in the flesh, I live by the faith of the Son of God, who loved me, and gave Himself for me" (Galatians 2: 19-20).

The apostle speaks of the same thing in other terms at Romans 7: 1-6. As an illustration of the believer's liberation from the Law, he refers to the woman who by the death of her husband "is loosed from the Law of her husband," and is at perfect liberty to marry another. Then he adds: "Wherefore, my brethren, ye also are become dead to the Law by the body of Christ, that ye should be married to another, even to Him who is raised from the dead, that we should bring forth fruit unto God."

These two passages—Galatians 2: 19-20—treat of the soul's liberation from the yoke of the Law, its restoration from unbelief and selfrighteousness to a life of faith in Jesus. Simultaneously occurs the rebirth of the soul, whereby one becomes "dead unto sin," liberated from the dominance of sin, as expressed in the clause: "that I might live unto God." There are many strong declarations on this phase of the subject in Romans six. For instance: "Shall we continue in sin, that grace may abound? God forbid. How shall we that are dead to sin live any longer therein? Know ye not that so many of us as were baptized into Jesus Christ were baptized into His death? Therefore we are buried with Him by Baptism into death, that like as Christ was raised up from the dead by the glory of the Father, even so we also should walk in newness of life. For if we have been planted together in the likeness of His death, we shall be also in the likeness of His resurrection, knowing this that our old man is crucified with Him, that the body of sin might be destroyed, that henceforth we should not serve sin. For he that is dead is free from sin. Now, if we be dead with Christ, we believe that we shall also live with Him; knowing that Christ, being raised from the dead, dieth no more. Death hath no more dominion over Him. For in that He died, He died unto sin once; but in that He liveth, He liveth unto God. Likewise reckon ye also yourselves to be dead unto sin, but alive unto God through Jesus Christ our Lord" (Romans 6: 1-11).

All this is a part of the concept: "dead with Christ" and "risen with Him." The believer's conscience is "dead to the Law," and in his daily life and conduct he is dead unto sin. Luther says that he who is dead with Christ and risen with Him "bids good-bye to the dear old Law," saying: "I thank you for your services. You can do no more for me. I have now learned that I am not able to stand righteous before you. But there is another man who has done for me all that you demand of me. Now it is good-bye to your guardianship." The Apostle Paul writes: "When the fulness of time was come, God sent forth His Son, made of a woman, made under the Law, to redeem them that were under the Law, that we might receive the adoption of sons" (Galatians 4: 4-5). "But after that faith is come, we are no longer under a schoolmaster" (Galatians 3: 25). Nothing but the love of Christ now constrains me to do that which is good.

Similarly he who is dead and risen with Christ has said good-bye to the servitude of sin. He says: "I can no longer serve you, O sin. I refuse to yield to your allurements. I am done with you. Clear out! I am through with you." The apostle shows how we die from the Law by the Law (Romans 7: 7-13). "When the commandment came, sin revived, and I died." "Sin, taking occasion by the commandment, wrought in me all manner of concupiscence," and, says Paul, "I died." "I fought, I struggled, I labored, I prayed against my sins. I grew terrified, struggled against the evil inclinations and—sinned again. I became helplessly weak against the assaults of the devil. I was entangled in the toils of concupiscence. I followed sin voluntarily. 'Sin abounded,' and I despaired. I wished that I had the strength to resist, to fight the enemy of my soul, to pray; but I could not even do that. I was impotent. I 'died.' I surrendered to Satan. I was lost. I thought that God's eternal judgment had been pronounced upon my filthy soul.

"When now all my struggles under the Law, my

efforts to free myself from the shackles of sin, had proved abortive and futile, leaving me a slave to the devil in spite of my externally highly respectable life; while I lay as the traveller from Jericho to Jerusalem by the roadside, wounded, half dead, wallowing in my blood, the Good Samaritan came by, saw me, poured oil in my wounds, bandaged my lacerations, lifted me up, and carried me to the inn. I heard the Gospel of the Son of God, who had given Himself as a ransom for my soul, a sacrifice for all my sins, and He poured the wine of His pardoning love in the wounds of my soul, lifted me up, helped me to walk aright, and lo, now I live in Him. Happy day! From the procrustean bed of hell I was lifted up to the fellowship of the Christ of God."

"Wherefore, my brethren, ye also are become dead to the Law by the body of Christ, that ye should be married to another, even to Him who is raised from the dead, that we should bring forth fruit unto God" (Romans 7: 4). In Him you have all your hope, your life, your consolation, your strength and righteousness. The words of the apostle have been verified in your own personal experience: "For I through the Law am dead to the Law, that I might live unto God. I am crucified with Christ: nevertheless I live; yet not I, but Christ liveth in me: and the life which I now live in the flesh, I live by the faith of the Son of God who loved me, and gave Himself for me" (Galatians 2: 19-20). I was dead, and behold, now I live.

"I am as one who died and entered another

world. In the former world I trusted in vain to my own works, my will-power, my strength of character, my resolutions. In my former life Christ was at best nothing more than an ethical teacher to me. Now in this present life of faith, He is my Savior, my song and my glory, my only joy and comfort. In my former life I was solely occupied with the things of this material world. I adored my intellect and followed the leadings of my evil heart. Now I am concerned with the things that are not seen. A single word from the mouth of God is worth to me more than all the wisdom of men boiled together. In my former world, the things of the world —riches, honors, the lusts of the flesh and the pride of life, were my supreme good. Now these earthly things are my enemies on account of the concupiscence in my flesh. My wealth, honor, joy and rapture are in Christ alone. I am 'dead with Christ and risen with Him.' Blessed be His holy name!"

THE CHRISTIAN LIFE
(*Continued*)

THE TWENTY-FIFTH DAY

MY faith and my renewed mind are not by any means perfected. I am not a spirit: I also have flesh and bones. These new elements—faith and the new mind—are, however, predominant in the life of a Christian. I am not so dead to the Law that it does not accuse me: it even incarcerates and oppresses me. But I can not abide to remain

under the Law. I hasten to protect myself with the
pardoning grace of God. I am not so dead to sin and
the world but that they tempt me and sometimes
overwhelm me and cause me to stumble and fall. But
I can not abide in their service: I get up again and
start once more upon my walk in the newness of life.

But even though both my faith and my life are
defective and imperfect, I know that they are perfect and acceptable to God. Whether my faith be
weak or strong, I am still robed in the garment of
Christ's righteousness. I remember what the Apostle Paul says: "For ye are all the children of God
by faith in Christ Jesus. For as many of you as
have been baptized into Christ have put on Christ"
(Galatians 3: 26-27). I am entirely in the covenant
of grace with God. Not one sin shall be counted
against me. Though my poor, cramped heart is unable to comprehend in all its power the efficacy of
the blood of Christ, it is valued in all its saving
force in heaven. There, in the heart of God, it is
valid for time and eternity.

In the eyes of God, then, we are dead unto sin,
risen and justified with Christ from the moment
when we have "put on" Christ by faith. Before God
we are as free of sin as the Son of God was when
He rose from the grave. That is the reason why
there is nothing condemnable in them who are in
Christ. "There is therefore now no condemnation
to them which are in Christ Jesus, who walk not
after the flesh, but after the Spirit" (Romans 8: 1).
They are "delivered from the Law" (Romans 7: 6).
Where there is no Law, there sin is not imputed.

Christ has redeemed us from the guilt and penalty of the Law (Galatians 4: 4-5). Christ is the security and the defender of His believing disciples.

That is the reason why no sin is imputed to your soul. Your soul lives in a realm of such liberty that there is no Law, there are no Ten Commandments to terrify and condemn you. To you as a believer there is no Mount Sinai with its thunderings and lightnings. You are freed from the exactions of the Law. You live under the defense of the grace of God. Luther says: "A Christian is not a person who commits no sin, but he is a person to whom not one sin is imputed." He has not the exalted privilege of being without sin. But if he sins, the Law can not condemn him, for the Law has no jurisdiction over him. If we were still accountable to the Law, no flesh could be saved. Then we might as well say good-bye to any hope of salvation. In that case, the Gospel would be a delusion and a snare, Christ would have died in vain, and all believers would go down to eternal death under the Ten Commandments. "The soul that sinneth, it shall die," is the irrevocable sentence of the Law.

But the Scriptures say: "For what the Law could not do, in that it was weak through the flesh, God sending His own Son in the likeness of sinful flesh, and for sin, condemned sin in the flesh" (Romans 8: 3). Again they say: "Christ has redeemed us from the curse of the Law, being made a curse for us" (Galatians 3: 13). And again: "But after faith is come, we are no longer under a schoolmaster" (Galatians 3: 25). The reason, then, why God does not impute sin and guilt to the believer is, as David and Saint Paul testify, that "righteousness might be imputed unto them" by faith (Romans 4: 11). Note that the apostle does not say: In whom there is no sin, but: "Sin is not imputed where there is no Law" (Romans 5: 13).

Not only, however, are we freed from the Law, so that sin is not imputed to our account, but righteousness is imputed unto us through faith. "For Christ is the end of the Law for righteousness to every one that believeth" (Romans 10: 4). Again the apostle writes: "Even as David describeth the blessedness of the man unto whom God imputeth righteousness without works" (Romans 4: 6). Hence, in the eyes of God we are not only delivered from sin and guilt, but we are endowed with an eternally valid righteousness. "For He hath made Him to be sin for us who knew no sin, that we might be made the righteousness of God in Him" (2 Corinthians 6: 21). Believers are "a purchased redemption, unto the praise of His glory" (Ephesians 1: 14). God is well pleased with them and loves them with an unhindered love.

All this is the result of having "put on Christ." "Behold," says Luther, "what endless riches are in the possession of faith! All the merits and works of Christ are given to faith. A Christian can rely upon them as safely as if he himself had performed the works and gained the merits. Christ has indeed not done these works for Himself, but for us. He has no need of them. But He has won these treasures for us, that we might believe and possess them.

If the Law then comes and attacks me, I say in defiance: I have fulfilled all your requirements and more through my substitute, Christ. Though there is sin in my flesh, I have a perfect righteousness in Christ. He is mine. He gives me all that He possesses. Hence His righteousness is my righteousness. The Law has nothing to say about me. It has no authority over me.

"If, however, I look upon myself, I confess that I find much of sin and uncleanness. The Law is perfectly right about that. The Law says: You are a sinner. I answer: Yes, I am a sinner. The Law then says: Then you are damned. If I say no, I certainly must have a good foundation to stand upon. Where am I to find this No? I certainly do not find it in my own bosom. But I find it in Christ. Then I present this No to the Law. He can speak this No, and with reason. For He is holy and without sin. He grants me this No in granting me His righteousness."

That is what the Scriptures mean when they say: "My brethren, ye are become dead to the Law by the body of Christ" (Romans 7: 4), or, "For Christ is the end of the Law for righteousness to every one that believeth" (Romans 10: 4). "There is no condemnation to them who are in Christ Jesus" (Romans 8: 1). "Sin is not imputed where there is no Law" (Romans 5: 13). How we should rejoice in this royal liberty! How we should meditate upon this divine righteousness! If it be true that there is no condemnation to them who are in Christ Jesus, what a heavenly truth! If it be true that their sins are not imputed unto them, even though at times they may be ensnared by the devil, what grace, what pardoning love! But they are not under the Law but under grace, and that explains their righteousness. They are not accountable to the Law as long as they hold fast to Christ. Oh, if this be the truth, it is a most glorious truth. And it is the truth as surely as God's Word can not lie.

The Word of God is truth in spite of what the devil, the selfrighteous Pharisees and human reason may say in objection. It is the truth in spite of my feeling or lack of feeling. Here we would rejoice and be glad because our Immanuel has founded a Kingdom on earth wherein sinners are not sinners before God but holy, well-pleasing and beloved through faith in the Son of God. This is the significance of the term "risen with Christ." We are risen unto a new life in Him and transformed into His image. "He hath raised us up together, and made us to sit together in heavenly places in Christ Jesus" (Ephesians 2: 6).

The second glorious fact in connection with our spiritual resurrection with Christ is, that we also are "dead unto sin" and risen with a new, holy nature, "born of God," and that "His seed remaineth in us." Here comes the astounding fact that we are actually "partakers of the divine nature," as Saint Peter says very definitely (1 Peter 1 : 4). From this truth it follows that we do not commit any sin, as the apostle says. "Whosoever is born of God doth not commit sin, for his seed remaineth in him, and he cannot sin, because he is born of God" (1 John

3 : 9). But "if we say that we have no sin, we deceive ourselves and the truth is not in us" (1 John 1 : 8). If we deny that a Christian, left to himself, may be overtaken by sin, realizing therein the carnal love of sin, we deny the plain words of the Bible. We close our eyes to the many examples in the Bible of such saints as have fallen into heinous sins.

But the notable thing is that a Christian never can remain in sin, "commit sin"; that is, he can not make sin his habitual mode of life; he can not make sin a practice which he defends and excuses. As long as God's "seed" remains, sin is to him a torment and a cause of terror. Holiness is his soul's delight, the essential course of his life and walk. If he falls into sin, he falls, as it were, into fire and water. He finds no rest or peace before he is delivered from the sin which besets him. Such a soul must be said to be "dead unto sin." He is lost to a life of sin. He is no longer serviceable to sin. He is wretched and unhappy if he attempts to sin, as the example of King David shows. He finds no real heart-joy in sin and is unable to continue in sin. He is really through with the servitude of sin. That man was a Christian who understood the psychology of the situation, who said to his wife: "If you are sure that your maid is a Christian, you need not watch the keys. If she wants to steal, let her try it. She will be thoroughly whipped by her sin and soon bring back what she has pilfered from you. If she is able to keep the stolen goods, the seed of God is not in her heart. For whosoever is born of God cannot sin, for the seed of God remaineth in him, and he cannot sin, because he is born of God."

THE CHRISTIAN LIFE
(*Continued*)

THE TWENTY-SIXTH DAY

"WHOSOEVER is born of God doth not commit sin; for his seed remaineth in him, and he cannot sin, because he is born of God" (1 John 3: 9).

Here it is to be carefully noted that the apostle speaks only of such sins as are manifestly and notoriously sins. Otherwise we might, on the basis of this place, condemn many of God's children, because some regard as sin that which others do not look upon as sin at all. (See Romans, chapter 14.)

Then, again, it is to be noted that the soul of a Christian may at times be contaminated by sinful thoughts or suggestions even though the Holy Spirit may not have departed from him. A distressing bondage and servitude to one particular sin may occur, especially when he lapses into legalism, looking more to himself than to Christ. But even this condition does not preclude faith. But when faith revives, the sin is conquered and routed. He, on the contrary, who has not the faith which "overcometh the world," continuing in slavery to some particular sin, even under the compunctions of an uneasy conscience, is never "risen with Christ." "For whatsoever is born of God overcometh the world; and this is the victory that overcometh the world, even our faith" (1 John 5: 4).

To recapitulate: Even the believer is in many respects frail and weak; but everything depends upon the issue, whether finally the spirit or the flesh comes off victorious and retains possession of the soul; whether he adheres to the good or the evil, to faith or to bondage, to righteousness or to sin. "Know ye not that to whom ye yield yourselves servants to obey, his servants ye are whom ye obey, whether of sin unto death, or of obedience unto righteousness?" (Romans 6: 16).

We have now seen what it means to be "dead with Christ and risen with Him." We have learned the glorious truth, which God alone has revealed to us, that he who has been slain by the Law but revived by the Gospel, restored and "clothed" with the righteousness of Christ by faith, is for time and eternity delivered from the guilt of his sins, and freed from all accountability to the Law. The evil which is still to be found in his flesh and in his daily life, is not imputed to him. He lives continually in the pardoning grace of God by faith. He has "put on Christ," and is therefore "not under the Law but under grace" (Romans 6: 14-15; 7: 4, 6; 4: 8; Galatians 3: 13, 25; 2: 19-21).

A pardoned sinner ought then to live in perfect tranquillity of soul and conscience. He ought to be as free and happy as if there were no Ten Commandments on earth. This is the first great outstanding fact to him who is "dead and risen with Christ." The second fact is, that being dead to the Law, he is also "dead unto sin." He cannot remain in sin. He cannot "commit sin." He cannot serve sin. If he falls into sin, he falls as it were into fire and water. He has no peace or joy in his heart. He recovers himself and walks in the way of righteousness. He is lost to the life of sin. In a very true sense, sin is an unnatural thing to him.

We have now discovered the meaning of the place: "Blessed and holy is he that hath part in the first resurrection: on such the second death hath no power" (Revelation 20: 6). Note the words: "blessed" and "holy." Blessed comes first, then holy. Of a truth, blessed. For is it not blessedness to live in a kingdom where sin is not imputed to us? where we are not accountable to the Law? where we are not judged by the Law? where we are not condemned by the Law? where we are beyond the reach of the Law? where the Law does not apply? where we are justified by the righteousness of another, the righteousness of the Son of God? And is not that person holy who has the mind of Christ? who does not commit sin? who cannot serve sin? to whom sin is a plague and a torment? whose delight is in righteousness and holiness? Is not this passage through death and resurrection into a new world a new life? In truth it is a glorious life.

Here, again, we are confronted with our feelings and sad experiences. If I question my feelings in the matter, all is instantly lost. My reason protests. "You are deceiving yourself. It is irrational and foolish. How could the Holy Ghost dwell in me? How can Christ be my life? Then indeed the divine life in me must be a secret and hidden thing." Hid, you say? Why, that is precisely the case. Listen to what the apostle says: "For ye are dead, and your life is hid with Christ in God. When Christ, who is our life, shall appear, then shall ye also appear with Him in glory" (Colossians 3: 3-4).

Our life in God is hidden, hidden with Christ. Christ is our life. But Christ is hid; therefore our life is hid. Thus writes the apostle. Such is the experience of all the saints. But we are not satisfied to let it go at that. We object: "If a person has the life hid with Christ in God, surely that life ought to show itself very definitely. It would shine forth all over his life and conduct. He would realize the ecstasy of it at all times. The whole world would make a note of it."

Very well. Let us look at your strictures for a moment. It is true that the believer has the testimony of the Spirit in his heart. "He that believeth on the Son of God hath the witness in himself," says the apostle (1 John 5: 10). Paul writes: "The Spirit itself beareth witness with our spirit, that we are the children of God" (Romans 8: 16). It is true that John the Beloved in his First Epistle frequently uses the expression: "We know." For instance: "Hereby we know that we dwell in Him, and He in us, because He hath given us of His Spirit" (1 John 4: 13).

It is furthermore true that he who knows nothing of conversion; the awakening from the sleep of sin; the labor for righteousness under the Law; the liberation from the condemnation of the Law through faith in Christ; the new life in Christ and His fellowship, only deceives himself if he thinks that his life is hid with Christ in God. He will construe this place to mean that the new life with Christ has no definite marks to be seen of all men, no outward manifestation, no transforming power in the life of the believer.

But he is utterly mistaken. It still remains irrevocably true that the good tree is known by its good fruit. The fruits of the Spirit will be seen in the life of the Christian. The fact remains, nevertheless, that the life of the believer is hid with Christ in God. That is the result of the following circumstances: First, that our blind, fallen intellect does not understand what is meant by "the fruits of the Spirit," nor does it appreciate them when they are clear enough in the life of the believer. Reason does not believe in that which cannot be seen and handled. Reason would dissect life itself before it believes. Or we are not satisfied with the fruits of the Spirit indicated by the Scriptures. We insist upon determining what should be the fruits of the Spirit and how the life hid with Christ ought to manifest itself.

When, for instance, the Scriptures mention love, peace and joy as the chief fruits of the Spirit, there are many who say: "Why, how is that? It is true that a new love was born in my heart when my sins were pardoned. It is also true that peace and joy entered my soul such as I never had experienced before. But after all, these things seem rather vague and intangible to me. There ought to be something more virile and demonstrable in my life. The love, peace and joy ought to be more permanent and sensational."

At times we do not even look at the fruits of the

Spirit in our own lives as the Scriptures enumerate them. We permit our imagination to dangle before our eyes the dim outlines of something else which fascinates us with its glamor and glittering attractiveness. The great work of the Spirit seems commonplace and trivial by comparison with the products of our deceiving imagination. Or, again, if we do not find certain marks of our own fabrication to demonstrate the life hid with Christ, certain ecstatic emotions and marvellous feelings of bliss, we are swift to conclude that the life hid with Christ is not in us.

Secondly: Our life in God is most hid when God not only withdraws from us every realization of the power of faith, but also permits sin to overcome us, Satan to overpower us by the insidious wiles of temptation. We find Peter denying the Lord, and Paul quarreling with Barnabas. When we prove weak and unstable under the siftings of Satan; when to our horror we find ourselves slipping away from the Lord through cowardice or the lure of the flesh, we ask ourselves: "Where, now, is my life hid with Christ in God? I must be insane to think that the Spirit of God dwells in me. It is the devil that has taken possession of me. He dwells in me." In such perplexities our life in God is indeed hid in the lowest depths of the soul.

Thirdly: God permits all sorts of calamities and adversities to befall a Christian for His own wise purposes. Against Job the patriarch, all the powers of man and nature seemed to unite in attempting to bring about his discomfiture. Robbers, storms and other destructive elements deprive him of all his possessions. His children are taken from him. His body is racked and wasted by disease. His wife ridicules his faith in God. His fool comforters add heavy stones to the burden which he bears. His own heart rages and fumes against his lot, and finally he curses the day on which he was born. Where is now the great man so signally blest of God? Where is now the exemplary saint than whom there was none greater in the land? Where is now the peculiar friendship of Jehovah which had been his through long years of prosperity and public regard? Truly, his life in God must have been deeply hid.

But of all the evil which may conceal our life in God, nothing is to be compared with sin. Compared with sin, other ills are as golden scourges. We soon learn that they are the chastisements of the heavenly Father. We learn the sweet secret that "whom the Lord loveth He also chasteneth." But sin, the rage of Satan in the flesh, the powerful lusts of the body, and the resultant conviction that we have been deserted by the Spirit of God—these are the stings of death which poison the soul and leave us in darkness and despair. Nothing is left to us but to look to the unchangeable God Himself for help in our dire distress and utter helplessness.

However, when the clouds roll away and the azure skies spread over the soul, we realize that in our darkest night the loving heart of the Father was the same, that the garment of Christ's righteousness was still wrapped about us, and that the life hid with Christ in God had even then been warmly pulsating in the soul. It is good for us to know how God leads and disciplines His saints. We should understand how the life in Him may be hid under the pall of death. We should know that the righteousness of Christ does not desert us in the hour of our weakness and despair; that there is grace under God's wrath, heaven in our hell, and the light of God's pardoning love behind the blackest clouds. Like Jacob of old, let us wrestle with the Lord until the dawning of the day.

Luther says in a sermon on the Day of Saint John the Baptist: "You have often heard, my friends, that God permits the feeling of sin, death and the devil to remain with us. Sin assaults my conscience and nearly drives me to despair of God's grace. The judgment of God terrifies me. The devil tramps on my neck and tries to keep me down. At such times we feel only that we are sinners in the power of death and the devil. But even in this wretched condition the anchor of God's mercy holds fast. Innocence and victory over evil remain to the believers. The Lord reassures him: 'The gates of hell shall not prevail against the believers' (Matthew 16: 18). He does not say: 'shall not assail them'; for the assaults of the powers of evil upon the Church will continue. But He says: 'The gates of hell shall not prevail against the Church,' that is, against the believers."

THE CHRISTIAN LIFE
(*Continued*)

THE TWENTY-SEVENTH DAY

"WHEN the believer is tried, he feels the misery of it as long as the ordeal perdures. I must feel the wretchedness of the ordeal when sin gnaws at my soul, and the wrath of God terrifies me, and the fear of death assaults me. But it is a delusion if I imagine that these horrible things hold complete dominion over me. In the midst of these perplexities the Word and the Spirit are near me. They give me courage. They assure me that God is not angry with me. They say to me that all my sins are forgiven, and that the Holy Spirit has not departed from me." Luther, in describing how glorious, just and pleasing to God a Christian is, says:

"Do you not suppose that it would make us happy to see this perfect righteousness? I have never seen anyone who was holy and righteous in himself. Everyone has his faults. Think of anyone you please, and you will find no one without sin. Paul, the most saintly of apostles, confesses that he realizes the Law of sin in his members. 'For the good that I would,' he writes, 'I do not; but the evil which I would not, that I do' (Romans 8: 19). He would not sin, and yet he sinned. I and many with me would that we were rid of sin; but it cannot be done, though we try to overcome sin. When we fall in sin, we rise again, to be sure; but sin remains a plague and torment to us." Thus far Luther. Sin is certainly the greatest ordeal to the believer's life and communion with God.

Our life in God is hid, however, not only to ourselves but also to others. Others are offended by our faults and shortcomings. The world, of course, is also offended; for it is offended even with that which is good in our lives and conduct. But sincere Christians are often sorely grieved by the reprehensible weaknesses of their fellow-Christians. Sometimes these faults affect the true doctrine and faith; sometimes their daily mode of life and conduct; sometimes there is quarreling and bickering. Then, again, there are apostasies, defections and denials of the truth. Other Christians are amazed and ask: "Are these really the people of God?"

Concerning this matter of disharmony in the lives of Christians, Luther, in the preface to the Revelation of John, writes these precious words: "This sentence: 'I believe in the holy Christian Church,' is an article of faith as well as the others. No merely human reason can understand the Church, even though it placed any number of spectacles on its nose. The devil may cover the Church with all manner of scum, offences and factions, so that you may be grievously offended. And God may conceal the Church under all kinds of weaknesses and defects, so that you pass an utterly unfair judgment upon the Church. But 'Faith is the evidence of things not seen' (Hebrews 11:1). The Church and her Lord sing this song: 'Blessed is he, whosoever shall not be offended in me' (Matthew 11:6). A Christian is hid to himself to such a degree that he does not see his own excellencies. He sees only his weaknesses and shortcomings, his sins and faults. But you coarse wiseacres have the audacity to evaluate Christianity with your blind reason and impure eyes. Our holiness is in heaven, where Christ is— not in the world before the eyes of everybody, like a piece of goods in the marketplace." All this simply means: "Our life is hid with Christ in God."

But even when there is nothing to depress us or to hide our fellowship with God, how incomprehensible is it not that we have this blessed life with Christ in God, this honor and righteousness of God, and yet this life remains invisible! It is in the nature of man to look only at externals, at those things which may be seen with the physical eyes. We live in the midst of a multitude of visible things. That alone which is the greatest treasure of our hearts, the heavenly and eternal, can not be seen—it remains hidden.

There are times when this fact becomes an ordeal to us. It is therefore necessary that we keep in our hearts these words of the apostle: "Your life is hid with Christ in God." We need to remember the words of the apostle that "as Christ is, so are we in this world" (1 John 4: 17). How was not His life hid in the world? He was the only-begotten Son of the Father, "the brightness of His glory, and the express image of His person," and yet how hidden was not all this divine glory! (Hebrews 1: 3). How deeply was not His majesty hidden under "the likeness of flesh"!

It is certain that faith must have a solid foundation to build upon with security. It is certain that He performed works which no one else could perform. It is certain that He received of the Father honor and praise through the Voice which out of the heavenly glory said to Him: "This is my beloved Son, in whom I am well pleased" (Matthew 3: 17). It is certain that He had all the marks of the promised Messiah, the King of Glory; and yet He said: "For judgment I am come into this world, that they which see not might see, and that they which see might be made blind" (John 9: 39). In order that the proud mind of unbelief, which always demands signs and wonders, might be punished with blindness, and that He might become like His brethren and bear their burdens, He was on earth "despised and rejected of men, a man of sorrows and acquainted with grief, and we hid as it were our faces from Him" (Isaiah 53: 3).

How hidden, how concealed from the penetration of reason is not all this: The Son of God is born in a stable; laid in a manger; raised in a village with a name so insignificant that the pious Nathanael asks the question, "Can there any good thing come out of Nazareth?" (John 1: 46); the Son of God poorer than the birds of the air; owning nothing, not even whereon to lay His head; despised, scorned, persecuted, and finally bound, wounded, scourged, spat upon, smitten by good-for-nothing rogues, hanged on a tree outside the city walls between two malefactors to the malicious sneers of His executioners, "If Thou be the Son of God, come down from the cross"; crying out after hours of excruciating agony, "My God, my God, why hast Thou forsaken me?"—at last giving up the ghost, and then His torn body laid away in the grave!

Where was the divine majesty to be seen in all this sordid spectacle? Where was the power and glory of the Creator of the universe? Was there ever anything on earth so irrational as the claim that this Sufferer is the Son of God? He rose from the dead, however, as He had said; was seen by individual disciples and by groups, even by five hundred, at various intervals during a period of forty days after His resurrection; ascended to heaven before the wondering gaze of many witnesses; thus only at times flashing forth the divine glory and power under the general weakness and humiliation. "As He is, so are we in this world."

As the Head, so are the members. As is the bride, so is the Bridegroom. Poor and ridiculed is the bride, despised and contemptuously regarded. But beneath the poverty there is divine majesty; under the weakness, eternal righteousness; under the external humiliation, the power and dominion of God Almighty. We are not to be confused by that which we feel and imagine. It seems no more unreasonable that we are the children of the living God, God's elect, holy and beloved, than that Jesus of Nazareth, the Crucified and Risen One, is the Son of God manifest in the flesh. Ought we not be satisfied with Him, our Head, our Elder Brother? Ought we not to be ready to go with Him through the Valley of Humiliation to the beautiful City of God?

By faith alone are we the children of God, just,

righteous and well-pleasing to the heavenly Father. We would believe upon the authority of God's own Word. We would believe that as firmly as if we were already in heaven, whatever our feelings may be. God's Word remains when all else passes away.

THE CHRISTIAN LIFE
(*Continued*)

THE TWENTY-EIGHTH DAY

THE reason why our life is hid is that the Kingdom of Christ is a kingdom of faith. Faith is a narrow gateway to the proud children of Adam. "And Jesus said: For judgment I am come into this world, that they which see not might see, and that they which see might be made blind" (John 9: 39). No one is qualified to enter this invisible kingdom who is not prepared to submit to whatever conditions the King imposes. Gideon's army was not recruited by volunteers but by the humiliating test as follows: "Every one that lappeth of the water with his tongue, as a dog lappeth, him shalt thou set by himself; likewise every one that boweth down upon his knees to drink" (Judges 7: 5). So here. He who submits to the counsel of God and bows down upon his knees before His scepter, no matter what the ordeals imposed upon him may be, follows Jesus in His obedience and is a worthy member of His invisible kingdom.

But he who must see, feel and taste the sweetness of the fellowship with God at all times; he who al-

ways must be conscious of this life and see it clearly
in a spiritual development and constant manifestation; he who expects that his soul-life shall always
be warm, pulsating and vigorous; his daily life pure
and holy; his course of life as calm and gentle as a
brook among the meadows on a summer day; that
all Christians must be without fault or weaknesses;
united in the bonds of an unbroken love; with no
delinquencies in converse and conduct; who is not
satisfied with the life hid with Christ in God, yea,
at times entirely covered and submerged by sin and
shortcomings—he who looks for all this perfection
in his own life and in the life of others, is not qualified to become a soldier in the army of the Lord.

The believers in the crucified Christ must be content to walk in the dense fogs of faith, at times to
see and feel nothing whatever of the grace of God,
as if they were entirely deserted of God. As Christ
was forty days and forty nights in the desert, fasted
and was tempted by the devil with his murderous
suggestion: "If Thou be the Son of God" (Matthew
4: 3), so likewise we also shall be tempted in the
desert of our spiritual drouth and vacuity by abominable suggestions and the sneer of the devil: "Are
you a child of God?"

Frequently a Christian goes stumbling about in
this spiritual murkiness until he actually thinks that
he is the most depraved of sinners, while at the same
time he is in secret actuality God's own well-beloved
child, clothed in the righteousness and beauty of
Christ, with the angels of heaven smiling down upon
him. But do not think that he feels this glory. How

vital it is, that we at all times remind ourselves that our life is hid with Christ in God! It will remain hid in this mortal life. "When Christ, who is our life, shall appear, then shall ye also appear with Him in glory" (Colossians 3: 4).

Upon the basis of such a life the apostle gives the following exhortation: "If ye then be risen with Christ, seek those things which are above, where Christ sitteth on the right hand of God" (Colossians 3: 1). He continues the admonition on the ground that "ye are dead, and your life is hid with Christ in God" (3). By their death and resurrection with Christ, the Colossians had entered a new world, begun a new life, a life of the spirit, in which "Christ is all, and in all" (11). He is their life, their consolation, their glory, their Head, the Chief of their salvation, their friend and brother. "Seek, therefore, those things which are above, where Christ sitteth on the right hand of God." Where the Bridegroom is, the bride would also be.

Christ is your life and joy. He draws your hearts to heaven. Through regeneration by the Holy Ghost you have received a new nature, which is so dead to the life of the world of sin that it has no attraction for you. Furthermore, your life in God, which is your true life, is hidden. It cannot fully develop in this world, nor can it freely expand, because you are still in the body of limitations and humiliation. Here you are not at home. You are pilgrims and sojourners in a foreign land. Not only that, but you are among enemies, you are in a country where your Lord and all your spiritual family never have enjoyed peace and tranquillity, but have been driven like refugees from place to place. Hence all you may expect in the world is a temporary shelter, not a permanent abiding-place. You have another destination than the inn by the wayside. Your home is in heaven.

"Seek therefore those things which are above, where Christ sitteth on the right hand of God." Seek not those things which are but earthly and perishable. He who has learned to know himself as a sinner, wretched, lost and condemned by the holy Law of God; but restored by faith to life with Christ, pardoned and justified by the merits of the Son of God, living no longer after the flesh but after the Spirit, has the heavenly mind and longs to be where Christ is in the home not made with hands.

Friend, seek those things which are above, where Christ is. Be not deceived into trying to create for yourself a paradise on earth. A Christian who has found peace and joy in fellowship with Christ cannot find any joy on earth to compare with the life in God. If any earthly thing produces greater joy, the spiritual life declines. If you would have a joyful life on earth, with peace and contentment in your heart, and the light of God's love shining upon your journey through life, then be not too absorbed in the unstable and vanishing riches of this mock-world, but seek the heavenly treasures which remain when all else passes away from your grasp. You will never find real joy and peace before you find happiness in God. If you find greater joy in the things of earth than you do in the friendship of God, there is something radically wrong with your relation to God.

Friend, you have a calling upon earth. You have a stewardship to discharge. You are accountable to God for all that He entrusts to your care and custody, use and enjoyment. You have labor to perform, daily tasks to meet. But your heart—your heart should be in heaven, where Christ is. The desire of the Bridegroom of your soul for your undivided love is that your heart be with Him—in heaven. When God grants you a special joy on earth, receive it with thanksgiving, but let it not turn your heart from seeking first the heavenly treasures. The grace of God is your chief treasure and joy. A comfortable living, prosperity, wealth, honors and emoluments, as well as intellectual gifts, education, experience and a stainless character—all these are precious benefactions, for which you are to thank God above all; but receive them with fear lest they entice your heart away from God, the Giver of every good and perfect gift.

Since a Christian has his supreme joy and happiness in fellowship with God, he will not sell his heart to any earthly treasure. If he gains the earthly things, they become a peril to his soul; if he fails to win them or loses them after he has secured them, they become a curse to him. If earthly things become a greater joy to him than is his joy in God, his soul is lost. If the earthly is of less joy than the heavenly, then he will not care to gain for himself more of this world's goods than he needs for daily sustenance.

Considering the thirst of the human heart for this world's goods, we are reminded of the words of Pretorius: "The greatest fortune of a Christian is to have no fortune at all." The Christian prays with the wise King Solomon: "Give me neither poverty nor riches; feed me with food convenient for me, lest I be full and deny Thee, and say, Who is the Lord? or lest I be poor, and steal, and take the name of the Lord in vain" (Proverbs 30: 8-9). For "ye are dead and risen with Christ."

He who is risen from death with Christ lives another life beside the physical life. He is born of God, lives and moves and has his being in fellowship with God, and is in heavenly places with Christ. Otherwise it would be too onerous to bear the burden of the cross of Christ. For the heart desires the things of this world. It argues glibly enough: "A bird in the hand is better than ten in the bush." It naturally seeks the things of this earth—wealth, honor, preferment, the gratification of the lusts of the flesh, the pride of life, and the like. Sincere Christians also have the carnal law of their members, the greed for that which is earthly and material. But they are "crucified with Christ." Hence they mortify the body with its evil lusts and proclivities.

The Psalmist Asaph confesses: "I was envious at the foolish, when I saw the prosperity of the wicked. They are not in trouble as other men, neither are they plagued like other men. Their eyes stand out with fatness, they have more than heart could wish" (Psalm 73: 2, 3, 5). But he adds:

"Nevertheless I am continually with Thee: Thou hast holden me by my right hand. Thou shalt guide me with Thy counsel, and afterwards receive me to glory. Whom have I in heaven but Thee? and there is none upon earth that I desire besides Thee. My flesh and my heart faileth, but God is the strength of my heart, and my portion forever" (Psalm 73: 22-26).

The apostle goes on about as follows: Since you are dead to sin and alive in Christ, continue steadfastly in mortifying the flesh. Do not divide yourselves between God and the world. Look not back upon Sodom. Be not seduced by the desires of the flesh. You are dead to sin and the world. Your real life is with Christ in God. Your home is not here. Your home is where Christ is. You are pilgrims and sojourners on the way to the heavenly home.

THE CHRISTIAN LIFE
(*Continued*)

THE TWENTY-NINTH DAY

AS risen with Christ and heavenly-minded, the Apostle Paul warns the believers against the sins and vices which too often characterize the unbelievers. He admonishes the Christians: "Mortify therefore your members which are upon the earth: fornication, uncleanness, inordinate affection, evil concupiscence, and covetousness, which is idolatry; for which things' sake the wrath of God cometh on the children of disobedience" (Colossians 3: 5-6).

These and other vices constitute "the old man with his deeds" (9). "The old man" is the natural depravity of man, inherited from Adam with all its lusts and evil propensities. The apostle continues: "In which ye also walked some time, when ye lived in them. But now ye also put off all these: anger, wrath, malice, blasphemy, filthy communication out of your mouth. Lie not one to another, seeing that ye have put off the old man with his deeds, and have put on the new man which is renewed in knowledge after the image of Him that created him" (Colossians 3: 7-10).

From these places I learn that Christians are not perfected saints in whom no evil is to be found, since they need an admonition like this. The apostle admonishes those who are "risen with Christ," "God's elect, holy and beloved," to mortify their members for sins so shameful as to make it hard for me to believe that such things were possible among Christians. First of all he speaks to them as true Christians: "If, then, ye be risen with Christ," etc. He designates them as "saints, and faithful brethren" (Colossians 1: 2), as "the elect of God, holy and beloved" (3: 12), and admonishes these saints to mortify and root out of their lives such things as adultery, fornication, uncleanness, inordinate affection, concupiscence, covetousness, wrath, malice, blasphemy, dirty language, lying, and the like.

Horrors! What do I see among these saints whom Paul addresses in such fine terms? I had supposed that those whom an apostle would recognize as sincere evangelical Christians must be so far removed from such gross and vile sins that even a warning against them would be an insult. Here, however, I learn that it is an utterly false conclusion to think that true Christians by the work of the Holy Spirit are so purified and cleansed that they are holy in themselves and free from sin. I learn from this epistle to the Colossians that Christians not only have the law of the flesh with its lusts and concupiscence, but also that they are in danger of falling into the vilest sins and crimes. I realize the truth of what Luther says in his commentary on the fifty-first Psalm:

"It is an unfounded and fictional statement to declare that any human being is holy. It is quite as unfounded as if one should say that God had fallen in sin, which is an impossibility. Therefore we must get rid of the delusion that, for example, Paul and Peter were without sin. In themselves they were sinners like other men. God alone is holy. 'And one cried to another: Holy, holy, holy is the Lord of Hosts' (Isaiah 6: 3). But we and all believers are called 'saints' because Christ has sanctified Himself for us and imparted to us of His holiness. The penitent thief upon the cross is quite as holy in Christ as the Apostle Peter. Holiness does not depend upon the circumstance that Peter and Paul have done greater works than the thieves and you and I. For by nature we are all sinners: in Christ we are saints."

From this epistle to the Colossians we learn how these two discordant facts are harmonized, namely, that the believers in Colosse, on the one hand, were such vile sinners as is indicated in the warnings of the apostle, and on the other hand, God's elect, holy and beloved. You who walk about, silent in the knowledge of your shame, thinking that no Christian can be as disgraceful as you are, come out from your dishonor: You have many brethren in your sorrows and sufferings. Remember that you may still be one of God's elect, holy and beloved. The fact that you feel sin in your flesh means nothing if you do not live in sin and cannot remain in sin; if only you rise from your sins through faith in Christ and begin once more to walk in newness of life. You are not under the wrath of God but under His pardoning grace. "There is therefore now no condemnation to them which are in Christ Jesus, who walk not after the flesh, but after the Spirit" (Romans 8: 1).

Hear what the apostle says to the Colossians in regard to the results of the sins enumerated in the black list which he makes: "For which things' sake the wrath of God cometh on the children of disobedience" (Colossians 3: 7). The children of faith are immune from the wrath of God. They are not under the Law but under grace. Their sins are forgiven even though they are not entirely cleansed from sin. There is this difference: The children of disobedience live and thrive in sin like fish in the water. Not so the believers. On this point the apostle says: "In the which ye also walked some time, when ye lived in them," that is, in the sins which he just has mentioned (Colossians 3: 7). Note: There is a "some time," a time passed away, for the believers. Then, in the past, they "walked" unhindered in a life of sin. It is not so now. Now they are "dead to sin." Never again will they come into the slavery of sin. Their new mode of life consists of "righteousness, peace and joy in the Holy Ghost."

The fact, however, that believers need the admonition constantly to mortify the works of the flesh by the power of the Spirit, is explained by the other fact, that the new spiritual life is not like a clock which, when wound up, goes on with regularity. It is a life, and as a life it is subject to manifold changes, to illness, danger and death. Saint Paul writes to the Corinthian church: "I am jealous over you with godly jealousy: for I have espoused you to one husband, that I may present you as a chaste virgin of Christ. But I fear, lest by any means, as the serpent beguiled Eve through his subtilty, so your minds should be corrupted from the simplicity that is in Christ" (2 Corinthians 11: 2-3). This "chaste virgin," this "bride" and "wife of the Lamb," is the believer, who in his conscience is dead to the Law, dead to sin, dead to the old life of sin, but now living in Christ, walking with Christ, knowing nothing but Christ crucified, which is "the simplicity that is in Christ."

And yet for such believers and followers of the Lord Jesus, the apostle fears that they may be lured away from the clean mind. This catastrophe had already occurred in the lives of many of those to whom he wrote. Their clean mind had been vitiated to the degree that they were not even offended by the incest committed by one of their church members: "It is reported commonly that there is fornication among you, and such fornication as is not so much as named among the gentiles, that one should have his father's wife. And ye are puffed up, and have not rather mourned, that he that hath done this deed might be taken away from among you" (1 Corinthians 5: 1-2). Such perversion of clean minds may occur even in our own day. The devil is not asleep. He has plenty of time and means. When the clean mind of Mother Eve could be vitiated, no one should feel secure. Admonition and warning are needed. Every Christian needs to take the lesson to heart.

"Mortify therefore your members which are upon the earth, fornication, uncleanness, inordinate affection, evil concupiscence, and covetousness, which is idolatry" (5). Here are mentioned essentially but two classes of sin—uncleanness and covetousness. These are two horrible abysses wherein numerous souls belonging to the Kingdom of God have fallen, never to rise again. They had been set free from the bondage of sin. They had "repented of the uncleanness and fornication and lasciviousness which they had committed" (2 Corinthians 12: 21). But they had fallen again and were now irretrievably lost.

These two classes of sin are dissimilar. The one is coarse and disgusting and arouses the condemnation of all decent people. The other is of such a quality that most people do not acknowledge it to be the heinous sin that it actually is. Greed is usually excused on a plea such as this: "I must provide for my family, and thrift is not greed." By the machinations of the devil, unchastity, which is so gross and abominable, may in the hour of temptation seem comparatively permissible. To a Christian this fact of the minimizing of sin is the surest sign that the devil is near and the hour of danger at hand. Whenever the sin which in your normal state of mind seems horrible to you begins to look innocent, then you may know that the time of temptation is at hand. The spirit of darkness is perverting your moral sense.

Hence, beware! You must either flee or fall. If you begin to higgle and haggle, to ponder and hesitate, you may soon be caught like a bird in the fowler's net. When Eve engaged in conversation with the devil and kept gazing at the forbidden fruit, she was on the way to disobedience. In this war we gain more by flight than by fight. It is one of the very common deceptions of the devil that he leads us to believe that we run no risk in going to the verge of sin, in trusting self-confidence that we will not fall over the precipice into the abyss below. When the soul is watchful, it keeps as far from the edge of sin as possible.

He who would avoid sin should avoid the temptation. He should avoid the opportunity for sin, the place, the time, the very thought. Jesus says: "If thy right eye offend thee, pluck it out, and cast it from thee; for it is profitable that one of thy members should perish, and not that thy whole body be cast in hell" (Matthew 5: 29). Even that which

in itself is innocent, as the eye, must be given up if
it serves as an instrumentality for sin. Though the
medium be as precious to you as is your eye, pluck
it out of your mind and heart and flee from the
temptation as you would from the pest. It is far
better to suffer deprivation on earth and save your
soul alive than to yield to sin and suffer from an
evil conscience here and agonize in hell hereafter.

For the purpose of inciting Christians to watchfulness, yea, to horror of the sin of unchastity in
all its forms, no more powerful warning can be
given than the following one by the Apostle Paul:
"Know ye not that your bodies are the members of
Christ? Shall I then take the members of Christ,
and make them the members of an harlot? God
forbid. . . . . Flee fornication. Every sin that
a man doeth is without the body; but he that com-
mitteth fornication sinneth against his own body.
What? Know ye not that your body is the temple of
the Holy Ghost which is in you, which ye have of
God, and ye are not your own? For ye are bought
with a price. Therefore glorify God in your body,
and in your spirit, which are God's" (1 Corinthians
6: 15-20).

You are bought with the precious blood of Christ.
You are not your own. You may not do with your
body whatever you please. Nor may you dispose of
your soul, heart and thoughts as you please. Believe in Christ, and your bodies are the temple of the
Holy Ghost. However mysterious it may seem to
you, that the Spirit of God dwells in you, it is nevertheless the truth, for God is true. "If any man

have not the Spirit of Christ, he is none **of His"** (Romans 8: 9). May I then take the members of Christ and make of them the members of an harlot? "Know ye not that ye are the temple of God, and that the Spirit of God dwelleth in you? If any man defile the temple of God, him shall God destroy; for the temple of God is holy, which temple ye are" (1 Corinthians 3: 15-16).

This sin of impurity, however, is overcome as a rule only through the process of despair. That it is an abominable sin, one may readily believe; but that it is forgiven and blotted out by faith in the cleansing blood of Christ and that I am God's beloved child and the temple of the Holy Ghost,—that is a hard thing to believe. For this reason many are overwhelmed by utter despair. They go about bearing the sin and the guilt silently in their hearts, waiting to conquer the sin. When this self-conquest has been attained, they intend to believe in the pardoning grace of God. Gaining in this manner no power to overcome the sin, they sink only deeper and deeper in the mire of desperation. As a drowning person struggles and strikes about in the water, rising only to sink again, finally sinking to rise no more, so the impure individual, with all his efforts at saving himself, sinks at last in the sea of despair. Having found pardon again and again and yet falling back in the same old sin or worse, he comes to the conclusion that God has deserted him and that no more grace is to be expected.

He who would be saved from the insidious power of this particular sin must learn the art of taking

God at His Word and of believing His gracious promises no matter how audacious such faith may seem to his distracted soul. No rules, no regulations, no prayers, no struggles will avail to break the shackles of this sin. Nothing can perform that miracle but the faith which, in the midst of a life of sin, trusts to the blood of atonement shed for the liberation of mankind by the Son of God. Christ alone can conquer the dragon of sin in the heart.

Furthermore: when you truly believe that your sins, no matter how heinous, have been taken from you and laid upon the Lamb of God; when you realize that the very sins which you find to your horror that you have committed, were laid upon the Son of God on Calvary; when you really believe this, the light of hope and freedom will arise in your soul; and that simple faith will break the bands of the sin which held you in its dreary servitude. "The joy of the Lord is your strength" (Nehemiah 8: 10).

In order to attain to such implicit faith and such joy in the Lord, it is not enough that you want to believe. You need to make use of the means which God has provided for the creation and sustenance of faith and joy. You need the Gospel, the Holy Supper, prayer, the intercession of sincere Christians for you at the Throne of Mercy, the intercession of the great High-Priest on the right hand of God, the humility to confess your sins, and the surrender of your soul and your life to God. You shall discover that your salvation in the last analysis depends upon the grace of God alone. That we may learn this profoundest lesson of life, God permits temptations to crowd upon us, trials to befall us, and sins to demonstrate our utter helplessnesss against the assaults of the devil and all his servants. Some day you shall realize most vividly that nothing can set you entirely free but the infinite compassion of God.

The experience of Saint Paul is in its main features the experience of every soul that comes to faith in Christ: "And lest I should be exalted above measure through the abundance of the revelations, there was given to me a thorn in the flesh, the messenger of Satan to buffet me, lest I should be exalted above measure. For this thing I besought the Lord thrice, that it might depart from me. And He said unto me: My grace is sufficient for thee: for my strength is made perfect in weakness. Most gladly therefore will I rather glory in my infirmities, that the power of Christ may rest upon me. Therefore I take pleasure in infirmities, in reproaches, in necessities, in persecutions, in distresses for Christ's sake: for when I am weak, then am I strong" (2 Corinthians 12: 7-10).

THE CHRISTIAN LIFE
(Continued)

THE THIRTIETH DAY

THE second abyss against which the apostle warns his readers is the sin of covetousness (Colossians 3: 5). It swallows men all the easier from the circumstance that the approach to its precipitous edge is hidden in flowers of wondrous beauty and fragrance. Greed covers its hideousness with fine feathers and expert explanations. Who wants to admit that he is covetous and greedy? A Christian who is becoming ensnared by the love of money scarcely realizes the first faint beginnings of the sin. He speaks volubly of the necessity for economy and thrift. He explains that one must care for one's own and for old age. His increasing lust for this world's goods is defended on the euphemistic ground that it is a Christian duty to appropriate as much as possible of the gifts of God, money included. Money, stocks, bonds, farms, securities—are not all these the gifts of God, to be received with thankfulness? Who has the right to reprimand him for the craving after riches? Who is to determine the line of demarkation between thrift and avarice? The Christian who would not share the damning judgment passed upon Demas must not deceive himself. Let him keep a sharp watch upon the disingenuous excuses manufactured by his own evil heart lest he fall over the precipice into the yawning chasm of covetousness. Let him take warning from the Word of God and save his soul from this most insidious and sneaking lust for money.

What says the Lord Jesus? You console yourself with the fact that all these earthly things which occupy your mind and heart, well-nigh to the exclusion of spiritual and eternal things, are in themselves entirely innocent. I would have you observe, however, that when Jesus points to the hindrances that prevent souls from being saved, He mentions certain material things which are in themselves entirely innocent: "I have bought a piece of ground. I have bought five yoke of oxen. I have married a wife" (Luke 14: 18-20). These things are not evil in themselves. And no one will admit that these and similar innocent things may so fill up the heart, soul and mind as to exclude entirely God, salvation and heavenly things. They do this precisely in the lives of millions of people, many of whom claim to be Christians.

When Jesus would indicate the things that choke the good seed of the Word in the hearts of men, He mentions only "the care of this life and the deceitfulness of riches" (Matthew 13: 22). He does not mention the gross sins and crimes, dishonesty, theft, fraud, swindling and the like, as reasons for the destruction of souls and lives. He simply says that the good seed of the Word of God sown in the hearts of men is choked by the sordid lust for material things. In this parable you see the dead-line between proper stewardship and avarice. The one is our duty, the other our danger. Few Christians there are who do not sense the peril of care and love of temporal riches. The watchful Christian asks himself: "Am I still living in God? Have the earthly cares choked the seed of the Word in my heart?" Jesus says that the weeds, thistles and thorns of love for material goods, the cares of life, the deification of money, are the elements in the soul that bring about its death.

How does this come about? As the two main elements in the Word of God are the Law and the Gospel, so their effect in the heart is twofold:

1) The work of the Law is to produce a broken and a contrite heart, a heart which keenly feels its disobedience to God and is driven to find peace and rest in Christ. Even after faith has been generated in the soul, the work of the Law continues in the life of the believer. It keeps alive the consciousness of sin and threatens at times to overshadow the light of the Gospel in the heart. It regulates his life and conduct in conformity with the express will of God as revealed in the Ten Commandments. It warns him against the way of the world and the machinations of his own sinful heart. It does not permit him to throw off the restraints of the Law, or to live in sin and disregard of the Law on the plea that he is not under the Law but under grace. It admonishes him to mortify the flesh, with all its evil lusts and propensities, and to walk in newness of life. It intensifies his realization of the law of sin in his body, and deepens in him an intelligent recognition of his own weaknesses and sins. It drives him to look more and more to Christ for salvation.

2) The unique work of the Gospel is that it communicates peace to the soul by the medium of faith in the merits of Christ. Together with the righteousness of Christ and peace with God through Him, comes the love of Christ which constrains the heart to surrender itself completely to Him and His service.

In a summary it may be said that repentance, faith and sanctification, the daily renewal, are the fruit of the seed of the Word in the hearts of men. From this fact it is easy to understand how the good seed is frequently choked in the heart by the cares of life and the deceitfulness of riches. This deplorable destruction of the work of the Holy Ghost in the hearts of men comes about when they grow so absorbed in the accumulation of wealth or in anxieties for daily bread, that the heart is filled to overcrowding with the things of earth and their minds have no place or time for the interests of their immortal souls. Communion with God in prayer and the contemplation of His Holy Word are side-tracked for the deceitful interests in the earthly things of life. The heart is hardened in gross materialism. Sin means nothing. It is only a notion thin as air. Carnality, vice, filthy habits hidden under the guise of respectability, dissimulation and hypocrisy, take the place of a sturdy crucifixion of the old man of sin in the soul, and he flourishes to the ruin of the soul and the delight of the imps of Satan. Thus the good seed is choked, conscience is chloroformed into insensibility, and the heart is covered with the noxious growths of sin and disobedience to the voice of the Spirit.

When the Law has lost its authority and power over you, when sin no longer makes you ashamed of yourself, what has become of your faith? What meaning has the Gospel to you? It is to you nothing more than an old story which you have heard a thousand times and means nothing in your life. For where the Law does not create sorrow for sin, the Gospel can do nothing by way of restoration.

Hence you are neither abased by the Law nor rejoicing in faith. But if you would cover yourself with the mantle of the Gospel while still worshiping false gods, you make of yourself a hypocrite, completing the hardening of your heart and quenching the last spark of grace in the soul. A soul like that resembles the smooth pebble on the beach which has been worn down by the constant wash of the waters and the sand. The heart that has been scoured on the one hand by the cares of this world, the lusts of the flesh and the deceitfulness of riches, and on the other by a hypocritical use of the Means of Grace, becomes finally so smooth, hard and cold, that nothing affects it but the loss of its idols. Once upon a time this same heart was receptive of the grace of God, realized its sinfulness and rejoiced in the pardoning grace of God. Now the good seed has been choked and bears no fruit. There is nothing but thorns and noxious weeds. How art thou fallen from the heavens, thou beautiful star of the morning!

The world is full of the examples of such wretched apostasy. I call to mind a merchant who by the mercies of God had been rescued out of a life of licentiousness and double-dealing in business. However, he soon discovered that by his new system of scrupulous honesty he was not prospering as formerly, and he began to reason as follows: "I have a family to support. My business is being ruined. My competitors are taking my customers from me. Either I shall have to go into some other business

or get back to my former methods of doing business."

He quit going to church; neglected family worship; laid aside good books and indulged himself
in questionable practices; drank with his customers
and prospects; gave them banquets and jolly parties,
using the Lord's Day for straightening out his ac-
counts or sleeping off the consequences of his end-
of-the-week carousals. If a Christian friend warned
him, he turned his back upon the friend in resent-
ment. He was set upon making friends with the
world. They soon became far more attractive to
him than his former Christian associates, whom he
now dubbed as "narrow-minded" and "strait-
laced."

Thus the mind is subverted, the conscience para-
lyzed. It begins with the hunger for this world's
goods and the pleasures of the flesh. How terribly
are the words of the apostle verified! "But they that
will be rich fall into temptation and a snare, and
into many foolish and hurtful lusts, which drown
men in destruction and perdition. For the love of
money is the root of all evil, which while some
coveted after, they have erred from the faith, and
pierced themselves through with many sorrows"
(1 Timothy 6: 9-10).

"Many sorrows." What a sad truth! Does not
every newspaper tell the sordid story of men who
would be rich and "have pierced themselves through
with many sorrows?" The jails, the penitentiaries
and the suicide's grave tell the actualization of the
warning words of the apostle. Like Judas with his

thirty pieces of silver they that would be rich ultimately go to their "place." Here belong the words of the Apostle James: "Go to now, ye rich men, weep and howl for your miseries that shall come upon you. Your riches are corrupted, and your garments are motheaten. Your gold and silver is cankered, and the rust of them shall be a witness against you, and shall eat your flesh as it were fire. Ye have heaped treasure together for the last days" (James 5: 1-3).

What a blessed philosophy of life to receive the good things of life with gratitude at the hands of God, to attend faithfully to one's daily tasks, to be content with daily food and clothing, and to trust God for the future! These are the happiest people on earth. "Godliness with contentment is great gain" (1 Timothy 6: 6). "Having food and raiment, let us be therewith content" (8). The wise King Solomon said: "A faithful man shall abound with blessing; but he that maketh haste to be rich shall not be innocent" (Proverbs 28: 20).

THE CHRISTIAN LIFE
(*Continued*)

THE THIRTY-FIRST DAY

POVERTY and care are mighty thorns to choke the good seed of the Word in the heart, especially when they are succeeded by prosperity and affluence. A young convert remained pious and exemplary as long as he was poor and hard-working. A rich marriage, however, translated him into a new social world, a world of pleasure and dissipation, of fashions and follies. Very soon the splendid Christian young man had been metamorphosed into a consummate worldling and an intolerable rogue. A zealous teacher in the Church, who labored faithfully for the salvation of souls under the strain of poverty and privation, finally was inducted into a high and lucrative position, when lo and behold, his former zeal evaporated and he became a drowsy watcher on the walls of Zion. He who formerly had been humble and warm-hearted now became arrogant and formal, exceedingly conscious of his influential office and great wealth. The sudden transition from a modest station in life to one of power and large influence had turned his head, and with the new outlook his spiritual life was giving way to external formalism. His sermons, which formerly had been vitalized by the Spirit, now deteriorated into essays with no vital interest in the saving of souls.

Numerous examples of a similar character might be cited, but these two are sufficient to illustrate the terrible truth that the cares of this world and the love of money too often choke the good seed of God's Word in the hearts of men. We are wise if we heed the words of the apostle: "Mortify, therefore, your members which are upon the earth, fornication, uncleanness, inordinate affection, evil concupiscence, and covetousness, which is idolatry" (Colossians 3: 5).

The words of the Lord Jesus about the mighty temptation to avarice are worthy of constant re-

membrance: "Woe unto you that are rich, for ye
have received your consolation" (Luke 6: 24). As
if He should say: If money is all the consolation you
have, you will soon be utterly disconsolate for time
and eternity. God have pity on the grovelling money
worshipper! Considering the intensity of the words
of our Savior in warning against the insidious, soul-
destroying power of wealth, we wonder if the old
saint Pretorius was not close to the truth when he
said: "The greatest fortune is no fortune." The
Law given by Jehovah to the tribe of Levi
read thus: "And the Lord spake unto Aaron, Thou
shalt have no inheritance in their land, neither shalt
thou have any part among them. I am thy part and
thine inheritance among the children of Israel"
(Numbers 18: 20).

The sins which the apostle further enumerates at
Colossians 3: 5-9 — "anger, wrath, malice, blasphemy, filthy communication out of your mouth, lying" etc.—are so palpably vicious and inexcusable
that not much needs to be said about them. In a
general way, the loving words of our Savior apply
to them: "Watch ye and pray, lest ye enter into
temptation. The spirit truly is ready, but the flesh
is weak" (Mark 14: 38). Every Christian is afraid
of falling into the sins of anger, malice, blasphemy
and lying; but let him beware! Let him be watchful.
Irritation readily creates bitterness, and bitterness
harsh language, wounding words and acts, malice
and lies about our neighbor. "The tongue is a little
member, and boasteth great things. Behold how
great a matter a little fire kindleth. And the tongue

is a fire, a world of iniquity. So is the tongue among
our members, that it defileth the whole body, and
setteth on fire the course of nature, and it is set on fire
of hell" (James 3: 5-6). Hence King David says:
"Be ye angry and sin not. Commune with your own
heart upon your bed, and be still" (Psalm 4: 4).

When anger arises in the heart—bide a wee. Control yourself. Remember how God has forgiven you.
Nothing so conduces to the suppression of anger as
the memory of the pardoning love of God in Christ.
Nothing is so effective a mental stabilizer and tran-
quillizer as the parable of the debtor whom his master forgave the "ten thousand talents." Repeat the
Lord's Prayer to yourself, and stop at the Fifth Petition: "Forgive us our trespasses as we forgive
those who trespass against us." In this manner "Ye
through the Spirit do mortify the deeds of the body"
(Romans 8: 13).

Similarly, if tempted to lie, remember that God is
an auditor and a witness. Think of the fate of
Ananias and Sapphira (Acts 15). Consider also
that you are a child of God among whom such sins
ought not even be mentioned. "Lie not one to another, seeing that ye have put off the old man with
his deeds, and have put on the new man which is
renewed in knowledge after the image of Him
that created him" (Colossians 3: 10-11). Note
here that the "new man" of faith in Christ is formed
and patterned after God. He grows more and more
like God in love, righteousness and peace. The image of Christ is reflected in his life and walk. "Here
is neither Greek nor Jew, circumcision nor uncircum-

cision, barbarian, Scythian, bond or free; but Christ is all in all" (11).

It matters not whether I belong to this school or that school, whether I am in high or low station, learned or unlearned. Everything depends upon whether Christ is to me all in all. The fact that Christ is my only wisdom, righteousness, sanctification and redemption, renders me "a new creature in Christ Jesus," "a new man," and the image of Christ will in clearer or dimmer outline be reproduced in my life, according as I walk with Him. Have a care, friend, that in confessing Christ as being all this to you, you do not dissemble and act the hypocrite, praising Him with your lips and denying His power in your life and daily walk. Pray God that Christ may become more and more a living, controlling reality in your life, that He may speak in your words, live in your life, direct your thoughts and your conduct. Then are you leading the life of a disciple of the Lord Christ. May God grant us all this grace. Amen.

AT THE CLOSE OF THE DAY

IT was a dark and stormy winter evening. The heavens were covered with heavy black clouds. The rain fell in torrents. The roads had become almost impassable, and one could not help but pity those who might be abroad on a night like this. It was late, and in every house a cheery wood-fire crackled in the fireplace.

Deep in the woods was a cottage where but seldom any traveller sought a shelter. But this evening a wayfarer rapped at the door. He entered and requested lodging for the remainder of the night. The friendly habitants bade him a cordial welcome, gave him the best place near the fire, dried his wet clothes, and at last invited him to share their frugal repast. The stranger told them how he had lost his way in the forest as the darkness fell, and how he had prayed God to guide him to some friendly shelter, and that at the same moment he had discerned the light from their window through the darkness and the storm.

After the meal, the stranger looked about uneasily as if in expectation of something. The host then remarked that it was time to retire and opened the door to a small chamber for the guest. The children were already preparing to go to bed.

"What?" stammered the guest, "have you not forgotten something before going to rest?"

"Nothing whatever, sir," answered the host in surprise. "We are through with the day's work. We have eaten our supper, and now all hands are ready for bed."

"In that case I must thank you for your hospitality," quickly responded the stranger, "and proceed on my journey, in spite of the storm and darkness. For I dare not sleep in a house where the family does not close the day by commending themselves to the hand of God and praying for His protection and blessing upon them, I should be afraid that the roof might fall upon me in the night."

"We have never thought of that," said the wife in a trembling voice.

"But God in heaven has thought about it," replied the stranger, preparing to depart, "and if His patience had not been as great as it is, I suspect the roof would have caved in long ago. For a house without prayer is built on the sands. Please help me with my horse. I must be going. I have not the courage to remain in your home."

"Please stay with us overnight, sir," now pleaded the cotter, "and teach us how to end the day as we ought to do. Will you not pray with us and for us? We have never had family worship and I would not know how to conduct it."

The visitor did not hesitate, but immediately produced a pocket Bible, read a few verses, fell on his knees at the side of a chair, and prayed fervently for himself and for the benighted souls of that isolated home in the depths of the forest. He prayed that they might learn to bring all their cares to the heavenly Father, and realize their dependence upon Him for every good and perfect gift. He prayed that they might seek the most precious gift of pardoning grace in Christ, and that the Holy Ghost might be shed abroad in their hearts. Finally he prayed for God's merciful protection during the night, commending them all as well as himself to the heavenly Father's keeping and closed his petitions with a fervent "Amen."

The prayer in the backwoods cabin that stormy night was not offered in vain. It found its way to the heart of God and was answered, as every prayer in the name of Jesus is answered. The Lord through that prayer opened the hearts of the inmates of the home, hearts that had long years been closed against Him. That prayer was the key which unlocked the door. Like Lydia of old, they "received the Word with gladness."

The night was far gone when the guest was permitted to retire. The supreme question, "What shall I do to be saved?" now displaced the tiresome, hackneyed ones: "What shall we eat? What shall we drink? Wherewithal shall we be clothed?" The weary stranger, like his Master at the well of Sychar, was glad enough to give up his sleep that he might "work the works of Him that sent him." That work was better than sleep to the guest.

By morning the rain had ceased; the storm had abated, and the sun shone through the drifting clouds. The stranger continued on his journey after he had led the family in morning worship. They never saw him again. But from that day a new life was begun in that little home in the forest. Jesus became the Master in that house, and parents and children served Him with delight. Prayer was as the breathing of their new life: it grew natural and spontaneous. It was to them the source of tranquillity and peace and contentment. The new man cannot live without breathing the clean air of God's heaven.

In their daily prayers the family never forgot to include the visitor of that stormy autumn night, although they never learned his name. On the Great Day of the Lord, when that which is hidden shall be revealed, the two shall meet, the family in the forest hut and the stranger visitor, and they shall know one another and marvel at the ways of God with men.

Dear reader, how are conditions in your home? Do you need to fear that the house may tumble about your ears because there are no uprights to support it? It is dangerous to go to sleep and to arise in a house like that. A home without prayer is a joyless home, an outlawed home, a Christless home. If you have not had family worship before, gather your household about you this evening and pour out your heart to God in prayer for them and for yourself, and your rest will be under the wings of God's eternal love. Now you have the time. Possibly you may not have time to-morrow.

A WORD IN PARTING

Dear Reader, Brother or Sister:

We have now come to the end of our book—but will you not read it again? You might find more in a second reading than you found in the first. Possibly you might find even more in the third and fourth readings than in the former two readings, providing you read in the right manner. That means that you not only read the sentences and chapters as they are printed before you in the volume, but that you read with a prayer in your heart for the enlightenment of the Holy Ghost; that you, secondly, meditate earnestly and with a hungry soul upon the contents of your reading; and, thirdly, apply the truths which you discover to your own heart and life. Too many read thoughtlessly and carelessly, and miss the best part of the reading.

Reading the Bible is not like the reading of any other book. An ordinary book you read once, and you have grasped its content. But the Bible is written by God Himself; its contents are therefore unfathomable. No matter how deep you dig in this goldmine, you will always find more golden nuggets to add to the treasury of your heart and mind. Tell others what you have found in that Wonder-Book, and ask others to tell you what they have found. That will help you to find much gold which otherwise might remain hidden to you.

Do not read for the purpose of showing off your knowledge of the Sacred Scriptures. That is the way the Old Adam in your heart would have you read. Read with the purpose of applying the truth which you find to your own life and conduct. Thus your reading will prove a blessing to yourself and a benediction also to others with whom you share your treasures.

Will you promise to read God's Word after this manner? Make answer to the Lord. I know that you need to read that Sacred Book, it matters not who you are. With equal certainty I know that the Lord through the reading will grant you grace, intellectual expansion, spiritual light, righteousness, peace of heart and joy beyond measure. He will guide you into all truth and confirm you in the truth. Only be sure that these are the treasures that you are looking for in the reading.

And now—farewell! Pray for the conversion of souls. Pray for the perseverance of the saints. Pray also for me, will you not? I am but a pilgrim and shall soon meet you. I am a member of the same Body as you are. I am a laborer in the same harvest as you are. But the fields are so great that we have not met thus far. Let us be faithful to the Lord of the Harvest, and we shall be manifested to each other on the Great Day of Ingathering.

You rejoice that many in our day are leaving the broad way to destruction for the narrow way that leads to eternal life? You mourn because so many of the redeemed do not hearken to the call of the Spirit, reject the salvation of the Lord and find no joy in His fellowship? You love the Lord and His Kingdom, do you not? You love the brethren, do you not?

In our meditation upon the Word of God, let us keep two things in mind: 1. The recognition of our natural depravity and sinfulness, and 2. The strengthening of our union with the Lord Jesus. In His name

Farewell!

THE WAY TO PEACE

To Thee, O dear, dear Savior!
  My spirit turns for rest,
My peace is in Thy favor,
  My pillow on Thy breast;
Though all the world deceive me,
  I know that I am Thine.
And Thou wilt never leave me,
  O blessed Savior mine.

In Thee my trust abideth,
  On Thee my hope relies,
O Thou whose love provideth
  For all beneath the skies;
O Thou whose mercy found me
  From bondage set me free,
And then for ever bound me
  With threefold cords to Thee.

My grief is in the dullness
  With which this sluggish heart
Doth open to the fullness
  Of all Thou wouldst impart;
My joy is in Thy beauty
  Of holiness divine,
My comfort in the duty
  That binds my life in Thine.

Alas, that I should ever
  Have failed in love to Thee,
The only one who never
Forgot or slighted me!
O for a heart to love Thee
  More truly as I ought,
And nothing place above Thee
  In deed, or word, or thought.

O for that choicest blessing
  Of living in Thy love,
And thus on earth possessing
  The peace of heaven above;
O for the bliss that by it
  The soul securely knows
The holy calm and quiet
  Of faith's serene repose!

JOHN S. B. MONSELL, 1863.